Culture & Liberty

Culture & Liberty

Writings of Isabel Paterson

Stephen Cox
editor

Transaction Publishers
New Brunswick (U.S.A.) and London (U.K.)

This book is printed on acid-free paper that meets the American National Standard for Permanence of Paper for Printed Library Materials.

Library of Congress Catalog Number: 2014032470
ISBN: 978-1-4128-5600-3 (cloth); 978-1-4128-5679-9 (paper)
Printed in the United States of America

Library of Congress Cataloging-in-Publication Data

Paterson, Isabel, author.
[Works. Selections]
Culture and Liberty : writings of Isabel Paterson / edited by Stephen Cox.
pages cm
Includes bibliographical references.
ISBN 978-1-4128-5600-3 (acid-free paper) 1. American literature--Women authors. 2. Criticism--United States. 3. Libertarian literature. 4. Libertarianism--United States. 5. Paterson, Isabel. I. Cox, Stephen D., 1948- editor. II. Title.
PS3531.A774A6 2015
818'.52--dc23

2014032470

To the memory of Muriel Welles Hall
Friend, scholar, individualist

Contents

Introduction

Today, Isabel Paterson is best known as an advocate of radical individualism, a prophet of the libertarian movement. She is known as a person who influenced (and antagonized) a wide variety of libertarian and conservative writers and public figures, from Ayn Rand to William F. Buckley, Jr. Her best remembered work is *The God of the Machine* (1943), which presents a theory of history and political economy from a libertarian point of view.

In her own time, Paterson was noted as a literary critic and novelist, and as one of the most dangerously witty writers in America. It was said that some people loved her and some people hated her, "but everybody reads her."[1] She combined individualist ideas with an individual and provocative style, a style that made people look forward to whatever her next pronouncement on American culture might be.

These various forms of fame, contemporary and historical, are monuments to a complex but strongly unified personality, always recognizable by a special approach to ideas and life. Paterson said that "only the most accomplished writers possess a sufficiently distinctive style for recognition."[2] The observation applies to her. She remains one of the most distinctive voices in American literary history—as this selection of her writings will indicate.

Frontiers

Isabel Paterson was born Mary Isabel (or perhaps Isabel Mary) Bowler on January 22, 1886. Her birthplace was a region of Canada that had only recently been opened to white settlement, Manitoulin Island in northern Lake Huron. The Bowler family was large and poor. There were nine children, a hardworking, intelligent mother, and a feckless, lazy father—"useless," in Paterson's estimation.[3] Her childhood was spent on a series of frontiers: backwoods Canada, lumber-country Michigan, desert Utah, and ranchland Alberta, where her family arrived in 1894. She had about two years of formal schooling and regarded its brevity as more of a convenience than a deprivation. She left home to work when she was seventeen or eighteen.

Out on her own, she held a series of jobs—most memorably, to her, that of a "hotel diningroom girl"—and began to form her own complicated view of life, simultaneously romantic and wryly skeptical. Learning shorthand and typing enabled her to get work with bankers and lawyers in western American and Canadian towns. One of her employers was R. B. Bennett, the principal lawyer in Calgary, Alberta, and a future premier of Canada. She was one of many independent young men and women finding their way in the new civilization suddenly called into being by the Canadian Pacific Railway. She had no money, but with the help of a CPR pass she could travel down to Minneapolis-St. Paul whenever she wanted, just to buy a hat.[4]

In 1910 she married, for reasons that were probably uncertain even to her, one of the nice young men of her acquaintance in Calgary, Kenneth Birrell Paterson. The wedding took place on April 13; by midsummer, husband and wife had separated, seemingly without anger, except perhaps at themselves. By 1918, Isabel had lost track of Kenneth, but they were never divorced. Divorce was hard to get in Canada, and although Paterson enjoyed romances (and flirtations) and would have enjoyed having more of them, she never found anyone compatible enough for a second marriage. Not only did she remain Mrs. Paterson, but in her middle and old age she was known to most of her friends as "Pat." The mystery of her husband haunts her last novel, *Joyous Gard,* completed three years before her death.

After the breakup of her marriage, Paterson traveled to Spokane, Washington, where a job turned up with a newly started paper, the *Inland Herald.* She began as a secretary, but because her writing was so much better than her boss's, she was soon transferred to writing editorials. She moved on to newspaper jobs in Vancouver, writing editorials, dramatic reviews, and short stories. Later she had jobs in San Francisco and New York, where she was on the staff of the *World,* the *American,* and *Hearst's Magazine.* She worked as an assistant to Gutzon Borglum, the sculptor. Then, in 1922, she was hired as an assistant to Burton Rascoe, literary editor of the *New York Tribune.* This was the crucial event of her career.

Rascoe was one of America's most important young critics—an energetic exponent of modernist literature and a person who seemed to know and like almost everyone in the literary world. Paterson, as Rascoe put it, was much more "conservative" in her tastes; as she put it, she couldn't "enjoy, for any length of time, a book in which it is impossible to be sure what the author means." And on first meeting

Rascoe, she found it impossible to enjoy him, either. They had difficulty even being in each other's presence. Still, she insisted on working for him, and he felt "afraid not to hire her."[5] From this strange beginning came a lifelong friendship, and a job that lasted to the end of Paterson's salaried life. In 1924, Rascoe left the paper, and the *Tribune* joined with the *Herald* to become the *Herald Tribune*; but Paterson survived as a staff member and columnist for the Sunday literary supplement, *Herald Tribune "Books."* Her weekly column, "Turns with a Bookworm," continued until 1949.

"Books" had a national circulation of about 500,000, and "Turns" was one of its most prominent features. It established Paterson as a literary personality.

The Shaping of I.M.P.

The column began as a collection of book news. The news element was present to the end, but very soon Paterson began shaping the acronymic signer of the column, "I.M.P." (Isabel Mary Paterson), into an investigator of any issue, literary, philosophical, historical, or political, that happened to interest her. I.M.P. roved the literary world, asking unexpected questions and delivering her own unpredictable answers; she was a woman alternately bemused, sardonic, enthusiastic, nostalgic; a woman who was sophisticated but down to earth, a woman who knew everything and wasn't afraid to say it frankly. As I.M.P. pushed, then overwhelmed, the limits of her genre, she transformed the column into a miniature republic of letters, in which all issues of intellectual importance could be considered, and all authors or public figures accorded equal rights to praise or blame.

In this community, Paterson herself was free to take any job she thought other writers weren't doing well enough. She might appear as the modest inquirer into the truth of things (a common pose), the dutiful provider of information that leading intellectuals had somehow never learned, the insistent recommender of good books, new or old, that would otherwise have gone unnoticed, or the "little grandmother," dragging erring authors to the woodshed to administer appropriate punishment.[6]

Readers came to expect all these forms of I.M.P.—and more, many more—to materialize within a single 1,800-word column. I.M.P. was instantly identifiable by her argumentative agility and virtuosity of tone. Her rhetorical skill was backed by a large and varied experience of life, and by enormous reading. In one of her columns, Paterson revealed the dark secret of American literature: "Authors themselves, as a rule, don't read a great deal. Readers read." But for her, reading was a necessity of life; and unlike many self-educated people, she was a catholic, not a special-interest reader. Her idea was that "any book is better than none." She also thought that "a writer should know absolutely everything in the most minute detail."[7] People who wanted to debate with her, particularly specialists in this and that, usually found that she had enough facts about their own fields to keep the argument going for as long as she wanted it to go. Although she did not become an American citizen until 1928, she had an encyclopedic knowledge of American life and language. She knew the American vocabulary in all its regional, occupational, and historical variations. She might misstate a reference; she could not mistake an idiom.

Paterson didn't try to simplify her ideas for the benefit of her audience, which she did not see as a mass but as a great many people with a great many individual interests. She never imagined that anyone's culture or interests were simple. Nevertheless, she thought that important ideas could be represented clearly to anyone. She valued direct words, succinct and luminous, the crystallization of truths as she saw them. While using rhetoric in complicated ways, she was capable of denying its importance. "After all," she declared, "truth is more effective than rhetoric."[8] Yet a crystal is a complex thing.

The brightest crystallizations of Paterson's ideas are her brief observations, maxims, and aphorisms. Many of them are mordant comments on books and people. "Nothing," she claimed, "is worth reporting if it doesn't cause the subject to deny and repudiate it violently." Her readers (if they were not also her "subjects") enjoyed her unfavorable reports. She had a reserved respect for Ernest Hemingway—"he is as good as one can be without being a great writer; and that's better than most of us"—but the remark that people quoted was, "His characters have no histories and no backs to their heads." She confided that America's self-consciously "lost" young intellectuals could "stay lost" as far as she was concerned: "Nobody would go to look for them."[9] Convinced that "it would be well if the skeptically inclined were more numerous right now all over the world," she did not hesitate to demystify the oracles of the age.[10] Of Oswald Spengler, hailed as the great explainer by some on the American Right, she complained, "The trouble with Spengler . . . is that any one can write like that. In fact, the main problem is how not to write like that if one has a typewriter." Inspecting the political failures of Leon Trotsky, a hero for many intellectual leftists, she suggested that besides revolution, "there must have been something else he didn't quite understand. Now we wonder what that could have been? People? Yes, that must be the answer; for there are no people in Marx's system."[11] As for America's own political pundits, some of them were "unable to write even a cliché accurately."[12]

Paterson's skeptical remarks weren't limited to particular people or movements; they extended to the whole tribe of authors, including herself—the person whom her columns, following the custom of the time, always designate as "we": "Authors are human—at least, we will not admit they aren't." If the hypothetical humans objected to the charges she made against them, they could always be reminded that "the one thing that no writer has ever failed to produce is a good alibi."[13]

Politicians and political ideologues were even better targets than authors, especially if they were supporters of the modern state. Writing of World War I, in which "the values of a thousand years were felled," Paterson said that this war, which was supposed to have been fought "to make the world safe for democracy," was actually fought by politicians "to make bureaucracy safe for themselves." Then along came the communist intellectuals, who wanted "to make the world safe for catchwords, on a capitalistic endowment." Addressing the perennial argument that the Marxist philosophy isn't invalidated merely by the experience of the Soviet Union, she asked, "No? Then what have you got against Fascism? Surely you wouldn't judge it by the way it works?"[14]

She found that battles could be won with only an aphorism, an anecdote, or a rhetorical question. James B. Reston, an important journalist who was always growing more important, offered the portentous, though commonplace, observation that "it is a 'dangerous illusion' that 'freedom comes easy.'" Paterson replied: "Does slavery come any easier?" She responded in a similar way to "the most dim-witted attempt at argument ever heard in this mortal world"—"the supposed retort to any advocate of freedom 'Do you mean free to starve?' We mean, do you think you can't starve with your hands tied?"[15] By way of comment on the presidential election of 1940, which resulted in victory for what she regarded as the party of big government and big spending, she mentioned a small, apparently irrelevant anecdote about President Washington's household management: "Washington paid his own expenses. And by the way, does the name mean anything to you?" Faced with the contention that a once-backward country was now "as civilized as [Fascist] Italy and as well policed," she replied, "Civilized is such a nice word."[16]

One common Paterson tactic is to support an argument by emphasizing the rightness of an obvious aspect of the counterargument, then to turn on the counterargument with an unexpected flank attack. Born a Victorian, Paterson always argued that the achievements of the nineteenth century were essential to civilization. It was in the nineteenth century that ordinary men and women were first able to do all the strange and amazing things that men and women want to do. Indeed, "if you don't understand the Victorians, human nature must remain a sealed book to you." But she knew the Victorians were tasteless and silly on a grand scale; their modern critics, ignorant and feeble though she thought them to be, were right about that. Still, their critique was inauthentic, because it refused to recognize that the Victorians had created their successors' opportunity to criticize. She won her point with a single sentence: "Such was the bequest of the Victorians to their immediate heirs—some sentimental souvenirs in grotesque bad taste, and a substantial bank balance."[17]

Her contention was, broadly speaking, political: Victorian capitalism had built the modern world's "bank balance." But politics was only one of Paterson's concerns. Some of her most memorable statements are comments about the many twists of human nature ("She lived only for others, whether they liked it or not"; "Nobody would be or is quite satisfied to belong to the leisure class"[18]) or about humanity's long process of self-understanding:

> "Problems" become problems only when there is some chance of solving them; until then they are accepted as quite natural conditions.[19]
>
> It took ages to get whales believed in at all, although they would be seen from time to time. . . . On the other hand, people will believe almost anything that isn't so.[20]
>
> The great body of literature and of information handed down in books actually comprises the world we have lived in, both mentally and physically. Every one who lives in this country lives in books; and that would be true even of an illiterate person. He is living in books he has never read.[21]

Paterson was ideologically opposed to the suppression of anyone on ideological grounds: "When we say free speech, we mean free speech, even if you don't know what we mean."[22] But she was in favor of variety on cultural grounds as well. She enjoyed America's panoply of ethnic and regional cultures and did her best to advertise local histories and other accounts of what Willa Cather called "obscure destinies." Informed that America's immigrant groups were advancing together on a program of "national unity" and "homogeneity," she objected: "This sounds so noble we hate to mention the fact that they really got along on the principle, not of 'homogeneity,' but of individualism."[23] She appreciated communal and utopian experiments that few people, particularly their neighbors, were able to tolerate. She didn't agree with the participants' ideologies or approve of their practices, but as long as they didn't try to impose their way of life on anyone else, she wasn't bothered. Far from it. When she wrote about the Oneida community, a bizarre experiment run by someone who "was sure he knew the answer to everything," an apparently certain object of Paterson's satire, her thoughts turned instead to the attitude of the surrounding society:

> Since his hold on [his followers] was limited to persuasion, he really wasn't doing any harm, but the neighbors wouldn't mind their own business and finally drove him away from his community. We suspect that what exasperated the neighbors was that the Oneida Communists seemed to enjoy their peculiar way of life. They could not rest till they had reformed the reformers. We think, to the contrary, that any notion, however eccentric, that can be put in effect within a group, without duress or infringement of the freedom or belongings of non-participants, is nobody else's business. Let 'em alone. Nothing is more salutary for theorists than contact with reality in working out their ideas.[24]

Yet while relishing individuality—in fact, eccentricity—Paterson understood the need for customs and appearances, and she found a way of describing them as things that are not basic but not superficial either:

> Formality is wearisome, and a good time is a good time; but there is a positive reason for certain formalities, and when they are abolished you may look for something else to go with them. It might be that the structure is crumbling when the facade drops off.[25]

When one views a troubled urban landscape, it is difficult not to think of that remark, and the complex analysis of culture it implies.

Many of Paterson's salient comments express her libertarian-conservative view of culture and history, but others are less easy to classify; they are simply the kind of things that only Paterson would say. As she remarks in one such passage, "it is singular that when you take things apart very thoroughly, the main ingredient can't be found." Nobody has an ideological interest in the strengths or weaknesses of

Babylonian civilization, but when Paterson writes of the Babylonians, "Where no adequate error existed, they invented one promptly," the reader can laugh and imagine all those other people to whom the statement might apply.[26] It is harder to explain exactly how some of her other observations work: "If one could bring the moon down to earth it would no longer be the moon," or even, "A cat is always around if there is a chance of the spotlight."[27] Still more irreducibly Patersonian is the passage in which, commenting on speculations about the afterlife, she refers to death as "the greatest of all riddles, the final sporting chance."[28] Death as a "riddle"—that was a cliché of the late Victorians. But death as a sporting chance? That idea was all her own.

Paterson the Novelist

Paterson was always her own best character, but while establishing herself as a columnist she was also gaining recognition as a creator of characters in fiction. Her first published novels were *The Shadow Riders* (1916) and *The Magpie's Nest* (1917), stories that exploited her experience as a young woman in the Canadian West. These works were interesting and fairly well received but did not establish her significance as an imaginative writer. Her next three novels did. All were historical fictions: *The Singing Season* (1924: medieval Spain); *The Fourth Queen* (1926: Elizabethan England); and her best historical novel, *The Road of the Gods* (1930: barbarian Germany), a beautiful production.

She followed *Road of the Gods* with her most commercially successful book, *Never Ask the End* (1933), an account of life as seen and remembered by a group of North Americans sojourning in Europe. The method was stream of consciousness—"sort of Virginia Woolf, but worse."[29] Neither the method nor the subject seemed likely to attract a large audience; but, to Paterson's own surprise, the book succeeded. In the next year she published *The Golden Vanity*, a story of life in the Great Depression. This is an active, robust novel, enlivened by social satire but generous in its sympathy even to people—some people—whom Paterson habitually disliked. It provides a consistently interesting perspective on the winners and losers in America's financial games.

Paterson herself was migrating from the edge of poverty to the insecure middle class. During the 1920s she lived in a respectable apartment in a not-respectable neighborhood of Manhattan, aptly called Hell's Kitchen. She attended the parties thrown by Lee Meader, a wealthy, free-living architect, and although she was not a free liver herself (she didn't have enough money, and Jazz Age activities usually bored her), she developed warm friendships among the eccentric or just plain interesting people she met. At the end of the decade, the group dispersed. Close friends died. Paterson lost money in the financial collapse that began in 1929. She began to feel old, and she did not meet advancing age without complaint. But her finances were improving. In 1931, she decided that "Hell's Kitchen isn't what it used to be," and two years later, on the strength of her recent book sales, she built a house for herself in Stamford, Connecticut.[30] In 1942, she built another house, in Ridgefield, Connecticut, and lived there until 1952. She scraped together enough money to make two short visits to Europe, in 1929 and 1933. She never visited Europe again, and after the death of her mother in Alberta in October 1933, she probably never left the United States again. She was still a working woman who needed to show up at the office, and when she traveled she took her typewriter and a large collection of books.

Limited Government

By the time World War II arrived, much of Paterson's life was absorbed in the elaboration of her philosophical and political ideas. Her basic views about politics and economics had been formed long before. Unlike many other creators of the individualist Right—the libertarian and libertarian-conservative movements so much in evidence today—Paterson was not a disappointed modern liberal, reacting against the New Deal, or a disappointed communist or socialist, reacting against the suddenly perceived failures of collectivism. In her words, "a whole lot of people in recent years have minded acutely seeing their own ideas carried out."[31] But she wasn't one of them. She had been agitating against big government when Herbert Hoover still occupied the White House.

Hoover was called by his admirers "the Great Engineer." Paterson took the name seriously but unfavorably, detesting him for his efforts to engineer prosperity and moral well-being. His administration began with attempts to defend Prohibition and ended with attempts to control prices and keep bad investors from going broke—an economic program that was precisely wrong, in her opinion. But it wasn't just his specific measures that were wrong; it was the idea, shared by virtually all political sects and movements, that the role of government was to structure and restructure society, until it got things right. Where others saw a benevolent conservatism or an idealistic progressivism, she saw an absurdly intrusive state.

Paterson believed that the purpose of government had been accurately identified in the Declaration of Independence, which stipulates that "governments are instituted among men" to "secure" individual rights—just that, and nothing more. In her interpretation, the operative concept was "minimum government," government used not as a means of reforming morals, running the economy, or creating an empire, but solely as a means of preserving people's freedom to work, trade, own, and enjoy as they wish.[32]

She had held this idea for a long time; it may have been simultaneous with her first systematic thoughts on political and historical issues. In *The Singing Season*, one of her characters expresses the additional idea, which is emphasized in much of her later work, that nations prosper when their government is limited. He describes the role of a political leader in this way:

> Keep the roads open, the ports clear; make . . . a safe haven for the merchants of all nations, and your neighbor states will ask for shelter under your protecting hand. It is better to make than take.[33]

Political ideas are also prominent in *The Golden Vanity*, which ridicules the popular idea that modern societies should be planned, managed, or "engineered" by an elite group of intellectual or economic leaders. The novel examines the social and psychological effects of this modern notion, none of them good, and of both leftwing and rightwing attempts to modernize America in accordance with it.

But it was her columns and reviews in the *Herald Tribune* that made Paterson notorious for her political ideas. She found innumerable ways of stating them.

> The power of the state is always in inverse ratio to the power of the nation.[34]

> The law of civilization is contract law. The government of a civilized country is a limited government. The economy of a civilized country is private capitalism.[35]

> The power to do things for people is also the power to do things to people—and you can guess for yourself which is likely to be done.[36]

> The highest civilization affords the greatest latitude for variations in conduct.[37]

> Fire burns, water is wet, and unlimited government is tyranny.[38]

> A lot of American principle is contained in the two words: "'Just don't." Much of the rest is encompassed by the suggestion of minding one's own business. The whole is summed up in the word "liberty."[39]

A few days after the electorate voted Herbert Hoover out of the presidency, Paterson reminded readers of her own position:

> We hold obstinately to the political principles of the Founding Fathers, who sought to safeguard only "life, liberty and the pursuit of happiness." They did not expect any system to make people happy; all they said was, Go ahead and try. We are constantly being told that "conditions have changed," so these principles are no longer applicable. Conditions do not alter principles and their consequences. We have more elaborate machinery now than Archimedes ever dreamed of, but the principle of the lever remains the same, and any engineer who proceeded on the idea that it is obsolete would be surprised.[40]

Paterson greeted Franklin Roosevelt's first full day in office in 1933 with a lecture about "the rights of man, personal liberty and private property," the need "to get out from under the heavy load of taxes and too much government." She had voted for Roosevelt because he was against Prohibition, but she did not like him. Nevertheless, she had seen bad economic times before, and she had high hopes for the resilience of the American people: "In the next ten years, there will be the queerest resurgence of private adventure-capitalism any age ever saw—something like San Francisco after the earthquake and fire. . . . It's going to be wild."[41] That didn't happen. Roosevelt inaugurated the greatest attempt in American history to manage the country's economy and reform its ways of life. Paterson spent the next ten years as a social critic surveying what she considered the political and intellectual ruins of the 1930s.

She didn't try to comment on every passing political incident; she reserved her column space for events that were especially useful in illustrating broad patterns of history—thereby ensuring that her work would be interesting far in the future. In her view, the political events of the 1930s were a continuation and enhancement of destructive tendencies that began before the Great War:

> A World War precipitated by irresponsible power vested in incapable hands was followed by the establishment of dictatorships wielding

> even more irresponsible power. The growth of widespread organizations, which came down in the crash, induced a burning zeal for even more comprehensive organization.

The "prevailing contemporary delusion" was

> that human affairs, nationally, internationally and privately, can be planned and regulated, in whole and in part, with perfect smoothness and order, so that everybody will have everything and be satisfied.[42]

This "delusion," prevalent throughout the Western world, had become the guiding spirit of American politics. In 1936, Paterson's fellow citizens ("a well meaning electorate") voted overwhelmingly for continuation of the New Deal—or, as Paterson put it, "for bad debts, bad money and bad faith," with "the amiable intention" of giving "everybody something for nothing."[43] They wanted government to save them from their bad investments and keep wages up while somehow keeping prices down. They wanted fiat money instead of gold, so they could satisfy their debtors with inflated currency. The effect was more or less what Paterson expected from these impulses: new investment stagnated, unemployment remained high, and, as she frequently pointed out, working people who had saved their money had to pay the debts of wealthy people who unloaded failed investments on the government.[44]

Even more significant was the change she felt in American cultural values. Because the United States was formed on the idea of individual freedom, it was originally "a great romance, a heroic age, springing from a fresh apprehension of the relation of man to the universe." She thought it "very strange" that Americans had now "lost sight of their own adventure." How had it happened? She suspected it was her own people, the "literati," whose imaginations had failed. "This," she said, "is essentially a romantic country—discovered, settled, and carried on as a great romance"; the planned, regulated, and collectivized America, the America envisioned by her fellow intellectuals, was anything but romantic.[45] Their emphasis on "material conditions" was reductive, anti-intellectual; their sense of human possibilities was ridiculously restricted and contrary to all precedents in real American life; their conception of humanity was hypocrisy itself, since they regarded all people as blindly conditioned by their circumstances but assumed that they themselves saw clearly what to do.

This was supposed to be progressive thought. To Paterson, it sounded as medieval as an authoritarian church or the divine right of kings. People who prided themselves on being part of the wave of the future should be informed that "what a wave brings ashore is wreckage."[46] The wreckage of the Depression era was not just political and economic; it was human, and it was emphasized by what Paterson saw as a vast surrender of intellectual integrity and authenticity. In a typical column, written during the last few days of the Hoover administration, she defended the socializing intellectuals' right to be heard but insisted that others' rights be recognized as well. People had a right not to be treated as units in an economic scheme: "The Economic Man is useful as an abstraction, but the individual man is not an arbitrarily transferable unit. . . . [A] civilization or a society inevitably contains within itself many cultures, many ways of life; it is an organism—not a machine." The "ideologist" who wants the power to change it all shows his ignorance about himself: "If he clamors for 'a strong man,' he never asks himself how he'd like a sock in the jaw from that strong man. He thinks only his opponents will be socked. If he wants the power of government extended, he assumes innocently that those powers will then be used only as he suggests. He is a simple soul, and so was Torquemada." Another way of putting that was to say that "the craving for power is in itself a sign of inferior abilities and unfitness for responsibility," or simply, "It is the inferior man who clutches at power."[47]

Paterson grew especially concerned about the spread of communism among America's authors and intellectuals. It touched, or enveloped, many people she knew and some people she admired. This was a time when organizations sponsored by the Communist Party had thousands of intellectual adherents, many of them important names in literature, science, and the arts. It was also a time when many liberal intellectuals saw no enemies to the left and could not decide how seriously to take large claims about Soviet accomplishments, in the meantime giving Stalin the benefit of the doubt. Paterson could decide, and her decisiveness earned her many enemies. She was immune to the idea, strongly visible in communist intellectuals' many attempts at folksiness, that communism was latter-day Americanism:

> Now the original American principles are individualism, limited government, and private property. Indeed, strictly individual private property was first defined and recognized in this country. The American idea then was the absolute antithesis of Communism. In so far as it remains it still is so.[48]

Just as obstinately she ridiculed the idea that material progress can result from the sacrifice of liberty, or that liberty is, after all, hard to define.

> Freedom is just freedom from restraint. And what Communism, government control, brings about is freedom from soap, freedom from shoes, freedom from food.[49]

She would not entertain the idea that economic well-being—a "fair distribution of wealth"—was incompatible with individual freedom and the minimum state. Quite the contrary:

> Destitution is easily distributed. It's the one thing political power can insure you.[50]

The notion of a prosperous Soviet Russia seemed as absurd to Paterson as that of a prosperous Nazi Germany.

Unlimited Possibilities

But for Paterson, the larger issue was still American intellectuals' inability to understand, and enjoy, their own mental and spiritual heritage, which was the romance of "the individual soul . . . gifted with the divine spark," free to work out its own destiny in a world of facts it could know and understand. Writers and thinkers had lost the facts as well as the romance, and Paterson was there to tell them what they were missing. Quoting Joseph Conrad, she said that the novelist's job was "to make you see, to make you feel."[51] She evidently thought the same about the job of the political commentator. And the challenge went beyond politics; it was a question of getting people to see and understand America's special historical culture.

The challenge arose even in connection with such apparently non-political matters as people's relationship to the natural world. Paterson was an intense enjoyer and observer of nature, and a scholar of its history in America. She thought "the intrinsic beauty of the American landscape, its exquisite variety and charm, is just beginning to be appreciated; for centuries Americans looked rather wistfully to the Old World for beauty, while it was spread lavishly under their noses." She built her houses in areas that were still somewhat rural and spent as much time there as she could, appreciating the trees and sympathizing with the flowers, which, like her, wouldn't do anything just because somebody told them to: "Whatever a plant does, you have to let it."[52] She loved books about plants and flowers and said of one such book:

> Maybe we found special merit in Donald Culross Peattie's *Flowering Earth* because it is essentially an exposition of life as freedom—the vital process being always unpredictable even in the plant world, inasmuch as it would have been impossible to foresee the course of evolution at any given previous stage.... [A] granite boulder is actually feeble and without effective resistance, compared to the apparently delicate and perishable lichen which grows on its surface. The boulder is inorganic. The lichen is alive.[53]

She found the same unpredictable vitality and power in the lives of men and women. A partisan of human progress, she was contemptuous of people whose ideal of nature was that of a material world cleansed of human life. That ideal appears to be a permanent characteristic of America: seven decades ago, the antithesis between "man" and "nature" was as forcefully drawn as it is today, and the outrage about the former's invasion of the latter was almost as loud. Paterson refused to share it. Discussing a book that was advertised as "a reminder of our pampered, wasteful past," she made her own position clear:

> For years this has been the do-goods' theme song, and it's largely tosh. Americans have been the most productive people on earth, by virtue of invention and industry in a free economy. Naturally they have used wood, coal, oil, metals and the like. They have grown crops and eaten them. Why not? Would there be any merit in letting the trees die, fall and rot as they had been doing throughout the ages, or leaving the ore in the ground, or the land unused? American agriculture has been infinitely better, in respect of the permanent use of the land, than the agriculture of the medieval economy. As a matter of fact, really good farming developed with the development of America, with the institution of private property. It is true that coal and oil will presumably be used up in time; but only by their use in a free economy and with apparent lavishness could science advance to the point where fuels may be manufactured—which is now a practical possibility and an outcome of the age of industry. The trees the pioneers cut down would have been dead of old age before now. More are growing, and can grow. With those used, Americans built houses, and for the first time in the world's history they made comfortable houses, mastering the problem of heating and bringing in water for the ordinary domestic establishment. They built soundly, beautifully and conveniently. No "medieval craftsman" could compare with a capable American in handling material to a useful end and making it artistic quite incidentally. We are plumb tired of the continuous insinuation that this country

> was just a mistake. It was—and still is, in spite of the accumulated deadheads—the most wonderful country, with the most wonderful people and the happiest life, the world has ever seen—or will ever see again, if we let it go. Americans were not pampered; they worked. They were not wasteful; they made something.[54]

During the past two or three decades, American conservatives and libertarians have grown increasingly interested in their own history, and in Paterson's. Unfortunately, they are often interested only in general views of her political thought. Yet her political ideas were part of a broader vision of life, which she communicated with a complex organization of words and experience.

Her columns were written quickly, often in an hour or two on a Friday afternoon; but many of them are formal essays with the verbal complexity one sees in the passage just quoted. Colloquial terms and slang ("do-goods," "tosh," "plumb tired") are arranged in an intricate dance with solemn propositions; rhetorical questions alternate with personal observations; history is invoked by the mention of things that contemporary Americans ought to know but few of them see or feel ("for the first time in the world's history they made comfortable houses"); facts of life are stated as facts of life ("more are growing, and can grow"); generalizations are emphasized by antitheses ("Americans were not pampered; they worked"); three-fold emphasis is summoned at the right place ("soundly, beautifully and conveniently"); and the reader is told what to do about it all (don't "let it go"). The impression is that of a complex and vital spontaneity, the spontaneity with which Paterson marshals her rhetoric but also the spontaneity of American culture, the spontaneity that is also skill, skill that "masters the problem." It is the sense of a world that is open to all the patterns of human life.

This is the sense Paterson tries to communicate in her novels, the sense that also emerges in her letters and political arguments. One instance will illustrate. In 1940, Paterson commented on Robert Nathan's *Portrait of Jennie*, a novel about an aspiring artist who, from time to time, encounters a young woman who inhabits a different dimension. Inspired by these strange meetings, he becomes a great artist. Paterson interpreted the story as

> an imaginative presentation of the life one doesn't live, of the curious intimations and chance meetings which may come to nothing in fact, but which seem to have had a meaning none the less, far beyond that of many of the completed events, the obvious successes and tangible rewards. After all, every one meets thousands of persons in a life-

> time. One may very well fail to remember the very name of a person encountered daily for years. Yet a face seen only in passing, a voice heard once, an hour's conversation, or perhaps a short friendship interrupted by distance or by death, will remain in memory, with a strange significance attaching to it. Books also have peculiar properties for different individuals. There is no telling what odd volume may determine a destiny—or perhaps it doesn't, but it serves as a peg to hang the event on. We don't mean that books "influence" any one as they are commonly supposed to do, or that they exercise much moral or immoral influence; but a rather dull and conventional booklet of a missionary's reminiscences, read at a given moment, might, for example, set the spark to a latent tendency and ultimately contribute something to the making of an explorer. That is one reason why censorship seems to us intrinsically absurd. If anything is allowed in print at all, it will somehow defeat the censor. The only censor who did know what he must do to effect his pestilential purpose was the one—we forget who it was, he succeeded so thoroughly—who ordered the wholesale and total burning of the books.[55]

Left to themselves, to read what they want and do what they want, individual people create what today's libertarians call a "spontaneous order" out of the multitude of possibilities surrounding them. "There is no telling" what meanings they will find. Adventure, achievement, progress, romance, mystery, reflection on the mystery of oneself—all arise from the unlimited potential of individual life.

In another discussion of human possibilities, Paterson speaks of "something special and important to our times, a sense of the necessary diversity of life when we are threatened with regimentation and bureaucracy. All the ways of life are in it, and a recognition that they are ways, not ends; and that each has its own obscure end, beyond any definable satisfaction."[56] Life isn't politics or government programs; it is unplannable possibility. Its enemy is regimentation, coercive planning, force that blocks the paths and tries to restrict the possibilities. The function of government, as Paterson saw it, is always to halt, stop, destroy; and that is defensible, she thought, if what is destroyed is aggression and force itself. But everything beyond that is a way of death.

The God of the Machine

It was mainly because of Paterson's writings in the *Herald Tribune* that American conservatives adopted the saying, "Isabel Paterson is always right."[57] At the beginning of the 1940s, however, she was working on a more theoretical statement of her ideas. She was inspired by the idea of the Founding Fathers as literal "framers" of a constitutional order—and, because their framing could accommodate the utmost extent of human liberty, of an authentic manner of living in the world. She used the architectural concept as one of the two main pillars of her own large framing of ideas, the theory of politics and history embodied in *The God of the Machine* (1943).

The book analyzes the American constitutional system as a structure deriving its strength from the way in which the "thrust" of each part is resisted by the other parts. The framers never intended the political system to move or "progress": to the contrary; they intended it to stay put, to form an enduring shelter for the liberties of individual people. Paterson's idea resembles the familiar "checks and balances" image of the Constitution, but she provided it with many original extensions and applications. Some of the applications were historical, such as her analysis of the mid-nineteenth-century crisis of the Union as resulting from an imbalance of "thrusts," South against North, that were permitted by the defect in the structure, which was slavery. Other applications were unusual versions of political theory, such as Paterson's idea that every political structure needs a resistant "base." In the constitutional system, the base is formed by a wide distribution of local political bodies—the states and smaller units—that offer resistance to the central edifice of the federal government. One essential form of resistance is the "mass veto" exercised by people qualified to vote because they hold property in the several states. According to Paterson, the early federal structure, in which virtually all states had property qualifications for voting, provided more stability than the current one, which gives votes to everyone in the "dislocated mass" of a mobile population.[58]

Paterson's idea of suffrage, which like many of her other ideas is simultaneously "reactionary" and "radical," is part of a larger theory encouraged by her reading of the *Federalist* Papers, where a sharp distinction is made between a democracy and a republic. She was also mindful of dictatorships, such as Nazi Germany, that were "wanted" by their people: "The fact that they want it doesn't make it all right; it only puts those who accepted it in wrong."[59] The voice of the people was not the voice of God. Voting must not be arbitrarily limited by race, gender, or social class; only a little real property should suffice to enfranchise a person. But voting must not be used to destroy the structure of liberty it exists to serve, with the excuse that the democratic populace is getting what it wants.

The second conceptual pillar of *The God of the Machine* derives not from architecture but from electrical engineering. She pictures human societies as "circuits" of production and exchange, along which human energy is routed and put to use. The earliest circuits involved the trading of goods from hand to hand; later, the circuitry was expanded by the use of money and protected by laws and customs that guarded the mechanism from force and fraud. When such institutions are based on the idea of individual right—the right to do what one wants, so long as one allows others to do the same—they allow individuals to invest securely at great distances of space and time. New resources are identified; new technology is developed and applied; new wealth is generated. The circuit embraces the globe. But when government—which is an "end appliance," using energy but not producing it—begins to channel energy for purposes other than the protection of production and exchange, the energy is "short circuited." There is a gradual "leakage" or contraction of the circuit, or a revolutionary "explosion" that destroys it.

Paterson finds many useful applications of the "circuit" idea and many examples of economic and political circuitry, reaching back to the Romans and Carthaginians and ahead to the dynamic economy of the future. She was not surprised by the failure of the Nazi attempt at rewiring Europe, and she would not have been surprised by the final blowout of the Soviet Union. But despite the attention she pays to economic and political machinery, her emphasis is always on the constructive power of human beings, who are *not* machines: "a machine economy cannot run on a mechanistic philosophy." The "dynamo" of the economic machine is the individual human mind.[60]

In her own day, many conservative and libertarian intellectuals failed to appreciate, or perhaps to understand, her engineering "metaphors," as they called them, or to see their significance to her arguments for limited government. But they found other things to appreciate in *The God of the Machine*—chapters on regulation of the economy, on the American educational system, on the effects of statist humanitarianism, on the evils of slavery, on sound money, and on other topics. The book did not sell as well as Paterson wished, but it sold fairly well for the kind of book it was. It touched an emerging audience on the intellectual right, and it won many intellectual sympathizers.

Survival

In 1940, Paterson published an eighth novel, *If It Prove Fair Weather*, the story of a failed romance. The book had a moderate success, but it must have disappointed her general audience, which by now expected her to write about politics, not love. She would write one more novel,

Joyous Gard. Completed in 1958, it is in some ways her most interesting work of fiction. Partly a modernization of medieval romance, partly a study of the interior life of a person much like herself, partly an analysis of her regrets and feelings of displacement, partly an idealized vision of the triumph of life, it is a beautiful and touching book, quite unsuited, as prospective publishers were pleased to tell her, to the conditions of the 1950s.[61] For now, it remains in manuscript.

Paterson's last column was published on January 30, 1949. Management of the *Herald Tribune,* a "Republican" paper, had been modern-liberal for a long time, and far-leftists had proliferated on the staff. During the second half of 1943, the length of Paterson's columns had been severely cut; now she herself was cut—"retired" on a tiny pension, from which subtractions were made for the Social Security payments she refused to collect. She didn't believe in government-enforced "insurance."

From 1952 to 1959, she lived on a farm she had purchased near Princeton, New Jersey. Modest investments supported her in modest comfort. She rose when she wanted, read what she wanted, wrote what she wanted. She corresponded with people who appreciated her work, some of whom became leaders of the conservative and libertarian movements. She restored some friendships, lost others. When William F. Buckley, Jr. founded *National Review* (1955), the most influential journal of modern conservatism, she rejected his offer to pay for regular contributions but contributed several long articles anyway. She left his orbit when he insisted on relatively slight edits of an article he had commissioned (pages 79–93, below). In the late 1940s she had quarreled with her disciple Ayn Rand over a number of issues, most notably belief in God: Rand was an atheist, Paterson a self-labeled deist whose speculations went considerably beyond the chilly assumptions of ordinary deists. Paterson discusses these conflicts in a letter in this volume (pages 196–201).

One friend she did not lose was Muriel Hall, a young mother working in the research department of the Time Inc. magazine empire. Muriel and her family—her husband Ted, also a journalist, and their two young children—became the center of Paterson's interest in people. In late 1959, when Paterson was between houses (she had sold her farm but was waiting for a tenant to move out of a house she owned in Greenwich, Connecticut, so she could occupy it herself), the Halls insisted that she sojourn with them in their large old house in Montclair, New Jersey. It was there she died on January 10, 1961. She is buried in Muriel's family plot at St. Mary's Episcopal Church, Burlington, New Jersey.

After Paterson's death, Muriel collected and preserved her papers and arranged for the republication of *The God of the Machine.*[62] In the late 1980s, when the editor of this volume arrived to do research, Muriel shared with him her records, her memories, and something of her enormous strength of personality. One result was a new edition of *The God of the Machine*; another was a biography of Paterson, published one day after Muriel's death on July 13, 2004.[63] Since then, discussions of Paterson have multiplied in print and especially in the electronic media—means of communication that closely approximate Paterson's notion of the "long circuit" to which anyone can "hook up."

Paterson said of herself: "The only thing we can be sure of is that whatever the majority thinks it will not be what we think." That was true during her lifetime, but today another of her statements seems more appropriate: "Nobody knows the future; but the past has generally belonged to those who went against the tide, to those who acted as if they had free will, and who cared more for freedom than for 'belonging.'"[64] Libertarian ideas are now common currency in America's political marketplace, and interest in Paterson herself continues to grow. Clearly, people don't have to agree with all, or even most, of her ideas to admire her as an exponent of the idea that "people are not gadgets nor bundles of odds and ends; they have minds and souls of unreckonable potentiality, and the most important thing in the world is for that fact to be recognized, so they won't allow themselves to be packed into containers and labeled for a given use."[65]

This selected edition of Paterson's writing is a response to many requests for publication of works long out of print, or never before printed. Selection has been difficult, because Paterson wrote so much, on so many topics, in so many moods, and to such a consistently high standard. The best an editor can do is to offer some of her words on some of the themes she favored, words that illustrate some features of her accomplishment, and of herself. That is at least a start.

Notes

1. Anon., "'Books' Covers the World of Books," *Publisher's Weekly* (September 30, 1939) 1341.
2. Paterson, "Turns with a Bookworm" (hereafter referred to as "Turns"), *New York Herald Tribune "Books,"* July 10, 1932.
3. Stephen Cox, *The Woman and the Dynamo* (New Brunswick NJ: Transaction Publishers, 2004) 9–10. Hereafter abbreviated as WD. This is the Introduction's main source of information on Paterson's life.
4. Paterson, "Turns," July 24, 1932.

5. Burton Rascoe, *We Were Interrupted* (Garden City, NY: Doubleday, 1947) 140–43; "Turns," February 13, 1938.
6. "Turns," March 6, 1932.
7. "Turns," December 29, 1940; October 1, 1933; October 16, 1932.
8. "Turns," January 27, 1935.
9. "Turns," November 12, 1933; June 12, 1933; May 13, 1934.
10. Paterson, review of William Plomer, *Cecil Rhodes*, *"Books,"* May 21, 1933; see below, page 17.
11. "Turns," April 25, 1937; January 24, 1937.
12. "Turns," December 16, 1934. Said of Rexford Guy Tugwell, a member of Franklin Roosevelt's "brain trust."
13. "Turns," July 4, 1943; June 13, 1937.
14. Paterson, review of *The Laurels Are Cut Down*, by Archie Binns, *"Books,"* April 18, 1937; "Turns," June 11, 1939.
15. "Turns," January 10, 1943; July 16, 1939.
16. "Turns," November 17, 1940; November 22, 1936.
17. "Turns," November 26, 1939; Paterson, review of *Family Album*, by Humphrey Pakington, *"Books,"* August 13, 1939.
18. "Turns," December 13, 1936; December 31, 1939.
19. Paterson, review of *Pamela's Daughters*, by Robert Palfrey Utter and Gwendolyn Bridges Needham, *"Books,"* November 29, 1936.
20. "Turns," March 29, 1942.
21. "Turns," December 21, 1941.
22. "Turns," April 5, 1936.
23. "Turns," June 16, 1940.
24. "Turns," February 16, 1936.
25. "Turns," March 22, 1942.
26. "Turns," December 14, 1941; September 4, 1938.
27. Paterson, review of Maude Meagher, *The Green Scamander*, *"Books,"* April 2, 1933; "Turns," January 21, 1940.
28. "Turns," September 20, 1931.
29. Paterson to Garreta Busey, undated [October 1931].
30. "Turns," July 5, 1931. Paterson moved into her house in Stamford in spring, 1934 ("Turns," May 13, 1934).
31. "Turns," October 26, 1941.
32. Paterson, *The God of the Machine* (hereafter referred to as GM) (New Brunswick NJ: Transaction Publishers, 2004) 69–70.
33. Paterson, *The Singing Season: A Romance of Old Spain* (New York: Boni and Liveright, 1924) 33.
34. "Turns," May 23, 1943.
35. "Turns," February 21, 1943.
36. "Turns," October 27, 1935.
37. "Turns," February 16, 1936.
38. "Turns," May 7, 1939.
39. "Turns," June 16, 1940.
40. "Turns," November 27, 1932.
41. "Turns," March 5, 1933. Paterson had discussed her dislike for Roosevelt as well as Hoover in a letter to Garreta Busey, undated [late November 1932–early December 1932].

42. "Turns," January 5, 1936.
43. "Turns," November 22, 1936. Paterson took this opportunity to prophesy that four years later, Roosevelt would seek a third term.
44. "Turns," June 30, 1935; March 8, 1936; March 17, 1940.
45. "Turns," October 11, 1942; April 28, 1935. Anticipating by many years Ayn Rand's idea of romantic realism and rationalism, Paterson wrote, "Here the great romantic-rational vision took form; and it's been a good life, even though a hard one" ("Turns," February 14, 1932).
46. "Turns," February 23, 1941.
47. "Turns," February 26, 1933; Paterson, review of Joan Haslip, *Lady Hester Stanhope, "Books,"* June 28, 1936; review of *The Memoirs of the Marquise de la Rochejacquelein*, ed. Cecil Biggane, *"Books,"* April 22, 1934.
48. "Turns," March 19, 1939.
49. "Turns," July 19, 1942.
50. "Turns," September 29, 1940.
51. GM 69–70; Paterson, review of Morley Callaghan, *Such Is My Beloved, "Books,"* February 18, 1934.
52. "Turns," February 16, 1936; November 24, 1940.
53. "Turns," December 3, 1939. Peattie (1898–1964), a renowned naturalist, published *Flowering Earth* in 1939.
54. "Turns," February 15, 1942.
55. "Turns," January 28, 1940. Robert Nathan (1894–1985), remarkable for his wry, speculative fiction, received many good notices from Paterson. *Portrait of Jennie* (1940) was made into a notable film by the same name (1948).
56. "Turns," July 16, 1933.
57. Ayn Rand to Isabel Paterson, July 26, 1945, *Letters of Ayn Rand*, ed. Michael S. Berliner (New York: Dutton, 1995) 176; Whittaker Chambers to William F. Buckley, Jr., December 16, 1954, *Odyssey of a Friend: Whittaker Chambers' Letters to William F. Buckley, Jr., 1954–1961*, ed. William F. Buckley, Jr. (New York: Putnam's, 1969) 94. Chambers (American conservative writer, 1901–1961) indicated that he did *not* agree with the common saying.
58. See GM at, for instance, 122, 124, 138–39, 159–60.
59. *The Federalist*, No. 10; "Turns," February 21, 1943.
60. GM 156, 130.
61. R. T. Bond to Paterson, September 10, 1958.
62. Caldwell ID: Caxton, 1964.
63. GM (1993); WD (2004). Muriel Hall read and thoroughly discussed the biography before its publication. For the story of Muriel Hall, see Stephen Cox, "Muriel Hall, R. I. P.," *Liberty* 18 (October 2004) 21–22; and "Representing Isabel Paterson," *American Literary History* 17.2 (2005) 244–58.
64. "Turns," November 22, 1936; February 2, 1941.
65. "Turns," June 15, 1941.

A Note on the Text

Paterson's text has been reproduced as she wrote it, with the following exceptions:

> Editorial interpolations appear in square brackets.
>
> Obvious typographical errors are, for the most part, silently corrected.
>
> In general, current conventions are used in italicizing or quoting titles and in the choice of single or double quotation marks. Paterson usually conformed to current American usage about quotations, but she seldom used italics for book titles. The *Herald Tribune* house style was to put them in quotation marks. In her correspondence, virtually all of which is typed, she also preferred quotation marks, so she could avoid going back to underline.
>
> Paterson's *Herald Tribune* columns have spaced periods between sentences, to lighten the appearance of the long blocks of small type in which the columns are set. Paterson said that her "polka dots" were derived from poet and editor William Rose Benét: "though his were asterisks, which are much more swell" ("Turns," February 10, 1929). The current edition does not reproduce this feature, but it does reproduce all spaced periods used by Paterson for other purposes, in print or typescript.
>
> Editorial omissions from Paterson's writing are indicated by the symbol >>, except in the introduction and notes, where ordinary marks of ellipsis (. . .) are used. The >> mark appears for omissions at any point in Paterson's letters and for any internal omissions in other material.
>
> Many titles of the essays and reviews included here are provided by the editor. Paterson's columns did not have individual titles, and the titles of her reviews are usually simple journalistic signposts, not certain to have originated with her. Original titles, if different from those editorially supplied, appear at the end of selections.

Paterson made few corrections in her typing, but whenever words that she crossed out are interesting in some way, they are reproduced in footnotes.

Sources of previously published material appear at the end of each selection. Grateful acknowledgment is made in regard to the following manuscript material:

> Isabel Paterson letters to Lillian Fischer. Manuscripts and Archives Division. The New York Public Library. Astor, Lenox, and Tilden Foundations.

> Isabel Paterson letters to Burton Rascoe. Rare Book and Manuscript Library. University of Pennsylvania.

Grateful appreciation is expressed to the repository of the Isabel Paterson Papers, the Herbert Hoover Presidential Library and Museum, West Branch, Iowa, for permission to publish Paterson's correspondence and other work in manuscript. Unless otherwise indicated, the Isabel Paterson Papers provided the texts used here.

Abbreviations and References

"Books": *New York Herald Tribune "Books,"* the literary supplement of the *Herald Tribune.*

GM: Isabel Paterson, *The God of the Machine,* Transaction Publishers, 1993.

"Turns": Paterson's column in *New York Herald Tribune "Books."*

WD: Stephen Cox, *The Woman and the Dynamo: Isabel Paterson and the Idea of America,* Transaction Publishers, 2004.

Asterisks refer the reader to the list of People Mentioned, which provides information about names better known to Paterson's original audience than to her current one. This list supplements information provided in notes on specific passages.

People Mentioned

John Dalberg-Acton, 1st Baron Acton (1834–1902): English historian; Roman Catholic exponent of liberalism in church and society.

Alexander Agassiz (1835–1910): Swiss American marine zoologist and mining engineer.

Amos Bronson Alcott (1799–1888): New England transcendentalist, educationist, reformer, and experimenter with ideas; father of novelist Louisa May Alcott (1832–1888).

Richard Aldington (1892–1962): English novelist, poet, and biographer.

Maxwell Aley (1889–1953): American journalist and editor.

Thomas Aquinas (1225–1274): seminal Roman Catholic philosopher and theologian.

Guillaume Sylvan Casimir Phiquepal d'Arusmont (died c. 1855): French educational reformer and husband of Frances Wright.

Mary Austin (1868–1934): writer of fiction and nonfiction, especially about the American Southwest.

Newton D. Baker (1871–1937): American secretary of war (1916–1921).

Mikhail Bakunin (1814–1876): Russian anarchist.

Angelica Balabanoff (1878–1965): Russian Bolshevik and rebel against Bolshevism; lifelong proponent of various socialist movements.

Earle H. Balch (c. 1894–1977): executive vice president (1932–1947) of G. P. Putnam's Sons, publishers of Paterson's *The God of the Machine*; later a cultural attaché for the US State Department.

Clive Bell (1881–1964): English art critic.

William Rose Benét (1886–1950): American poet and editor; founder of the *Saturday Review of Literature*.

Arnold Bennett (1867–1931): English novelist.

William E. Borah (1865–1940): Republican senator from Idaho (1912–1940); a leader of Western progressivism.

Gutzon Borglum (1867–1941): American sculptor, most noted for his work on Mt. Rushmore.

James Boswell (1740–1795): Scottish author of *The Life of Samuel Johnson* (1791).

Florence Wattles Bowers (c. 1888–1947): friend of Paterson; publicity director for E. P. Dutton, publishers; socialist activist and onetime director of the socialist Rand School of Social Science.

Kay Boyle (1902–1992): American novelist; participant in expatriate and bohemian culture and leftist political movements.

Braxton Bragg (1817–1876): Confederate general.

Berton Braley (1882–1966): American reporter and short-story writer but best known as a maker of popular verses, often extolling work, modern industry, and the capitalist system.

William Cowper Brann (1855–1898): owner and editor of *The Iconoclast* (Waco, Texas), specializing in abuse of persons disliked by Brann.

Aristide Briand (1862–1932): several times prime minister of France.

Henry Herschel Brickell (1889–1952): columnist and editor.

Courtney C. Brown (1904–1990): statistical economist, director of corporations, dean of the Graduate School of Business at Columbia University (1954–1969).

John Brown (1800–1859): abolitionist who in 1859 attacked the federal armory at Harpers Ferry, Virginia, in an attempt to start a slave rebellion.

William Jennings Bryan (1860–1925): Progressive politician; Democratic nominee for president in 1896, 1900, and 1908; secretary of state under Woodrow Wilson; advocate of "free silver" and other populist and reformist causes.

William F. Buckley, Jr. (1925–2008): leading American conservative intellectual; essayist and novelist; founder of *National Review* (1955).

Buffalo Bill (William Frederick Cody; 1846–1917): Western adventurer and impresario of Buffalo Bill's Wild West Show, which toured America and Europe.

Edmund Burke (1729–1797): Irish statesman and philosopher; an intellectual founder of conservatism.

Garreta Busey (1893–1976): associate of Paterson at *Herald Tribune "Books"*; returned (c. 1928) to her hometown, Urbana, Illinois, where for many years she taught English at the University of Illinois.

James Branch Cabell (1879–1958): American novelist and creator of satirical-mythological romances.

Walter S. Carpenter, Jr. (1888–1976): career executive with the du Pont company; president (1940–1948); chairman of the board (1948–1962).

Alexis Carrel (1873–1944): French scientist and surgeon; recipient of the Nobel Prize (1912).

Robert Stewart, Viscount Castlereagh (1769–1822): British foreign secretary and leader of the House of Commons (1812–1822).

Willa Cather (1873–1947): major American novelist.

John Catron (1786–1865): associate justice, United States Supreme Court (1837–1865), an appointee of President Jackson; sided with the Union when his state (Tennessee) seceded.

Houston Stewart Chamberlain (1855–1927): English writer, known for his racial theories.

John Chamberlain (1903–1995): American literary critic and friend of Paterson, who influenced his transition from leftist to conservative and libertarian views.

Stuart Chase (1888–1985): friend of Paterson in the early 1930s; writer on social and economic subjects; exponent of "technocracy"; author of *A New Dea*l (1932).

Emily Clark (Balch) (c. 1890–1953): friend of Paterson; author; co-founder of *The Reviewer* (1921), which encouraged the "Southern literary renaissance"; wealthy widow of artist and explorer Edwin Swift Balch (1856–1927).

Alta May Coleman (died 1931): press agent for theatrical companies; Paterson's best friend during the 1920s.

Mary and Padraic Colum (1884–1957 and 1881–1972, married 1912): Irish writers and important figures in the Irish Literary Revival; friends of Paterson.

J. Gordon Coogler (1865–1901): South Carolina poet used by critic H. L. Mencken to exemplify the South's lack of culture.

Charles Alfred Coulson (1910–1974): prominent British mathematician and chemist; exponent of Christian belief.

Noel Coward (1899–1973): British playwright, composer, and actor.

Jasper Elliot Crane (1881–1969): vice president of the du Pont company; supporter of the libertarian Foundation for Economic Education (see "Leonard E. Read," below).

Kyle Crichton (1896–1960): author, editor at *Scribner's* and *Collier's* magazines, and writer (under the name Robert Forsythe) for the communist *New Masses*.

Oliver Cromwell (1599–1658): leader of Parliamentary armies during the English Civil Wars; lord protector of England (1653–1658).

John Crosby (1912–1991): American radio and television critic.

Will Cuppy (1884–1949): humorist and "mystery and adventure" columnist for the *New York Herald Tribune*; friend and literary protégé of Paterson.

Benjamin Robbins Curtis (1809–1874): associate justice, United States Supreme Court (1851–1857), an appointee of President Fillmore; resigned from the Court in the wake of the Dred Scott decision, on which he dissented.

Ethel M. Dell (1881–1939): English author of popular romance novels.

René Descartes (1596–1650): French mathematician and philosopher.

John Dewey (1859–1952): American philosopher and educationist.

William S. Dix (1910–1978): university librarian, Princeton University (1953–1975).

John Dos Passos (1896–1970): avant-garde American novelist. A leading literary leftist in the 1930s, he afterward became a conservative.

Theodore Dreiser (1871–1945): prominent American novelist.

Gustav Eckstein (1890–1981): American medical doctor and psychological researcher; prominent writer and intellectual.

Jonathan Edwards (1703–1758): New England preacher; Calvinist theologian.

Harvey Fergusson (1890–1971): novelist, most noted for his writing on the American West.

Lillian Toffelmire Fischer (Farley) (1896–1987): showgirl; fashion model; later Paris editor of *Harper's Bazaar*.

Nathan Bedford Forrest (1821–1877): Confederate general.

Fern Forrester (Shay) (d.1931): artist and book illustrator; first wife of Frank Shay, bookseller.

Anatole France (1844–1924): French novelist; recipient of the Nobel Prize (1921).

John Galsworthy (1867–1933): British novelist; recipient of the Nobel Prize (1932).

Lewis Gannett (1891–1966): book reviewer for the *New York Herald Tribune* and other journals.

Grace George (1879–1961): American stage actress.

Henry George (1839–1897): radical American economist; author of *Progress and Poverty* (1879) and advocate of the Single Tax.

Edward Gibbon (1737–1794): author of *The Decline and Fall of the Roman Empire* (1776–1789).

Etienne Gilson (1884–1978): French philosopher; historian of medieval and Roman Catholic philosophy.

Ellen Glasgow (1873–1945): American novelist.

Henry Grattan (1746–1820): Irish statesman; proponent of Catholic emancipation and an Irish parliament.

Horace Greeley (1811–1872): founder and editor of the *New York Tribune*; Democratic candidate for president in 1872.

Crawford H. Greenewalt (1902–1993): chemist; president of E. I. du Pont de Nemours Co. (1948–1962), chairman of the board (1962–1967); authority on hummingbirds.

Isabella Augusta, Lady Gregory (1852–1932): Irish writer; patron of the Irish Literary Revival.

Edward Matson (Ted) Hall (1921–2003): journalist and friend of Paterson; husband of Muriel Hall.

Muriel Welles Hall (1921–2004): journalist and researcher for *Life* and other publications; wife of Edward Hall; friend of Paterson and executor of her estate.

Rebecca Hall (Metzger) (1947–): daughter of Edward and Muriel Hall.

Thomas Hall (1956–): son of Edward and Muriel Hall.

Henry Hazlitt (1894–1993): American economic journalist and literary editor, influential especially among conservatives and libertarians.

William Randolph Hearst (1863–1951): American newspaper magnate.

Heinrich Heine (1797–1856): German poet and essayist.

Robert Selph Henry (1889–1970): vice president for public relations, Association of American Railroads; historian, especially of the 1840–1880 era.

Joseph Hergesheimer (1880–1954): American novelist, much acclaimed in the 1920s.

Granville Hicks (1901–1982): influential literary critic; exponent of communism and editor of *The New Masses,* later anti-Marxist college teacher and figure in publishing.

Richard Hofstadter (1916–1970): prominent American historian.

Elisabeth Sanxay Holding (1889–1955): novelist, chiefly of "hard-boiled" detective stories; the person to whom Paterson dedicated *Never Ask the End,* "For Her Long-Suffering Sympathy."

Joseph Maunsell Hone (1882–1959): Irish publisher, writer, and editor.

Harry Hopkins (1890–1946): close advisor and aide of Franklin Roosevelt.

Peggy Hopkins (Joyce) (1893–1957): actress, adventurer, and celebrity, noted for marriages and affairs with wealthy men.

Cordell Hull (1871–1955): United States secretary of state (1933–1944).

Aldous Huxley (1894–1963): English novelist.

Thomas Henry Huxley (1825–1895): English scientist and advocate of Darwinism.

John Jay (1745–1829): jurist and diplomat; first chief justice of the United States (1789–1795); an author of the *Federalist* Papers (1787–1788).

James Hopwood Jeans (1877–1946): English physicist and contributor to modern debates on cosmology.

Oakley Johnson (1890–1976): American communist activist.

Samuel Johnson, often called Dr. Johnson (1709–1784): English poet, lexicographer, essayist, and conversationalist; subject of James Boswell's celebrated *Life*.

George Kennan (1845–1924): American journalist and explorer (most notably in the Russian empire). He attacked both tsarism and Bolshevism.

Nikita Khrushchev (1894–1971): premier of the Soviet Union (1958–1964).

Frol R. Kozlov (1908–1965): first deputy chairman of the Soviet Council of Ministers, sometimes regarded as the likely heir of Khrushchev; visited many places in America in June and July 1959.

Thomas W. Lamont (1870–1948): partner in the banking house of J. P. Morgan & Co.; advisor of presidents; represented the United States Treasury at the Paris Peace Conference after World War I; involved in the Dawes Plan (1924) and the Young Plan (1929)—failed attempts to settle the problem of German war reparations—and in the lending of money to Mussolini; active philanthropist; father of Corliss Lamont (1902–1995), a communist writer.

David Herbert Lawrence (1885–1930): English novelist and poet, noted for his explorations of sexuality.

Edward Lear (1812–1888): English artist and comic poet.

Pierre Lecomte du Noüy, often spelled du Nouy (1883–1947): prominent French biophysicist and admirer of Paterson; author of *Human Destiny* (1947); husband of Mary Lecomte du Noüy (1891–1974), his biographer (1955).

Isaac Don Levine (1892–1981): Russian American journalist, most commonly remembered as an opponent of communism.

Sinclair Lewis (1885–1951): American satirical novelist; recipient of the Nobel Prize (1930).

Norman Lindsay (1879–1969): Australian artist and novelist.

James Linen (1912–1988): advertising manager for *Life*, later publisher of *Time*; major collector of toy soldiers.

Walter Lippmann (1889–1974): influential commentator on American politics and theorist of communication in modern society; advisor of presidents and shaper of elite opinion.

John Locke (1632–1704): English philosopher; influential theorist of individual rights and liberty and of limited government.

Huey Long (1893–1935): populist politician; governor of Louisiana (1928–1932); United States senator (1932–1935).

Frederick Lonsdale (1881–1954): English playwright, author of successful musicals and comedies.

Robert Morss Lovett (1870–1956): academic and journalist; associate editor of *The New Republic* (1921–1940); secretary and acting governor of the Virgin Islands in the early 1940s, until dismissed for associations with communism.

Henry R. Luce (1898–1967): publisher of *Time*, *Life*, and other journals.

Maurice Maeterlinck (1862–1949): Belgian playwright.

Curzio Malaparte (1898–1957): Italian journalist and fiction writer; once a fascist, he became a communist.

Clarence E. Manion (1896–1979): dean of the Law School at the University of Notre Dame (1941–1952).

Marie, Grand Duchess of Russia (1890–1958): granddaughter of Tsar Alexander II; princess of Sweden (1908–1914); exile and autobiographer.

Samuel S. Marquis (1866–1948): dean of St. Paul's Episcopal Cathedral, Detroit; pastor and friend of Henry Ford.

John Marshall (1755–1835): chief justice of the United States (1801–1835).

Lenore Guinzberg Marshall (1899–1971): American author and editor.

Robert Marshall (1901–1939): prominent American forester, conservationist, and socialist activist; explorer and student of Alaska.

Guy de Maupassant (1850–1893): French artist of the short story.

Helen Davies McGlade: Boston bookseller.

John McLaren (1942–2002): cousin of Edward and Muriel Hall, informally adopted by them.

John McLean (1785–1861): associate justice, United States Supreme Court (1829–1861), an appointee of President Jackson; dissenter in the Dred Scott case.

Bruce McRae (1867–1927): British American stage and film actor.

Herman Lee Meader (1874–1930): American writer, architect, and host of elaborate parties.

Henry Louis Mencken (1880–1956): influential critic of American literature and culture.

Robert Andrews Millikan (1868–1953): American physicist; Nobel laureate (1923); shaper of the California Institute of Technology; believer in the complementary relationship of religion and science.

George Monk (1608–1670): English general who enabled monarchy to be restored in 1660.

George Moore (1852–1933): Irish poet and novelist.

Hannah More (1745–1833): English poet, essayist, philanthropist, and Christian moralist; once a writer of great popularity and influence.

Thomas More (1478–1535): chancellor of England under Henry VIII; defender of Roman Catholicism; author of *Utopia*.

John Pierpont Morgan (1837–1913): leading American banker.

Christopher Morley (1890–1957): American author of works in many genres, including poetry, journalism, essays, and novels.

Horatio Nelson, 1st Viscount Nelson (1758–1805): British naval hero of the wars against Napoleon.

Hoffman Nickerson (1888–1965): American military historian.

John O'Leary (1830–1907): Irish nationalist leader.

Robert Owen (1771–1858): British industrialist and social theorist; founder of a utopian colony at New Harmony, Indiana. His son Robert Dale Owen (1807–1860) was an American politician and social reformer.

Howard Madison Parshley (1884–1953): American zoologist; writer on reproduction and sexuality.

Blaise Pascal (1623–1662): French philosopher and mathematician.

Dr. Charles Griffin Pease (1854–1941): American dentist and homeopathic physician; anti-tobacco zealot and agitator for anti-tobacco laws.

Alice Jane Grey Perkins (1865–1948): private-school history teacher; a socially well-placed American, engaged in the women's suffrage movement in the United States and England.

Josephine Pinckney (1895–1957): American novelist and poet, active in preservationist causes.

William Plomer, pronounced "Ploomer" (1903–1973): South African author in many genres.

Praxiteles (4th century B.C.): Greek sculptor.

Marcel Proust (1871–1922): French novelist, author of *À la recherche du temps perdu* (1913–1927).

Bonnie Prudden (1914–2011): American physical fitness activist and vendor of exercise programs; she inspired the formation of the President's Council on Youth Fitness.

James Putnam: editor and executive with the Macmillan publishing company.

Burton Rascoe (1892–1957): editor and literary critic; friend of Paterson; Paterson's department head at the *New York Tribune* (1922–1924); married (1913) to Hazel Luke.

Leonard E. Read (1898–1983): general manager of the Los Angeles Chamber of Commerce; the creator, with Henry Hazlitt, of the Foundation for Economic Education (1946), a libertarian research and advocacy organization.

James B. Reston (1909–1995): Scottish American journalist, for many years an eminent figure at the *New York Times*.

Quentin Reynolds (1902–1965): American journalist and foreign correspondent.

Cecil Rhodes (1853–1902): leader of British imperialism in southern Africa.

Nathaniel (Nat) Roberts (1880–1930): American engineer; official of Nippon Electric Company in Tokyo; technical director for Bell Telephone in Europe; friend and romantic interest of Paterson.

William E. (Bill) Robinson (1900–1969): American newspaper executive; president and chairman of the board of Coca-Cola; friend of President Eisenhower.

Bertrand Russell, 3rd Earl Russell (1872–1970): prominent British philosopher.

John Rustgard (1863–1950): Norwegian American lawyer; attorney general of Alaska Territory (1920–1933); later a writer on economics and political economy.

Dred Scott (c. 1799–1858): slave who sued for his freedom, initiating a case decided by the United States Supreme Court in 1857. Denied freedom by the court, he received it from an owner who opposed slavery.

Evelyn Scott (1893–1963): American novelist, poet, and autobiographer.

George Bernard Shaw (1856–1950): leading British playwright and advocate of socialism.

Stuart Pratt Sherman (1881–1926): prominent American literary critic; Paterson's department head at *Herald Tribune "Books"* (1924–1926).

William Tecumseh Sherman (1820–1891): Union general who devastated the South on his march from Atlanta to the sea.

Nevil Shute, full name Nevil Shute Norway (1899–1960): British pilot, engineer, and novelist.

Upton Sinclair (1878–1968): novelist and exponent of socialist causes; unsuccessful Democratic Party nominee for governor of California (1934) on the EPIC (End Poverty in California) platform.

Edmund Ware Sinnott (1888–1968): distinguished American botanist; professor and dean at Yale.

Alfred Emanuel (Al) Smith (1873–1944): governor of New York (1919–1920, 1923–1928); Democratic nominee for president (1928); opponent of Prohibition; representative of the conservative wing of the Democratic Party.

Claire Spencer (1895–1987): Scottish American novelist.

Oswald Spengler (1880–1936): German philosopher of history; author of *The Decline of the West* (1918).

Lawrence Stallings (1894–1968): American playwright, novelist, and critic.

Lincoln Steffens (1866–1936): American political journalist and "muckraker" of the Progressive era. His *Autobiography* (1931) flatters both Italian fascism and Russian communism.

Alexander H. Stephens (1812–1883): member of Congress, governor of Georgia, and vice president of the Confederate States of America; prominent intellectual defender of the right of secession.

Benjamin Stolberg (1891–1951): editor, columnist, and journalist specializing in labor issues.

John Strachey (1901–1963): English politician and writer; supporter of communism in the 1930s.

Algernon Charles Swinburne (1837–1909): English poet, associated with flamboyant post-Romanticism and "decadence."

John Millington Synge (1871–1909): Irish playwright.

Roger B. Taney, pronounced "TAWN-ee" (1777–1864): American secretary of war (1831), attorney general (1831–1833), and secretary of the treasury (1833–1834); chief justice of the United States (1836–1864).

Tomás de Torquemada (1420–1498): grand inquisitor of Spain.

George Macaulay Trevelyan (1876–1962): comprehensive British historian.

Benjamin Ricketson Tucker (1854–1939): American anarchist and publisher of the journal *Liberty*.

Rexford Guy Tugwell (1891–1979): economist, academic, member of Franklin Roosevelt's "brain trust," and governor of Puerto Rico; tireless advocate of government social planning.

Doris Ulmann (1882–1934): noted American photographer; friend of Paterson.

Mary Heaton Vorse (1874–1966): American journalist and activist of the Left.

Henry Wallace (1888–1965): United States secretary of agriculture (1933–1940); vice president (1941–1945); secretary of commerce (1945–1946); presidential candidate of the Progressive Party (1948).

Horace Walpole (1717–1797): English historian and epistolary artist.

Mary Augusta (Mrs. Humphry) Ward (1851–1920): well-connected and popular British novelist and essayist on religious and political subjects.

James M. Wayne (1790–1867): associate justice, United States Supreme Court (1835–1867), an appointee of President Jackson. A Georgian, Wayne sided with the Union in the Civil War.

Arthur Wellesley, 1st Duke of Wellington (1769–1852): British general who defeated Napoleon at Waterloo; twice Prime Minister.

H. G. Wells (1866–1946): British novelist and exponent of socialism and social planning.

George Frisbie Whicher (1889–1954): writer on history and literary history.

Emerson Whithorne (1884–1958): American pianist and composer, prominent in the pre–World War II period.

Eli Whitney (1765–1825): inventor of the cotton gin.

Wendell Willkie (1892–1944): attorney, businessman, and Republican nominee for president (1940).

Edmund Wilson (1895–1972): prominent American literary critic.

Theresa Wolfson (1897–1972): American labor economist and professor at Brooklyn College.

Virginia Woolf (1882–1941): English novelist and essayist.

Frances Wright (1795–1852): Scottish writer and reformer, active in America.

William Butler Yeats (1865–1939): preeminent Irish poet.

Part I

Essays and Reviews

1

The True Individualist: Thoreau

It is significant of Thoreau's genius that among writers of permanent value he loses least by brevity of treatment, so long as it goes to the point. The appropriate work of scholarship, admirably exemplified in this small volume, is that of selection rather than accumulation. Thoreau spent his life trying to strip off superfluities, as if to discover what would be left; should it not be the man himself? That is his final title to fame, for on the whole he succeeded. Singularly, though no one could claim intimacy with him while he lived—"as for taking his arm," a woman friend declared, "I should as soon think of taking the arm of an elm tree"—in the end he stands revealed, near and plain, in full day. If the ghost of Thoreau were now to walk across the fields and woods he knew, one cannot imagine that any one he might encounter need be startled. There should be rather an undisturbed recognition of a natural figure in the landscape, a man where he belonged. So Mr. Whicher* paints him, with fitting economy of description and quotation, using fewer than a hundred pages, yet achieving a full-length critical portrait.[1]

In the dry light he preferred for his own vision, the main events of his biography are defiantly matter of fact. Typically, in the Concord group of writers, Henry David Thoreau alone was actually native to Concord. He would be. The exotic French strain in his ancestry was subdued to the New England environment; his father was an independent "ingenious mechanic," his mother obviously a capable housewife, and the family ambition centered upon giving a superior education to the children. Out of their slender means, Henry was sent to Harvard; with the aid of a scholarship and his own earnings. After graduation, he set up a private school, with his brother John, and did well enough, until John's uncertain health terminated the venture. At home Henry learned his father's trade of making pencils, and proved his Yankee birthright by improving the process. He never exhibited any idealistic disregard of money at the expense of others, but paid his own way, and he had enough aptitude for industrial affairs to observe in passing the possibilities of a water power site for factories. Occasionally he did a job of surveying or resorted to tutoring to put himself in funds. Meanwhile, Concord supplied intellectual society. The ambient is perfectly indicated by Mr. Whicher with the compressed information that Thoreau contributed "a poem, and an essay on the Roman poet Aulus Persius Flaccus" to the first number of the *Dial*, while earning his keep in the Emerson household by "attending to Emerson's garden and woodpile." The Massachusetts version of the shepherd of Admetus[2] was the Transcendental hired man.

It is to be presumed that these desultory occupations were all secondary to an intention to be a writer. Otherwise he might have filled out a pattern of external success in various pursuits which were open to him, with his demonstrated skill of head and hand. Business or a profession, journalism or academic advancement, were within the range of possibilities. The times were propitious. From 1817 to 1862, his term of life, was a period of vast material expansion of the nation, with concomitant opportunity for enterprise, shrewdness and thrift. No doubt he felt the pull of that great spring tide, for he remarked that in his undirected rambles he always found his footsteps turning westward. Yet he refrained from joining the transcontinental migration, as he stepped aside from the industrial drive. Likewise there was a rising literary consciousness, not only the "flowering of New England" but the genesis of an American literature of continental character. Had he struck out to report the country on the grand scale of its physical growth, he might have gained popularity by the incidental flattery to patriotic pride. Instead, he took the back trails and published his first book, *A Week on the Concord and Merrimack Rivers*, in the year of the California gold rush, as if to insure that it should be heartily ignored. Seven hundred copies remained unsold, from a first edition of a thousand. He stacked them in the attic and concentrated all the more closely on his own backyard, to write *Walden*. Apparently nobody quite knew what to make of that either, when it appeared. Like its author, it did not fit into any exact classification. One may call Thoreau a naturalist and be right enough, but it does not describe him completely. He added little or nothing to factual knowledge of nature, or its scientific analysis. His observations are original only in being first hand, sharp and fresh. Neither can he be appraised strictly as an artist in the medium of words who seeks a subject for esthetic form. "Expression is the act of the whole man," he declared; and "the one great rule of composition is to speak the truth."[3] But the truth is something more than simple objective itemization of things. There was some truth he wanted first to get at, and then to affirm.

Much of his personal records consists of things he did not do; and those omissions were neither accidental nor trivial. He never married. He gathered no property and sought no formal honors or position. He would not follow, nor would he lead; consistently he refused to be counted in as a member of any group or sect. Cross-grained as a hickory knot, he even resented persuasion from Emerson to convictions he already held. Contrarinesss could hardly go further—nor be more absolutely justified. After all, Emerson compounded with the world sufficiently for modest comfort. Thoreau could do without comfort. Yet he expressly repudiated imitators of his experiment in the simple life. At the least hint of compulsion, coercion, or the mental servility of the second-hand, he shied and backed and braced himself for unconditional resistance.

It must not be overlooked that in certain aspects he presented a faintly risible spectacle. Physically he was no rugged outdoor type, being rather small in stature and perhaps always delicate in health, since he was to die of consumption at forty-five. There is a touch of humor in setting up such a hermitage as Thoreau's cabin by Walden Pond, so close to an organized community that it could not possibly escape general observation. "He liked to keep out of sight of houses." Maybe, but he must rather have liked to be seen doing so; for there was space enough in America for a man to get out of sight of houses altogether, if that had been his earnest wish. The hermit of Walden stayed well within the reach of the maternal pantry shelf. Indeed, one cannot but imagine him sauntering by adjacent homesteads in a fairly exasperating manner. A farmer could hardly put in an honest day's work without Thoreau leaning on the rail fence to inquire why the poor soul wasted his time so laboriously. If this picture is drawn from fancy, it is not unwarranted by Thoreau's reflections; and rural consciousness is acute for the implications of behavior. It is a slight failure of cosmic justice that none of the wretches thus detected in their sinful indulgence of making a hard living had a chance to read the astounding bit of humbug Thoreau set down in his journal when he let a campfire run wild and set their wood lots and hay meadows ablaze.[4] A truant schoolboy could have mumbled a better excuse, or at least something less self-righteous; Thoreau squirmed himself out of the responsibility.

For Thoreau was capable of sophistry. He fell into it in a greater matter, with his glorification of John Brown* as a hero; his choice of phrases showed a dangerous aptitude in that dubious art. If his pen had been for hire, he might have served the worst of causes only too well. But he did not set himself against his age without reason. His opposition constituted a true relation to history. Feeling in every fiber of his being the way the world was going, he did not mean to go along. And only a man who was civilized in grain could have become so immediately aware of the inward threat to civilization which was increasing steadily with the visible prosperity and progress of the nation. The moral obligation which prompted him to separate himself from society, as a living symbol of protest, arose from the very conditions which should tend to bring a man into easy contact with his kind. It derived from his sense of history, his classical education, his strong local attachment and his exquisite sensitiveness to personal relations. Reading and writing are not primitive accomplishments; they constitute the art of communication on a high level, the instruments of abstract thought and the means of its continuance in time, linking past and present. Further, Thoreau had taken pains to acquire a working knowledge of the elements of advanced technology, with mathematics and mechanics. In his emotional capacities he was also essentially a normal person. He wrote once in a haunting phrase that justified his ventures in poetry, that he had lost "a hound, a bay horse and a turtle dove" that he was forever seeking. He meant a dear friend, his brother who died young, and the girl he loved and sought to marry. He was never estranged from his own family; and he spent his later years in the house he had helped his father to build. These are the components of a good life within an established framework, open to progress.

Yet as a naturalist his keenest perception was for the scent of the wilderness, of virgin forest, untrodden earth, water from clean far springs, a landscape still largely unshaped by human agencies. The metaphysical overtone in his writings refers most often to this aspect of nature. He sought to take it unaware, to double back and see, as with the eyes of Adam, what kind of universe he inhabited, in order to find his true place in it. "Happy the man who observes the heavenly and the terrestrial law in just proportion."

What he took out of the social order, when he walked into the woods, was a developed human being, carrying within himself the resources of a complex culture, for an ultimate adjustment. He was re-enacting personally the discovery of the New World. The great idea which America represented was never that of a return to savagery. It was the logical conviction that since man is by nature a rational, moral and spiritual being, his *natural* condition must be that of a civilized person. And as those attributes can be exercised only in the highest degree of freedom, then clearly unless humanity had been sent to the wrong planet freedom should be attainable here and now. "One world at a time."[5] Thoreau's protest was an act of patriotism, a declaration of true faith and allegiance to his country as to the unique chance which had been offered mankind to become what it ought to be. Therefore he conceived it to be his duty to orient himself, to touch a reality of which he could say: "This is, and no mistake; and then begin."

Essentially the things he would not do were all one thing. He would not yield to the drift of expediency. He would set his course by compass and pole star.

For it was precisely during Thoreau's lifetime that the American mind swung away from principle to what is curiously called the practical, as a guide to conduct. The tendency was evident in many ways, from the tame external conformity to "public opinion" which amounts to no one having any opinion, to a decline in mental courage for systematic intellectual speculation. Because the problem was already in existence, the shift became most apparent on the issue of slavery. It would take a volume to trace the process of change on this one question, but the revealing word of the period is compromise.

Thoreau would have none of it. If he were expected to tolerate an avowed evil for material reasons, his answer was that he could live with a minimum of possessions, but not without self-respect. If it were for the sake of society, he asked what kind of society could be had on such terms. But his most acute insight was exhibited in his rejection of the cult of philanthropy. He was "revolted by humanitarian projects for doing good to one's fellow men."[6] The benefactor approached with a halter in hand. Every argument of the humanitarian—the plea of security, of uplift, of the duty of the privileged to assist their inferiors and the inability of the unprivileged to help themselves—was put forth in Thoreau's day to excuse slavery: and it fits the case as well as any other. Thoreau was neither to be trapped nor coaxed.

And he was quite practical enough to identify unerringly the means by which slavery must be instituted and maintained. It is the political power. Hence his fixed antipathy to government in such extension, as the manifest foe of all good men. He admitted no authority which would compel him to contribute to a wrong. His refusal to pay the poll tax was formal notice that he did not consent.

But a fatal result of compromise had already taken effect. When men govern themselves by principle, they can study disinterestedly the function of organization, having an end in view. That is truly practical, for practical action is that which serves a purpose. Expediency is the dodging of purpose, of a definite conclusion. Political science was practically forgotten by avoidance. Thoreau never got so far as to examine the positive means of preserving freedom in association. The example he gave was negative or passive—"civil disobedience." This is in fact a pre-political method. Gandhi borrowed "non-co-operation" from Thoreau. Political science is unknown to the Orient; such deficiency is the cause of the weakness of the East as compared to the West. The sole alternative is irrational violence. This again is the sinister alliance so often seen between the pure phrasemaker, the self-styled idealist, and the exponent of brute force. Thoreau's defense of John Brown's aimless raid (the act of a man scarcely sane, and involving sheer murder), was such a lapse. If John Brown had been right, Thoreau himself should have followed the same course. He never did. And one cannot but suspect that Thoreau knew there was something terribly wrong with his position at this point, else he would not have taken care to cloak his sanguinary protagonist with the fictitious authority of an official title, as "Captain" John Brown. Further, when the Civil War presently broke out, Thoreau "resented the fact that he was obliged to hear about it." He was a sick man, near to death; and he had got only half way to the truth he sought. One must know not only what not to do but what to do.

Likewise the mass of notes he had made remained unwrought into permanent form. He had cleared his site, gathered much honest stuff for building, but *Walden* was his one structural achievement—a lodge in the wilderness. There is irony in Mr. Whicher's prefatory comment: "Though Walden Pond is preserved as a state reservation, it is no longer a refuge of the spirit." *Hast thou found me, O mine enemy?*[7] Thoreau's Walden is not bounded by place or time. He deserved Emerson's eulogy: "His soul was made for the noblest society"; and he did not fail in his primary purpose. "I came into this world not chiefly to make this a good place to live in but to live in it." He lived, and is still alive.

"Henry David Thoreau, Native of Concord," review of George F. Whicher, Walden Revisited: A Centennial Tribute to Henry David Thoreau, Herald Tribune "Books." *From* New York Herald Tribune, *October*

Notes

1. A reference to George F. Whicher's *Walden Revisited* (1945), the book Paterson is reviewing.
2. In Greek mythology, Apollo was once employed as a shepherd by King Admetus.
3. "The one great rule of composition—and if I were a professor of rhetoric I should insist on this—is to *speak the truth*": quoted by Whicher 80.
4. Whicher does not discuss Thoreau's rationalization for the events of April, 1844, as delivered in his *Journal* for May 31, 1850: "It is as if the lightning had done it. These flames are but consuming their natural food" (*The Writings of Henry David Thoreau* [Boston: Houghton Mifflin, 1906], VIII. 23).
5. Other quotations in this article derive from Whicher's *Walden Revisited*, but this one does not. A likely source is Henry Seidel Canby, *Thoreau* (Boston: Houghton Mifflin, 1939) 434: "The anti-slavery orator Parker Pillsbury, an old friend of the Abolitionist Thoreaus, visiting him in the last weeks, wished to talk to him of the next world. Thoreau whispered, 'One world at a time.'"
6. Whicher 64.
7. 1 Kings 21:20.

2

The Reformer as Tyrant

If one were obliged to select a single specimen or case history to exemplify what happened to liberalism in the nineteenth century, how the name was appropriated and exploited by strictly authoritarian reformers, the life and works of Frances Wright* might stand for all the tribe. Here it [is] related fairly enough, and can be recommended for its sheer human interest as much as for instruction. An imperfect sympathy with the lady does not spoil the entertainment; it's a good action story too. Something keeps happening all the time. Something had to keep happening around Frances Wright; if there were a brief interval of quiet, she either started the wheels going, or threw in a monkey wrench, or went some place else where there was a ruckus already under way.

Frances Wright began with the prime requisite for an omniscient do-good; she inherited an independent income before she was twenty-one. The money came from her grandmother. Her father, a Scotch merchant of advanced views, went broke, and in the polite language of his daughter's biographers, "was reduced to the desperate expedient of putting all his real estate into the hands of his uncle and two other Dundee tradesmen to save it from his creditors." He was very progressive indeed, a splendid progenitor for a social fixer. Furthermore, Frances was orphaned in girlhood, and thus left absolutely free to pursue her own devices.

Her education as a young lady omitted all mention of the American Revolution. When she came upon a history of it, in Italian, she wasn't quite sure if it were fact or romance. Anyhow, it stirred her blood. She read up on it pretty thoroughly. And as soon as she was of age, she headed for the United States.

Letters of introduction made her first visit to New York socially agreeable. She had a Byronic blank verse tragedy produced in New York; and visited Niagara Falls. She wrote a book on her travels, largely enthusiastic. Returning to Europe with her literary reputation, she extended her acquaintance in distinguished circles, and formed a close friendship with the aged but perennial hero, LaFayette. When he made his final grand tour of the United States, Fanny Wright and her younger sister, Camilla, went along, more or less discreetly. The connection, undoubtedly innocent but slightly absurd, caused a mild scandal. LaFayette's family were annoyed. Fanny apparently wished to be adopted by LaFayette, or even perhaps to marry him, but he himself discovered scruples against the latter course.

Frances soon found a new objective, a cause of her own. Every one was founding communities. She followed the fashion, proposing to devote her colony to the solution of one special problem, slavery. She had met Robert Owen* and his son, Robert Dale Owen,* the patrons of New Harmony, Indiana. Frances fixed her community near theirs; she chose Nashoba as the site.

Her idea was to buy Negro slaves, educate them for freedom, and meantime have them work out the price of their redemption. The sum mentioned is $6,000 each with interest and "expenses of colonization," which sounds exorbitant, and may possibly be an error in transcription. Anyhow, what she expected was exactly what the ordinary slaveholder looked for from his slaves: capital, expenses and interest. But at the end of a year Fanny's slaves had earned less than their keep; if a slave could be worse off, they would have been so. All that Frances Wright and her Nashoba board of trustees could do was to "forgive" the debt solemnly, which might have been funny even to the slaves if they had understood accounting. The Nashoba enterprise altogether produced nothing but controversy, chills and fever, and several ill-assorted marriages. Finally Fanny freed her slaves and took them to Haiti, where she got the black republic to give them a start, with land and tools, or at least promises. What became of them there, deponent saith not.

Frances Wright then returned to France, and married one of her Nashoba group, a French pedagogue, Phiquepal d'Arusmont.* The marriage was prompted by expectancy of a child.

Motherhood did not hamper Fanny any more than it did Mehitabel, the cat—though the comparison may be misleading, for Fanny did not indulge in promiscuous affairs.[1] But she had her career. She was handsome in a big way, nearly six feet tall, designed for a public figure. She left her child in France with its father and continued roving across the ocean and back at intervals. She made lecture tours in America, usually arousing violent dissension. Some of her opponents were sensible, some merely abusive. Of course she was called a "free lover" and in theory, as far as the term has any meaning, she was one, though she married for convenience.

The proposed educational scheme of her community was significant. She would have given the government of her Almost-Perfect State absolute control over children, "to house, feed and educate them." The parents should be permitted only to "visit them at suitable times, but in no way allowed to interfere with the form of instruction carried on." In short, the children would be in custody, the parents barred out and held to the duty of producing and paying; and these conditions would be called "free education."

There would also be no more private property; it would be communized in some undefined form of holding. Of course, all this was to be called "democracy." The Nashoba practice of "democracy" was almost as bright as the proposals mooted today under that head. For example, when the slave plowman sprained his knee, a vote was taken to decide whether or not his knee really hurt him badly. The majority decided it didn't, and he must go back to plowing.

In all definite proposals of the pseudo-"liberals," the practical operation will be found to call for absolute power in the state. The basic idea of personal initiative is never entertained for a moment. Frances Wright revealed this most curiously in her complaint that she had never been taught domestic economy; she was one of the world's worst housekeepers. But there was nothing whatever to prevent her learning of her own accord. She never did. Nothing could be learned; it could only be taught.

It is obvious that Frances Wright never had the slightest comprehension of the political principles of the United States, the free enterprise, private property, society of contract, by which and not otherwise liberty can exist—the system which inevitably abolished slavery within a generation of the Nashoba futility. But Frances Wright would, given her way, have destroyed liberty altogether, quite unaware of what she was doing.

It is not to be supposed that she was a hypocrite. She was simply incapable of grasping the operative principles. She was also a woman of immense energy, of a natural oratorical talent, and with a natural craving for the limelight. Since liberty was the popular slogan, she repeated it; but it might just as well have been that blessed word Mesopotamia.[2] She would have organized expeditions and shouted, on to Mesopotamia.

Her husband, d'Arusmont, with the most lofty protestations of doing it for her own good, grabbed her property. The spectacle of one reformer reforming another is grimly edifying. A tragic accident terminated the contest; Frances Wright died, bravely enough, in her fifty-seventh year. Her biographers explain that "this book is a belated attempt to pay some measure of the debt we owe her." They do not mean to be satirical.[3]

"A Lively Professional Female Reformer," review of A. J. G. Perkins and Theresa Wolfson,** Frances Wright, Herald Tribune "Books." *From* New York Herald Tribune, *September 10, 1939*

Notes

1. Mehitabel, of the "Archy and Mehitabel" stories and poems, was the creation of journalist and story writer Don Marquis (1878–1937), whose work Paterson enjoyed.
2. A once common expression, often used to parody ignorant religiosity.
3. Future presidential nominee Wendell Willkie* wrote to Paterson (September 11, 1939) warmly applauding this review and its critique of false liberalism.

3

What Is Known as a Practical Man

Some thoughtful students of history have fixed upon the Boer War as the first breaking point or collision of those forces of the modern world which resulted in the grand smash of the World War. Three stages of culture were in conflict. Money and machines were frankly brought into action by an industrial empire to conquer a rural people who held by the land; and the primitive black warrior nations of Africa were pawns in the game.

From this point of view Cecil Rhodes* has a certain historical importance, as he was a conscious and direct agent in the whole process. Whether or not his role makes him a great man remains a matter of definition. He also evades personal classification as man of action or of imagination. His imagination was extremely materialistic, distinctly juvenile; he liked to think of large areas of red on a map,[1] and millions of money. His action was mostly through subordinates, not involving personal risk to himself, and mainly for financial reasons. Money power, on however large a scale, does not confer any heroic quality on its possessor. Rhodes seems to have had courage enough on occasion, however, when it was necessary for him to meet and confer with Zulu chiefs or hostile backveldt Boer intransigeants.

One cannot even say without qualification that Rhodes was a complex character. The blanks in his mental and emotional nature were extensive. His private life was thin, if he can be said to have had a private life. Women had no place in it at all. One woman tried to capture him and then tried blackmail. Rhodes kept out of her reach. Like many men who make a parade of iron will and large interests, he was afraid of women. He was much attached to a few men friends, employees, "yes men." He was said to have personal charm, persuasiveness, when he chose; but that seems to have been with people who are impressed by any ordinary word from an important man. His features and expression in all extant photographs are distinctly disagreeable. Though he was tall, he was never robust; the weakness of physique which resulted in a comparatively early death was the first cause of his going to South Africa.

He went out at seventeen for his health; an elder brother had preceded him and settled in Natal. The diamond boom at Kimberly began about that time. Both brothers went to the diggings. Cecil Rhodes was in business as a diamond speculator, with Alfred Beit as a partner, before he was twenty.

He returned to England to attend Oxford, continuing to spend his long vacations in Africa, and holding onto his business interests. The reason he was determined to have an Oxford education was no passion for spiritual values. He said: "Wherever you turn your eye—except in science—you find an Oxford man at the top of the tree." As a boy, the son of an Anglican vicar, he had thought of entering the law, and named the church as a second choice, "a clergyman's life is the nicest," but there again one gets no hint of religion as the deciding factor. It was simply a profession. He was what is known as a practical man.

For highly practical purposes he entered South African politics, meanwhile consolidating financial power in great combinations such as the De Beers diamond syndicate. At thirty-seven he was premier of Cape Colony; while his Chartered Company held almost unlimited powers of political territorial expansion on behalf of England, after the fashion of the old East India Company. The Cape to Cairo railway was already his "dream."

The Boers stood in the path. Instinctively one's sympathies are with the Boers; their rude and stubborn resistance to "progress" had the sanction of a genuine way of life. They cared for something more than money—for their personal dignity, for independence and room. They had, of course, ousted and exploited the natives quite frankly, with no pretence of philanthropy; Rhodes and his companies manoeuvred the blacks into peonage "for their own good."

The instigation of the Jameson Raid[2] is still counted against Rhodes as a major blunder. It ended his immediate and visible political career, and left a stain of hypocrisy and dishonor on his name. For all that, the humiliation touched the pride of England, though the worst aspect of pride; and must have had a considerable effect in working up English sentiment to support the Boer War soon after. So Rhodes might not, in the long run, have considered the Raid either a mistake or a failure. For it is more than doubtful if he would have seen any connection with the Great War, if he had lived till then.

William Plomer* has followed the main outlines of Rhodes's career skilfully, keeping a vigorous framework and a graphic quality. Of necessity he has omitted the complicated financial transactions by which Rhodes gained power, remarking only that they were not distinguished by scrupulosity.

Mr. Plomer is a South African born, of English blood; he understands both the terrain and the people, with an unusual, impartial sympathy for human values in any race. From that point of view he could not very well be an ardent apologist for Rhodes and he treats his subject with a temperate but undisguised irony that is distinctly refreshing. His attitude is that Rhodes may have been an inevitable channel of power, given the times, but he was in that respect more or less a protagonist of the forces of aggressive stupidity which have since found other outlets in Fascism and the Nazi movement. "To those at all skeptically inclined it will seem that a sense of public duty so closely allied with a progressive personal aggrandizement may possibly be suspect." It would be well if the skeptically inclined were more numerous right now all over the world.

"A Channel of Power, But Not a Great Man," review of William Plomer, Cecil Rhodes, Herald Tribune "Books." *From* New York Herald Tribune, *May 21, 1933*

Notes

1. Red signified the possessions of Britain.
2. An attempt, at New Years of 1895–1896, to instigate a pro-British revolution in the Boer state of Transvaal.

4

The Achievement of the Wright Brothers

In 1912, Paterson set a record for high flight by a woman, as a passenger in a flimsy biplane piloted by pioneer aviator Harry Bingham Brown (1883–1954). The invention of the airplane exemplified her ideas about capitalism, risk, and progress.

There were two Americans who asked nothing of anybody; they could earn what they needed, and mind their own business; and out of their native genius they solved a scientific problem which gave mankind the mastery of the air. They had a shed for a workshop and a pasture field for an experiment station. We like particularly the episode of the selection of Huffman's field. It was part of a farm owned by a Dayton banker. The Wrights asked the owner if they could rent it. Mr. Huffman said they could use it free; he only requested them incidentally to "drive his cows to a safe place and not run over them!" We shall never know whether Mr. Huffman thought anything would come of the Wrights' experiments; but that was the American way, too—let them use the field, they wouldn't do any harm. Oh, no, no charge. It was private property, so there was no red tape. At about the same time another man, the head of an endowed institution, with $50,000 of government funds and $20,000 as a special gift, was trying to invent a flying machine; and he got nowhere with it. But the two who needed nothing whatever except their own brains, their own earnings and their own leisure time at their own disposal, performed the feat.

That is what we are now urged to be ashamed of, to ignore, to repudiate and deny and destroy. That is the United States; that is the capitalist system. We are told, for example: "The Russians like everything about the United States except capitalism." Isn't that kind and condescending? They like everything about this country except that it is alive, that it is free, that it is productive and independent. They like everything about it except that it is the country of Washington, Jefferson, Madison, Franklin, Edison, the Wrights. Oh, certainly, we must fix that up—we really must be liked, mustn't we? So if any one doesn't like what we have been, we must scrap all that, and supply what is wanted—Henry Wallace* and Harry Hopkins.* You ought to like them if you don't like the Wrights. We aim to please. Try to overlook what Americans used to be; it was all a mistake. >>

Another striking aspect of the story of the Wrights is the often mentioned fact that plenty of people saw them flying and thought nothing of it. Why was that? Because the really significant events in human history happen in the mind. Merely seeing a thing happen means nothing, unless the one who sees also thinks about it, understands it in abstract terms. The Wrights didn't learn to fly by random "experiments"; they knew exactly what they were doing, and why. They didn't learn by having such interesting talks with every one they met, or by international cultural relations, or by buzzing around youth conferences. They were really quite anti-social. And they did invent the flying machine. So what will you have?

"Turns," May 23, 1943. From New York Herald Tribune, *May 23, 1943*

5

American Concepts

What this country needs is a stabilized vocabulary. Herschel Brickell* came back from the South and told us that he had got himself charged with radicalism by printing a letter of his which actually expressed sentiments of the purest classical Americanism. Then we met Burton Rascoe,* and he said he was behind schedule with his book on *Demi-Gods of Literature*, because he has to spend most of his time explaining any simple remark he may make; and, furthermore, the sight of the newspaper headlines day by day shatters his mental processes and derails his train of thought. There is practically no communication possible at present except between old friends who understand one another, anyhow, and they have to fall back on the sign language.

So we were walking along Forty-second Street, and Maxwell Aley* stopped us and asked, How is everything? And we went mad and tried to tell him!

Right now the world has reached a new low for all time in respect of intellectual honesty. During prosperity people stopped thinking because they were on a joy ride. Now they're afraid to begin again, and eagerly accept anything that they cannot understand just because they can't understand it, and it gives them the feeling that some one else is doing their thinking for them. But nobody is. Nobody will follow through his own theories to the full extent of their implications.

Maxwell Aley then said, why don't you? Well, maybe it would land us in jail, and maybe nobody would print it; but here goes.

People now want some sort of fool-proof social, political and economic system which will combine the advantages of all possible systems and the disadvantages of none. There ain't no such animal.

We believe in the classic American concepts of a purely political government, which shall not undertake to save people's souls or provide them an income. That means private property and personal liberty. The disadvantages are that you may not have any private property, and may at some time or another find yourself in a breadline; and, furthermore, that you must be prepared to risk your life for your liberty, and die for it if the odds go against you. This sounds like harsh doctrine, and it is. The conditions of life itself are nothing for nothing and little for sixpence. The harshness can be mitigated only by personal decency, a sense of obligation of human beings to help one another personally in times of stress. As for security, we do not expect it, because life is not secure. Life is a long series of risks and from one point of view an ultimate net loss; everything slips away by degrees and you die. On the other hand, the alternative to living is not having lived; so it is equally fair and rational to say that whatever you get out of life is net gain. We take it on those terms.

Moved by a genuinely benevolent and humane sentiment, during a generation past, people have thought and hoped to achieve security and take care of everybody all the time. Possibly it can be done. Only possibly; there is a considerable margin of doubt, for the management of such a world would require a broader intelligence than has yet been displayed. However, if it can be done, it means regimentation, the use of force to compel every one to fall into line. There will be that kind of a breadline—economic serfdom, an autocratic, bureaucratic, supreme state.

Even with the clear statement, there is always a paradox at the end of the logic. Personal liberty naturally is restricted by physical facts, individual abilities and accidents of immediate circumstance. That has to be understood.

The concept of security has the same inherent limitations. In the last resort it must depend on somebody's ability to run things and somebody's good will in handing out the work tickets or whatever the form of organization demands. So it is not security, it is dependence, quite another thing. Likewise it depends on the simple willingness of the unit to fit in. It assumes that every one wants to be secure. Or else that every one should want to, and therefore must be constrained for his own benefit. This is the same moral basis for authority as that of the Church in the days of its temporal jurisdiction. It assumed that every one wanted to be saved, and that if he didn't, he ought to, and must be at any cost to his own mortal frame. There is nothing the matter with the argument except that some people still refused to be saved. They obstinately went to hell. It's hard to get around that final retort. They did not want to be saved and they were not saved; in short, the theory did not work.

By whatever road, the logic of reality always gets back to the individual. And even in refusing, one must choose by default.

The "intellectuals" and revolutionaries are the worst in declining to analyze their own concepts. We open at random *Recovery through Revolution*[1] and read in Robert Morss Lovett's* introduction: "Wealth is relative. Welfare is absolute." This is tosh. One might say that wealth is absolute by limiting the definition to material objects, and overlooking that it is use makes those objects wealth. But "welfare" is wholly relative.

The world is in a horrible mess because we had a war and during the war blindly handed over authority to those who happened to be in high places at the time. We see what they did with it, and now we are asked to hand over still more authority so that their successors, whom we have no reason to suppose are any brighter, may fix it up again, by applying more of the same processes. Conscription, taxation, borrowing and regimentation were the means of making war. They are now advocated as the means of making peace. The great financiers and politicians brought about the crash. So now they calmly appropriate those powers which they so misused, as their permanent privilege.

It is a world-wide economic disfranchisement, and people are too bewildered to know what is being done to them. If we had children, we'd be rather ashamed to look at them and reflect that we were born free, and had sold them down the river—and at that, for "only a promise to pay." It was neither individualism nor industrialism nor democracy that got us into the present trouble; it was the abandonment of all three, for what was supposed to be a temporary necessity and the general good. Well, will anyone now say that the sheeplike docility of the people actually worked for the general good?

The truth that nobody will admit is that unlimited borrowing power, unlimited taxing power, and unlimited power to depreciate currency spells absolute expropriation, with no guarantees whatever. And to grant power and believe that it will not be used is sheer imbecility.

However, whether or not people are willing to think through their own ideas, history will do it for them. You don't have to face the facts; a brick will hit you just as hard from the rear as from the front. Here's a new book by John Dewey:* *How We Think*, with the subtitle, *A Restatement of the Relation of Reflective Thinking to the Educative Process*. Isn't that drawing it mild? The relation—isn't it the whole process?

Note

1. A collection (1933) edited by Samuel D. Schmalhausen.

6

But Is It True?

The John Reed Club[1] announces a series of sixteen public lectures on Sunday afternoons at 63 West Fifteenth Street, "to work out a complete proletarian theory of Art, Literature and Criticism." Which reminds us of the cowboy who got himself a brand before he had any cattle. But the cowboy explained—well, you get the idea. Oakley Johnson,* executive secretary of the club, adds a postscript: "The articles by Edmund Wilson* in [*Herald Tribune*] BOOKS were extensively discussed. We find his contributions very interesting, but not entirely representative of our point of view on certain essential points."

Taking the words right out of our mouth. As we were saying last week, we feel it our plain duty to do a little back-seat driving. And we had a discussion with Edmund Wilson, warning him that what he said would be used against him. Not that we expect to please the John Reed Club either.

Be it understood that we do not object to the airing of Communist opinion. It's been aired a good deal lately, and we are so thoroughly unconverted that we still hold to the original principles of the United States, that thought should be free and ideas freely examined. The regimentation of thought and forcible suppression of opinion are the most intolerable aspects of the proposed communistic state, and inseparable from it. And those who imagine such a state would be an improvement on our present political system had better begin to imagine the bare possibility that they won't be running the communistic show, and may not find it entirely representative of their views in certain essential points.

Mr. Wilson declared flatly, as we understood him, that he no longer believed in those antiquated documents, the Declaration of Independence, the Constitution and the Bill of Rights. He used to, but has lately decided that they were the work of impractical idealists, who at the same time were impelled by bourgeois group considerations. He believes in economic determinism; people think and act according to their "group interests." Jefferson represented the agrarian group interest, and so on.

Which we flatly deny. Jefferson then, as a landed proprietor, should have been the last person to abolish the laws of entail, which he did.[2] Washington as a slave owner should have been the last man to set his hand to a declaration of the Rights of Man, which he did. It is puerile to accuse men who risked their lives and, quite incidentally, their property, during seven weary years of war, and spent another seven years of arduous and unpaid toil setting up a government, of being impractical idealists, with no appreciation of the difficulty of putting principles and ideals into practice.

They knew what they meant, and meant what they said; and they solemnly warned us that nothing worth having comes easy: "Eternal vigilance is the price of liberty."[3]

The unique feature of their achievement is that they created for the first time in history a purely political government. It was their conscious intention to keep economics as well as religion out of it. Economics, property, is the basis of class government. Their object was to lift the weight of economic considerations from the political balance.

What Marx did was to write a new charter for feudalism. Men had been bound to the land as serfs in medieval Europe. Marx could not get rid of the idea that they must be chained, so the logical thing, in his view, was to chain them to the machines.

The theory of economic determinism puts the effect before the cause. Economics are created by intelligence; they don't operate automatically, and the skill and knowledge which Russia is now borrowing and hiring from the United States cannot be developed under communism. If they choose political communism—and they have the choice—they will get that, but not the free play of intelligence. They are determining their economics, not being determined by them. That is their own affair. Our present difficulty is that our "best minds," both big business men and intellectuals, have already got the political machinery dangerously entangled with the economic system, disrupting both; and they are now demanding that the government should save them from what they've done to it. They are infants yelling for pap.

They don't seem to have been around. Edmund Wilson astonished us by saying he had only lately read Henry George.* How any one could have escaped—the works of Henry George were strewn about the West like leaves in Vallombrosa.[4] Or Marx; had we read Marx? Good grief, didn't we have to proofread *Capital* once; and a dreary job it was.

As for liberty and equality, Mr. Wilson said nobody believed in those any more. And besides, is there free speech and freedom of the press in this country?

Yes. There is, to an immeasurably greater extent than under any other system. What Mr. Wilson seemed to find all wrong was that one cannot invariably get paid for writing what one pleases. Or, he said, get one's opinions printed except in obscure little magazines. As if the Little Magazines print what they don't want! And why should they? They get their fun by bouncing their unpaid contributors.

The intellectuals never draw the vital distinction between the inevitable result of any given system and the equally inevitable imperfections of its operation, arising from the fact that it has to work with imperfect human beings. But if they really hold to Marx's economic determinism, why argue about it at all? Why not save their breath to cool their porridge? Even if one doesn't care for liberty, surely it is a needless exertion to rivet one's own chains.

It is an interesting suggestion, that we are, as Mr. Wilson informed us, the last surviving person to believe in those quaint old notions on which the republic was founded. But is it true?

Notes

1. The John Reed Club, a Communist Party organization for intellectuals, was named for American communist journalist John Reed (1887–1920).
2. Entail was a legal device used to keep inherited land from being sold off or claimed in foreclosure.
3. A saying frequently but erroneously attributed to Thomas Jefferson.
4. Milton, *Paradise Lost*, 1.302.

7

What Went Wrong

Adeline Hohlfeld[1] brought an anthropologist to tea with us last week, and Gustav Eckstein,* author of *Kettle*, was present, and we all got into a knock-down-and-drag-out argument about social psychology. The anthropologist upheld the current view that everybody is just what he or she is "conditioned" to be, and human beings are nothing but so much protoplasmic dough baked in a mold of external influences. He said he had lived among the Maoris and became just like them. So after he had gone away, completely unconditioned by us, we looked at Gustav Eckstein and he looked at us and we exclaimed simultaneously that the anthropologist was just what he was and if he sold tractors or lived among the head-hunters of the upper Amazon, he would be no different. He could develop himself more or less, but he'd be himself. There is that catch in Behaviorism, its proponents never explain why some conditions do condition and some don't.

So then we went to a party given by Lenore Marshall* for Evelyn Scott,* author of *Eva Gay*, and for Robert Marshall,* author of *Arctic Village*. Talking of her travels, Evelyn Scott said she loved best of any place in the world the Southwest. We said it hurts our eyes; and we like a soft climate and a green landscape, having been brought up on the dry sunny prairies, and thus conditioned evidently to prefer something else. She said yes, she was brought up in Tennessee, and the desert light hurt her eyes, too; nevertheless, she loves the desert best and would rather live there than anywhere. >>

Robert Marshall, having been conditioned by an urban environment and a college education, went and lived a year in his chosen Arctic village and enjoyed it enormously.

Kyle Crichton* and Benjamin Stolberg* were among those present, and having once had a long and acrimonious dispute with Kyle Crichton we found ourself in complete agreement with his views on everything else, except in detail. He said he had gone to hear Bernard Shaw* and was saddened, since Shaw was once his greatest hero. We didn't, having considerable regard for Shaw as a first-rate playwright and none at all for his social ideas. The clew to Shaw's social theories may be found in his own account of the room he worked in for years, in his mother's house. He has described it as submerged in piles of undusted papers, and with the remains of lunch or breakfast left about all day by the indifferent servant maid. Now we can't take any stock in the economics or social program of a man whose unconscious hope is to get the state to come in and sweep his room and trim his whiskers for him. If he had tidied that room himself, we'd be willing to listen to him. Most of the "new economics" of today comes from young men who went to college on an allowance, and then came out in nice white collars to jobs on politely radical magazines supported by kind wealthy ladies. From them we get a mother's boy economic program with a kind maternal government taking care of everybody out of an inexhaustible income drawn from mysterious sources.

Benjamin Stolberg told us sternly: "You stand for a lost cause, a dying decency." All right, one has to die anyhow some day, and we'd rather die with decency than survive it. But Benjamin Stolberg represents a fairly tough survival of decency, because no matter what he labels himself, he really stems from the Germany of Carl Schurz, the last of the forty-eighters.[2] So maybe some flame of the human spirit will persist even through the Age of Gibberish we are now enduring.

Seeing Henry Hazlitt* deep in solemn converse with John Chamberlain,* we edged over in time to hear John Chamberlain say: "Economics must be entirely rewritten." We then uttered a low moan and swooned away while Henry choked on a pickled onion. Have we got to go through that again from the beginning?

If it's absolutely unavoidable, however, we will give John Chamberlain the recipe for rewriting economics. Remember, you must write your economics to obfuscate a situation that two or three honest words would make fatally clear. First the statesmen of all nations must start a war with loud hurrahs, to make the world safe for democracy. Then the financiers must step in and give the impression that war doesn't really cost anything, because you can do it all on loans, and, in fact, everybody will make a nice profit out of commissions on the bonds. The industrialists don't need to worry about taxes, because they will also make a profit out of the war materials paid for by the bonds. And stocks will go up, so everybody can make a profit out of margins in the stock market.

Then, mysteriously, the bonds begin to fall due. That was never expected. The immediate thing to do is to "refinance" them with new bonds, and new profits out of new commissions. This is called the New Economic Era.[3] After this has gone on for some time it begins to look queer, but nobody can think why. The fact can be obscured for a little while longer by calling interest "debt service" and non-payment of debts "stabilization of the currency." Bad debts must be called "frozen assets," and "credit" means new loans that cannot possibly be paid. Finally the international financiers discover with dismay that they have destroyed the value of their own invested commissions. There is then nothing to do but add noughts[4] to infinity on the credit side of the ledger, call for a dictator and inaugurate a rain of paper like the ticker tape hurled out of the Wall Street windows on a parade day. Announce that democracy will not work in a crisis, and grab whatever any individual has left. And you have a lovely economics in which nothing need ever be paid, and if you think you have any rights you'll give everybody a big laugh.

The main trick is never to face a balance sheet.

And keep on good terms with the Bernard Shaws, because they can give you an out.

If you do not think this is a good system, you will get a letter from Harriet Ashbrook, telling you kindly that in spite of her best efforts toward enlightenment you "seem to remain in darkness." So she sends you a copy of *We, the People*—and it won't do you any harm. "If you still believe that all's right with the world," she says cheerily.[5] Still? We don't believe it yet, in spite of having been "saved" forty different ways. We've been telling the children such bad news for a long time past that they don't even know what we're talking about. They still believe in Santa Claus. "We're telling them that one way or another everything has got to be paid for; some one must take the loss."

The end of our story possibly may be found in II Kings, Chapter 9, Verses 32 and 33. If you take the trouble to look up what happened to an irritating and obstinate woman, observe the description of the "two or three" who finally executed vengeance on her.[6]

"Turns," April 23, 1933. From New York Herald Tribune, *April 23, 1933*

Notes

1. Probably a publisher's representative.
2. Stolberg was a Marxist who became an outspoken critic of Communists. Carl Schurz (1829–1906)—Union general, United States senator, and secretary of the interior—came to the United States after participating in the failed European revolution of 1848.
3. "New Era" was a term often used to denote the seemingly successful economic regime of the 1920s.
4. Zeros.
5. Harriet Ashbrook (1898–1946) was a member of the leftist League of American Writers, as was Leo Huberman (1903–1968), American socialist academic and author of *We the People* (1932).
6. They were eunuchs.

8

The Devolution of America

Florence Bowers* came in this afternoon with a strange gleam in her eye and laid upon our desk a copy of *Coup d'Etat: The Technique of Revolution*, by Curzio Malaparte.* Should we read it, we asked timidly. Not necessarily, she said. Recommend it to the boy friends of communism. Here are full instructions for them. I'm tired of hearing them talk about revolution, she said; let's have a little action. They have only to follow the green line—and see where it gets them.

So then we spent two hours saving the nation; and another hour subsequently reading portions of the book. Meantime our work isn't done. And there may be a lesson in that, too. Possibly if everybody would stop saving the nation, some work might get done. But, as Florence Bowers pointed out to us, we have got in bad all around; and she said we really ought to state our own position more clearly. She took us for a hidebound reactionary. She herself is a pre-Marxian Socialist, and so is equally open to misconstruction; for the Marxian recruits cherish the naive delusion that Marx invented Socialism and furthermore that nobody ever heard of Marx until they did.

It's rather hot weather for position-stating; but perhaps an analogy will not add much to the general confusion. Even if it makes us a crusted Tory, we do believe that no matter how far people have gone *in the wrong direction*, the best thing to do is to go back and start right again.

Out West there are charming spots called gumbo mudholes. It is a good idea to keep out of them. If a dumb driver had got us in and then urged upon us the necessity for bigger and better gumbo mudholes, we shouldn't think any more highly of him. If he then insisted it would be narrow-minded to get out, that what we should do is to settle down permanently, bring the parlor melodeon and the kitchen stove and sink them after the wagon, we might almost lose patience. And if after that some beamish lads who had theretofore spent their carefree days picking daisies in the adjacent meadow came hurrying up and advocated "liquidation" of all the still solid portions of the road bed,[1] we'd feel just about the way we do now.

For that, in our opinion, is what our Big Men and Best Minds and Internationalists and Young Intellectuals have done for us. This country started on sound working principles. The main idea was that the Federal government was to be political, not economic. It was to protect human rights from the pressure of group interests and interferences, not to legislate people into either piety or prosperity or private morality. Within the political frame, groups might form and function for economic or religious or self-disciplinary purposes, so long as they didn't try to force individuals into conformity. States and cities and municipalities might try all sorts of experiments and see if they worked—there was nothing against civic ownership of public utilities, or communal holding of property, by free consent.[2] There isn't now. But the highest consideration was personal liberty, and therefore the highest power of government must be dedicated to that.

But the upliftters got their way, the Newton D. Bakers* who immediately wished conscription on us. Then the demand for a "business administration" was heard; and look at the darned thing now. After having boasted how well they could run the country, the bankers and business men are asking the government to rescue them from what they did to it. And meantime the internationalists set about saving the world, and what a swell job they did! And the moral legislators sewed us up in a sack with prohibition. After which the technicians got us—the Great Engineers.[3]

At this point we shall be told that republican-libertarian principles were well enough for a young country with a scattered agrarian population. If the objectors will look up the record they will find that the original opposition said those principles were impracticable because they had been borrowed from classical history and would work only for a small city state, composed mainly of traders.

Others will tell us that the United States used to be isolated; but is so no longer, and must now develop the international mind. They seem to forget that when it was founded the United States had Europe in the back yard and on both sides—French sovereignty in Louisiana, Spain to the South, and British troops garrisoned in Canada. It had had one European war fought on American soil—the French and Indian war, and George Washington fought in it. He couldn't have felt nearly so "isolated" as he would have wished.

Finally, we shall be asked indignantly, would you rather have people starve than have the Federal government extend or change its nature. The answer is the same as if they asked us, would you rather remain thirsty or carry water in a sieve.

Notes

1. Paterson was concerned that businesses that remained sound were jeopardized by Hoover's (and later Roosevelt's) use of their resources to stabilize and otherwise assist unprofitable enterprises.
2. In *The Shadow Riders* (1916) Paterson had described the corruption that results from government's attempts even to regulate public utilities. In later works (see, for instance, GM 166–72), she attacked government regulation or subsidization of such utilities as railroads. As she saw it, the experiments didn't work. Here she characterizes local-government experiments as constitutional, even as private experiments in communal holding are legal and constitutional, however badly they may turn out. In "Turns," February 12, 1933, she would write, "Government and business can be entwined only in the same way as Laocoon and the python, or whatever breed of snake it was. It doesn't do either of them any good."
3. Herbert Hoover was called the "Great Engineer."

9

A Question of Privilege

Any book by Virginia Woolf* we will read, but we don't know whether that is a general recommendation or not. For instance, *Three Guineas,* Mrs. Woolf's latest, interests us throughout by its style and wit, and unlike *The Waves,* it is a model of clarity in statement, yet we cannot decide whether or not it will be intrinsically intelligible to the average American. That is not a reflection on the intelligence of the reader, either; we suspect there is a double and contradictory premise in Mrs. Woolf's logic in regard to the particular subject she is treating.

She is protesting against the position of women in the English upper classes—the professional and aristocratic levels. She asks for equality of opportunity, of pay, of economic position generally, within those classes. It seems plausible, but is it not demanding a privilege as a right? The assumption destroys itself. All those privileges require the same inequality and favor within the groups as between the groups. You can't have an aristocracy, for instance, except by the favoring principle of primogeniture. The oldest son gets nearly everything in the way of property. Then the younger sons get the privilege jobs, to maintain the group as a whole, so it won't die out by the biological odds on the single line. The women folks get the privileged position of "ladies," because that is all there is for them; there isn't any more. Privilege exists by the principle of limitation. It's no use asking it to stretch any further. Those who do not like what they get of it within their own group must either take their stand with the great majority and demand the abolition of all privilege, or take their chance as simple outsiders, adventurers at large. The education Mrs. Woolf demands is education for the favor jobs in the professions. But there are never quite enough of those jobs to go around among the sons. Still, why not let the daughters have their share, one may ask? The reason why not is that there is no reason why; the group can be maintained most effectively by simply supporting the women. If privilege is admitted at all, it can be only on its own terms, its own principles.

Mrs. Woolf glances at the reality of the situation when she remarks: "It would be interesting to know what the true-born working man or woman thinks of the playboys and playgirls of the educated class who adopt the working class cause without sacrificing middle class capital, or sharing working-class experience." We know what some of them think, and they think right. It's a search for new privilege, and a pain in the neck to the objects of their patronage.

Mrs. Woolf also takes a sideswipe at the "teaching" of "literature." She says: "It is an obsolete practice dating from the Middle Ages when books were scarce," and she intimates that with books available educated persons should now be able to read at home. For them to "continue to sip English literature through a straw after the age of eighteen" strikes her as rather worse than silly.

We find an even more glaring discrepancy in the strange career of Angelica Balabanoff,* told by herself in *My Life as a Rebel.* She met all the professional revolutionaries, and was one of them. She became disillusioned with the others, one by one, and depicts them with unsparing candor; those who succeeded astonished her by becoming dictators, despots, under one label or another, but all alike in practice. Why wouldn't they? What other end could they compass? They claimed to be "intellectuals," and they professed to be devoting themselves to the "working-class movement." Did they want to become working men? Not at all; they could have done that, anyhow. Then what place would there be for them, when their revolution was accomplished, except as dictators? When any one engages in revolution the clue to his objective will be found in whatever other occupation he actually follows or demands the opportunity to follow. If a "counter revolutionary" comes out for aristocracy, of course, he expects to be an aristocrat. If a genuine working man does advocate a working-class revolution he is making an honest and open demand for the dominance of his group as such, and might be perfectly satisfied with his share in it as a member of the group. If a man joins a revolution for liberty, he wants to be free himself. But if there is no avowed place for him in the scheme he proposes, or rather, if he does not propose to take the same place as those on whose behalf he says he is agitating, then he is unconsciously expecting to take the place of God in that scheme. The one thing you can bet on is that he is not proposing to abolish himself—though sometimes he effects that, to his own surprise.

For our own part, a proposal to do us good, by some self-appointed "leader," is the one thing that instantly arouses our suspicion. We want to hear first what he is going to do for himself. You know where you're at when a man makes demands on his own behalf—whether you concede them or not, there's no shenanigan. And taking it all around, we'd pretty near as soon meet a thug with a blackjack as a do-good with a plan for our special benefit. The one insuperable difficulty which makes philosophic anarchy impracticable is the number of good folks who could not possibly be induced to mind their own business. The wicked could be dealt with much more easily.

"Turns," August 14, 1938. From New York Herald Tribune, *August 14, 1938 © 1938* The New York Times.

10

Save Us, at Least, from Boredom

Going to a dinner to T. S. Eliot seemed like a good way to Get Away From It All—that is, to lay off the Depression and Communism and Hitler for a few minutes. Not a chance. The dinner was at the New School for Social Research; and we were incautious enough to look at the Orozco murals[1] and ask Mr. Eliot why do people rave over them. And he told us. He said, and convinced us, that those paintings are the art of the new religion of the masses. They are admired and reverenced by those of the faith. We didn't like to corner him and ask if he enjoyed or admired them; besides, he could easily have dodged us with a metaphysical answer. But, anyhow, he afforded us a great relief; now we know why they look just like any other chromos[2] to us. They are what used to be called "subject paintings," at the other extreme from the nineteenth century school of sentimental subject paintings which celebrated the Sanctity of the Home, the Purity of Womanhood, and Kindness to Animals; but intrinsically the same thing. It's an awful thought; they are precisely the same thing as the old colored Sunday School cards. But, on the whole, having been conditioned that way, we prefer the Sunday School cards. So we may as well admit we are Dated.

After the dinner Mr. Eliot lectured on Edward Lear* and Swinburne,* giving the verdict to Lear.

So then we went to a tea given by the James Putnams,* and there was Granville Hicks* converting Stuart Chase* to Communism. He might have succeeded, only Stuart explained that he was a Communist of sorts fifteen years ago, so Mr. Hicks was a little too late. It's harder to re-convert people. Maybe the only solution to world problems would be to have zones or mandates or enough desert islands to allot to people of different generations and mental ages. It is observable that no matter what people think they think, they can get along well enough as long as they have a common vocabulary in which to express their disagreements. When the vocabulary changes, and everything means exactly the opposite of what it used to mean, all is lost. The mutations of communism are peculiarly rapid. We have yet to discover any one Communist who will admit that any one else is a Communist. Each one enjoys the unique distinction of knowing what a Communist is and being it. So perhaps it won't be the Communists who will get us but the Nazis, who have neither ideas nor definitions, and therefore nothing to cause dissension within the ranks. There are many signs of Nazi psychology in this country now, especially the repeated remark: "Well, anyway we're getting action"—regardless of the nature or consequences of the action.

Here's a queer literary tribute, from *Hound and Horn*, inviting notice of Robert Miller Smith as exhibiting "a striking new talent in a love story, of a cold brutality comparable to the best gangster pictures intensified into a work of art."[3] Think that over. Lately, in conversation with Helen Davies McGlade,* and again with Emily Clark,* we tried to figure out why human beings had gone out of fashion in literature. That is, the contemporary mode is to show purely "behavioristic" creatures; all the shades of feeling and personal relations which distinguish human beings are carefully eliminated. This seems to tie up at some points with the "literature of revolution," and yet it doesn't make sense; what good would a revolution be to anybody except human beings? If everybody really is like that, why do they matter at all? Why even write about them?

Personally, we have a very dark suspicion. In every period of literate history, immense quantities of boring books have been produced. There is, in fact, a large continuous demand for "the genre ennuyeux."[4] Why people want to be bored we do not know—whether they feel that anything improving must be boring, and vice versa, and they have a worthy desire for self-improvement; or whether they just don't know the difference, boredom being their natural condition; but anyhow, they demand ready-made boredom. The demand is always met, because there are also numerous people who love to bore others. It is their mission in life. They don't care to come right out and say so; they must have a high-sounding pretext. So they adopt whatever is the ethical fashion: religion, morality, sentiment, patriotism; and bore from within.[5] This accounts for the ten-ton volumes of sermons which filled the libraries of the seventeenth and eighteenth centuries; the hortatory works of Hannah More* and her successors which ushered in the nineteenth century; the "problem" novels of Mrs. Humphry

Ward* and her well-meaning kind which were read devoutly thirty years ago. Nowadays we are required to be bored in the sacred name of economics and the proletariat.

This is the really awful part of it; if you don't agree with all or any of the snake-doctors who are offering their cure-alls, if you merely mention that so far they have only succeeded in making things worse, you are frivolous, reactionary, and anti-social; you have no sympathy for the working classes. All our sympathy is with the working classes; belonging to that category, we still maintain that we are human, and do not relish having insult added to injury by our self-appointed saviors.

"Turns," April 30, 1933. From New York Herald Tribune, *April 30, 1933*

Notes

1. The frescoes, by Mexican painter José Clemente Orozco (1883–1949), made propaganda for Lenin, Stalin, and "universal brotherhood."
2. Chromolithographs—cheap color prints, very common in the late nineteenth century.
3. Paterson refers to an advertisement or press notice about "Love Story," by Robert Miller Smith, a young journalist and publicity agent. The story, which appeared in the elite arts and literature journal *Hound & Horn* ([April–June 1933] 420–38), concerns a failed love affair between a young woman and an escapee from a prison in Maine. It includes a number of brutal scenes.
4. The boring type of writing.
5. Political agitators trying to advance their cause by working unnoticed within existing institutions were said to be "boring from within."

11

The Nobel Prize in Politics

In her column of January 17, 1932, Paterson ridiculed the agitation to award socialist writer Upton Sinclair the Nobel Prize in literature. A petition to grant him the Prize had been signed by 770 "eminent ladies and gentlemen," including Albert Einstein, John Dewey,* George Bernard Shaw,* and Bertrand Russell*—on which Paterson remarked, "If they feel like giving a prize to Upton Sinclair, we have no objection; but why drag in literature? . . . Mr. Sinclair's work is about as 'distinguished' as* Ten Nights in a Bar-room[1] *and is not even in the next lot to the field of literature." The topic was important because, she maintained, "literature has more to contend with than any other art—or science, either—because so few people seem able to believe that it exists. They are always talking about two or three other things under the impression that they are discussing literature. No, we are not going to explain what it is. Explanation is either unnecessary or useless. But it definitely isn't the works of Upton Sinclair."*

Three weeks later, Paterson commented on the objections to her objections.

Here is a rather perplexing letter from Ernest S. Greene, who sent us the pamphlet recommending Upton Sinclair for the Nobel Prize.[2] "Either you know nothing at all about literature and the people who produce it, or teach that subject in universities or colleges or belong to academies of letters; or else you have tried to mislead your readers by intimating that the 770 signers (and the list of sponsors is now nearer 800) are people whose interests are far removed from literature."

On the contrary, we said specifically that some of them ought to know better. Mr. Greene's zeal has interfered with his accuracy. This often happens; Theodore Dreiser* has got more cock-eyed statistics in his *Tragic America* than we should have supposed was possible.[3]

Being as we are a hireling of the capitalists, Mr. Greene suggests that he doesn't expect us to "even understand the viewpoint of the liberal humanitarians. But some time, if you do not lose your job by a slip of some kind"—and wouldn't Mr. Green grieve for that!—"I suggest that you spend about a year going over the many favorable opinions of Upton Sinclair which have been expressed by literary people all over the world." Why? We can think of lots of better things to do than reading over the same stupidity—even a stupidity of clever people—for a year on end. Fifty thousand Frenchmen can be wrong fifty thousand times.[4]

"And can't the truth be 'literary?'" Sure it can. Also apples can be green . . . or red. Why does Mr. Greene ask such foolish questions? May poetry be rhymed? Of course it may. Are the rhymed works of J. Gordon Coogler* poetry? They are not.

Mr. Greene might look up, during the year, the favorable opinions once expressed by literary people and persons in authority in regard to the works of the pious Hannah More.*

"I say," Mr. Greene says, "that books without propaganda for a better social order are absolutely worthless." That's what Hannah's friends, and the Victorian moralists, said. Worthless to him, presumably; which indicates nothing except an absence of taste. Literature has no value at all for him. Then why does he insist on talking about it? Certainly all forms of art are worthless to persons without any esthetic sense. Science is worthless to those without intellect. They would probably confuse it with magic; or, if not, it would seem a sheer waste of time to measure the distance to Arcturus instead of digging potatoes, which can be eaten. Now if Mr. Greene chooses he is welcome to construe this into a denunciation of potatoes, or a denial of the usefulness of food.

What is more perplexing in Mr. Greene's furious epistle is that he, presumably a rebel against the established order, seems to set store by the opinions of academicians as such. "Maybe," he sneers triumphantly, "you are, or have been, a university college teacher, an academician, or a former Nobel Prize winner. If so, you are a peer, and have as much right to vote against Sinclair as the hundreds who voted for him." Will someone please give the rebel yell?

Literature can't be taught. If it could, perhaps Mr. Greene would know what it is.

There are many other confusions which constantly recur to becloud the literary judgment. Reactionaries fall into the same error as radicals. Creative ability in literature is very frequently, perhaps in the majority of cases, linked with revolutionary sentiment; because the writer must have vitality, curiosity, passion and sympathy, and therefore will be stirred to protest against whatever he considers wrong; and since many things are always wrong, the writer is quite likely to be right. But his social rightness is not what makes him a good writer. Nor contrariwise. If Shelley had been completely misinformed about Castlereagh,* his terrific verse on that statesman would still be literature: "I met Murder on the way; he had a face like Castlereagh."[5]

Coming to the rescue, Christine Chapman[6] suggests that the prominent Europeans who signed for Sinclair are moved by a subconscious irritation, "a slight envy," against the United States. "It is not taste; it is temper. A justification for their harsh feelings." An inverted patriotism. "No one of the group holds Upton Sinclair's work to the same criterion as he does his own." As for the function of literature, Miss Chapman summarizes it admirably: "The pleasure it gives is infinite." That it gives no pleasure to Mr. Greene is unfortunate for him, but otherwise neither here nor there.

Patriotism is not enough; morality is not enough; sociology is not enough; nor timeliness, nor sincerity, nor fervor. These things will not enable a man to write well, no more than they will enable him to play the violin. The Trojan War is no longer news; Milton's theology is outdated; the ethics of many of the great Greek dramas are insanity to us; one may be delighted by Pascal's* *Provincial Letters* without being either Jesuit or Jansenist; the *City of Dreadful Night* hymns pure despair; and "Come Unto These Yellow Sands" has no meaning except: It's a lovely day, let's dance.[7] But all these belong to literature.

"Turns," February 7, 1932. From New York Herald Tribune, *February 7, 1932 © 1932* The New York Times. *All rights reserved. Used by permission and protected by the Copyright Laws of the United States. The printing, copying, redistribution, or retransmission of this Content without express written permission is prohibited.*

Notes

1. An anti-alcohol novel (1854) by Timothy Shay Arthur (1809–1885), and the theatrical version that followed.
2. Greene was an associate of Sinclair's who became his "secretary in New York."
3. Dreiser's *Tragic America* (New York: Liveright, 1931) is a violent attack on capitalist society, with arguments as remarkable as its statistics. Finding, for example, that Sunday schools are "shockingly wide in [their] appeal" (21,000,000 people are said to be enrolled in them), Dreiser demands that churches be forbidden to teach anyone, and that no one under the age of sixteen be exposed to religious teaching: "as all informed persons already know, laws of this nature are working out very well in Russia now" (254, 422).

4. An allusion to "fifty million Frenchmen can't be wrong," a saying among American soldiers in World War I, referring to sex, and further popularized by a song (1927) of that name.
5. Paterson regards Shelley's verse (from *The Masque of Anarchy* [1819]) as "terrific" in the sense of "violently intense." Shelley's word was "mask," not "face."
6. This correspondent cannot be identified.
7. Jesuits and Jansenists were opposing intellectual and political parties in seventeenth- and eighteenth-century Catholicism. Pascal was a Jansenist. *The City of Dreadful Night* (1874) is a poem by James Thomson (1834–1882). "Come Unto These Yellow Sands" is a poem in Shakespeare's *The Tempest,* Act 1, Scene 2.

12

The Culture of Communism

Paterson frequently emphasized her belief that the government should never punish opinion, no matter how erroneous it was (see, for example, "Turns," March 15, 1936, pages 56–57, below). But she was concerned about the influence of American communists and communist apologists on public life. She was disgusted by such people as the famous "muckraker" Lincoln Steffens, who complimented both fascism and communism, hypocritically endorsing regimes he didn't have to live under: "Steffens was supposed to be quite bright for saying of Russia: 'I have been over into the future, and it works.' . . . Nobody noticed when Mr. Steffens was so lyrical, that his trip 'over into the future' was provisioned with canned food from the U. S. A."[1] Esteemed foreign correspondent Quentin Reynolds* was another, and perhaps more egregious, instance of a common intellectual phenomenon.*

Several weeks ago[2] we quoted from *Only the Stars Are Neutral*, by Quentin Reynolds, these extracts: "A few miles outside of Kuibyshev[3] we passed one of the big concentration camps reserved for political prisoners. Beyond that we saw a long line of them working on a new road. There were about 800. They were swinging pickaxes and wielding shovels, and on their faces there was no sign of hope. A few soldiers with rifles guarded them carelessly, for there was no place for them to run. Steele and I looked at each other and winced. . . .[4] We winced, I think, because these 800 prisoners were all women." After that Mr. Reynolds left "admiring and respecting Russia."

Bennett Cerf[5] then wrote us that we had "quoted the one paragraph in the whole of the book that painted an unsympathetic picture of the Russian people, in their time of crisis.[6] This has given several folks that I've talked to the idea that *Only the Stars Are Neutral* is anti-Russian in tone. The fact, of course, is that Reynolds was completely convinced, when he was in Russia, that it is in America's interest to help the Soviet government at this time to the very limit of its capabilities. I would appreciate your making this point clear. . . . I don't think it is fair to allow your own opinions of Russia and its place in the United Nations' defense line[7] to distort the intent of another author's book. Incidentally, I note that *Only the Stars Are Neutral* is eighth on the *Herald Tribune* best seller list for July 12. I wonder how many of the 20,000 purchasers of the book would have chosen the one paragraph that you selected for reprinting." In a subsequent communication Bennett Cerf adds: "You see, Quent and I belong to that quaint group who feel that the Russians are fighting our fight, too, at the moment, and are doing a magnificent job of it. We think that our enemies are Germany and Japan. You, evidently, don't."

We do not undertake to tell other people what they think, but we know with what country Japan has a "neutrality" alliance; and we quoted Mr. Reynolds's own testimony of admiration and respect, in his own words. We might have quoted from the context at greater length. Before he went to Russia, Mr. Reynolds relates, he did a commentary for a Soviet propaganda film, to get permission to go. He says: "I would have joined the Communist party, learned to speak Russian, and sold my two brothers into slavery to get that visa. . . .[8] We had a grand opening. . . . I made a speech and did everything but sing the Internationale. I wound up by talking of Maisky (the Soviet Ambassador) as though he were a combination of John the Baptist, Clark Gable and Albert Einstein." You see how amiably Mr. Reynolds comes by his convictions. To be sure, it's all in good humor, if only those 800 women could see the joke.

In Russia, Mr. Reynolds found, "one could not, for example, inquire too closely about the so-called enemies of the state. Once more, let me emphasize that this is no criticism of Communism." Seems to need a little emphasis, or something. "We had a good lunch to celebrate our imminent entrance into the plutocratic ranks of car-owners" with a second-hand Ford from the Afghan Embassy. "We had caviar and vodka and broiled chicken and a wonderful salad and excellent cheese. We felt so good that we had a bottle of champagne to celebrate." "General Anders had an army of 150,000 Poles, all of whom hated Germans so much that they were willing to forget the past two years they had spent in Russian work camps or prisons after the 1939 partition of Poland."[9] He knows what those 150,000 Poles think, too. Then Mr. Reynolds went on a conducted tour, in another car. "Russia bought the plans of the 1936 Buick" to copy. Mr. Reynolds did "feel bitter about the censorship." That actually incommoded him a little, not somebody else. As for the 800 women in just one camp, even if they do feel bitter, Mr. Reynolds explains that "of course, it wasn't as bad as the convict labor I'd seen in our own South, because these prisoners weren't shackled and they didn't wear stripes." Never mind whether they had committed any offense, had any trial, had no place to run to, and were simply political prisoners. Mr. Reynolds still had reason enough for admiration and affection: "Our party was received at the hotel as if we were royalty. . . .[10] We ate great quantities of cold meat and ham and drank many bottles of vodka. . . . It was fun that night." Mr. Reynolds also had dinner with "Uncle Joe," and a menu of luxuries too long to print here. He had a good look at "Vyshinsky,[11] the man who prosecuted and sent to either death or imprisonment at least 100,000 Russian citizens in the 1938 purge." Mr. Reynolds had a wonderful secretary in Russia, named Sophiana. For nothing whatever, in her younger years she had been sent to a concentration camp and spent seven years at hard labor, separated from her husband and two children. "She emerged from those seven years of agony without one drop of bitterness in her soul. Oh, they had been wrong, she admitted"—admitted, that's the word—"but they had made a natural mistake." You wouldn't suppose she was under any fear they might make another such mistake if she had any hard feelings, would you? Sophiana brought Mr. Reynolds tea and cigarettes when he awoke at 10:30 in the morning. American and English cigarettes; she just picked them up in somebody else's room. "She was indeed a jewel of rare price." Leaving Russia, by air—Sophiana didn't go along—there was more wonderful food: "I borrowed a detective story from Madame Litvinov[12] and read it while eating her lovely caviar sandwiches." Now we trust it is quite clear that Mr. Reynolds is extremely sympathetic. But to clinch the matter, he relates a conversation with a Soviet factory manager, who explained that they don't have strikes in Russia. They "have no need of strikes," said the manager. "'I wonder why you people are so afraid of Communism,' this strangely enlightened man in the interior of Russia said thoughtfully.[13] 'Well, were I the owner of a big factory in America and interested only in profits, I, too, would be afraid of Communism.'"

Some day perhaps some foreign correspondent will come to the United States and investigate this singular phenomenon, the working of the Communist party in the United States; how for years past they have been consistently organized to penalize by undercover methods all critical comment on any topic relating to Communism, and to suggest the discharge of any person making such comment. He may be surprised, not to say baffled, to find that this current week

Mr. Elmer Davis[14] has been saying candidly that no Communists or "fellow travelers" should be allowed in the government service, "as a matter of policy," because as a matter of fact the Communist party is a secret organization in this county obediently serving a foreign nation. Such an investigator might ask, as we once asked a candid ex-Communist, where are the signed membership cards of American Communist party members kept; and might learn, as we did, that they were always sent to Moscow.

He might recall that in the interest of a foreign power allied with Germany Communists in this country pulled strikes and committed sabotage in American defense-work factories.[15] He might ask himself whether Mr. Davis, for one, is not keenly alive to the possibility of a recurrence of such events in case of a new alliance, while Japan gains the advantage.

He might even wonder why any American should assume that the United States is not fully capable of fighting its own fight and doing at least a tolerable job of it. When he looked at Germany or Russia or Japan today, he might ask himself whether the alleged accomplishments of such nations are not owing to resources borrowed, stolen or copied from the free nations of the earth; and from a freer past even in Germany; and he might then ask himself whether it is such a wonderful achievement for Germany to have looted Europe or for Russia to have copied a 1936 Buick. Such a foreign investigator might, we submit, actually see something to admire and respect right here in the United States.

But if an American does that, naturally he ought to be fired, if not brought before a firing squad. Especially if any American should recall that the Communist vote in Germany put Hitler in power,[16] he may expect to receive, as we did, a letter (signed Schroeder Boulton),[17] intimating that "this comes pretty near treason." Treason to what country? He will be given the pure Nazi argument that an alliance with Hitler or an invasion of a small country may be "justified on military grounds."

These things are the instant concern of any writer, however obscure or unimportant. They touch the core of intellectual integrity. We know, and have always known, exactly what to expect from those "sympathizers" for the expression of American sentiments. But we belong to that large group who believe that the United States really means something, that it is always in America's interest for Americans to think like Americans; that many Americans have laid down their lives for that belief, and many are at present fighting for it; and that our sympathy, our admiration, and our respect belong to them, living or dead, now and forever.[18]

Notes

1. "Turns," December 22, 1940.
2. "Turns," July 5, 1942.
3. Reynolds characterizes Kuibyshev, a city on the Volga formerly known as Samara, as "the wartime capital of Soviet Russia, the news center of the German-Russian campaign and headquarters for most of the government figures" (*Only the Stars Are Neutral* [New York: Random House, 1942] 155).
4. Here Paterson omits: "Of course it wasn't as bad . . . and they didn't wear stripes" (Reynolds 187), which she quotes below. Above, she silently corrects Reynolds's style by omitting "of them" following "about 800" (Reynolds 187). Steele was Archibald Trojan (Arch) Steele (1903–1992), Canadian American journalist and correspondent for the *Chicago Daily News.*
5. Cerf (1898–1971) was the cofounder and moving spirit of Random House, which had published Reynolds's book. He was later Ayn Rand's publisher. Cerf tried, not always successfully, to stay on good terms with Paterson.
6. Soviet Russia had been invaded by Nazi Germany in 1941.
7. Before the current United Nations was founded, America and its war allies were often called the United Nations.
8. Here, and following the next sentence, Paterson elides material from Reynolds, page 66. She also inserts the parenthesis following "Maisky."
9. In 1939, Hitler and Stalin concluded a pact allowing them to divide eastern European countries, including Poland, between them.
10. Here, and following the next sentence, Paterson elides material from Reynolds, pages 219–20.
11. "Uncle Joe" was a common nickname for Joseph Stalin; Andrey Vyshinsky (1883–1954) was a leading figure in Stalin's purge trials and in many other Stalinist affairs.
12. Maxim Litvinov (1876–1951) was foreign minister of the Soviet Union during the 1930s and ambassador to the United States from 1941 to 1943. His wife was the British woman Ivy Low (1889–1977).
13. Here Paterson omits the following, from page 192 of Reynolds's text: "'It is a red flag in front of a bull to you. Yet there are only a handful of Communists in America. Who stirs up the people so that they think all Communists have long black beards and carry bombs under their coats?' He laughed. 'I have seen your newspaper cartoons.'"
14. Davis (1890–1958) was a distinguished journalist who in 1941 was appointed by President Roosevelt as director of the Office of War Information. Far

from an extreme anti-Communist, he responded with hostility to the rise of McCarthyism.

15. The foreign power allied with Germany from 1939 to 1941 was the Soviet Union. During 1940 and early 1941, the press frequently ran stories about sabotage attributable to Communists and sympathizers with Germany.
16. Paterson appears to repeat the common social-democratic accusation that the Communists preferred fighting other leftists to uniting against Hitler. She may also believe that her audience is aware of the fact that many urban votes that customarily went to the Communists were ultimately delivered to the Nazis.
17. Schroeder Boulton (1909–2000), grandson of a mayor of Brooklyn and a founder of the Germania Bank, and well placed throughout his life, was a Wall Street executive of strong modern liberal sympathies. The letter in question, which is in the Paterson Papers at the Hoover Presidential Library, is dated July 20, 1942; it was sent from Boulton's address at "Fifty Two Wall Street, New York," to the editor of the *New York Herald Tribune*. It complains of Paterson's column of July 19, 1942, in which she posed the questions, "Who made the treaty with Hitler which gave him the go-ahead signal for the war? Who invaded Poland simultaneously with Hitler and shared the loot with him? Who is asking for help from the United States while keeping on good terms with Japan? Who actually put Hitler in power by the swing vote delivered on the Party Line? Information, please." Boulton asks, "Don't you think the above paragraph comes pretty near treason in war time?" He defends the Hitler-Stalin pact and the Soviet invasion of Poland.
18. Paterson must have had great difficulty fitting her critique of Reynolds into the space available in her column; his book is actually much riper with communist propaganda than she indicates. In a manner that Reynolds clearly regards as clever, he introduces familiar charges of communist atrocities, only to dismiss them as empirically false ("there was no anti-religion in Russia that I ever saw"); or to say that it's all true, but all for the best (Sophiana "came out of her imprisonment in perfect health, mentally and physically"); or to claim that things are much worse in other countries, especially the United States: "Under Soviet law these [victims of Stalin's purges] and the other thousands who had been affiliated with them had been guilty of treason and deserved the death penalty. Had only the Low Countries and Poland and Norway and the other slave states eliminated their own traitors how much happier their fate would have been. Perhaps some day we will dig up the Congressional Record and see there the voluntary evidence given by our own Fifth Columnists and find a prosecutor as ruthless and relentless as Vyshinsky. But we are pretty soft." He advocates a crackdown on "anti-Soviet propaganda in our country" (*Only the Stars Are Neutral* [New York: Random House, 1942] 98, 119, 93, 99).

13

Freedom and Control

Though we know he didn't intend it for publication, we take advantage of a letter from Harvey Fergusson* (author of *Modern Man: His Belief and Behavior*)[1] for leave to print, as they say in the Congressional Record. Mr. Fergusson writes: "My remarks upon the ethics of sex evidently irritated you, and I think you misunderstood me a little. I did not mean to imply that women are dangerous, as women, any more than men are dangerous; but it is surely undeniable that men and women often scare each other and that fright is what creates nearly all the trouble. The test of anyone's fitness to live in a given social environment comes in sex relations."

Probably it was our fault if we gave such an impression, but we were not irritated; we were enlightened, amused, and resigned, being unable to follow Mr. Fergusson all the way to his optimistic conclusion, his sole concession to the ineradicable yearning for Utopia which infests the human breast. He thinks that if people can only understand what ails them, Something Can Be Done About It. They are afraid; very well, don't be afraid.

This is true to a very limited degree. One may cure certain ailments, genuine derangements of the presumably normal functioning of the body or mind; but plenty of our difficulties are intrinsic. "The troubles of our proud and angry dust are from eternity, and shall not fail."[2] Many of those troubles have little or nothing to do with social environment. When Brainless, our cat, comes home after a mysterious absence, as he did last week, with one eye closed and one ear considerably damaged, we do not believe he had bumped up against his social environment in the dark. And quite evidently he hadn't been afraid. The test of his fitness to live seems to be his conviction that living is worth the trouble. And it's no use arguing about that, either.

We liked Mr. Fergusson's book, especially his main thesis that all effective living or achievement is creative, and comes from individual impulse, little of which can be foreseen. The queer thing about the present mania for "control" of the future is that it goes with a complete disregard of the consequences and implications that can be foreseen—for example, the suppressions which are required to establish the power demanded for "control." People seem to have forgotten the difference between principles and material objectives. A principle may not have any material objective. It is an assertion of the value of imponderables, and may entail actual material disadvantages. A man may lose money by keeping his word, for instance. His own feeling about himself is worth more than the money to him, but the two factors are incommensurable in any strictly rational terms.

Here we pick up a booklet[3] which reads well enough until we come to the last page: "Is America in danger of losing her freedom? Should the subversive elements be put down with violence? Not unless they incite violence first. What should be the limits to tolerance? When facts warrant the conviction that a demand for tolerance is not made in good faith. Tolerance is no virtue where human liberty is at stake."

That is deplorably plausible and all wrong. Furthermore, it is ag'in the Constitution. Any Sedition Act is unconstitutional, and subverts the first principles of the American political structure. Any country is always in danger of losing its freedom. One of the best ways to lose it is to subscribe to the fallacy embodied in the above quotation. In the vernacular, it means: "I'm for freedom, so you shut up; or I'll put you in jail." The same fallacy may be concealed by various highbrow phrases, as, for instance, this from *The New Republic*: "Liberty is a positive purpose, not an absence of restraint." Bosh. Liberty is an absence of restraint. And nothing else whatever. It does not presuppose any purpose, good, bad, or indifferent. It is not a means, but an end. When we are enjoying what liberty we have, in aimless idleness, are we to expect *The New Republic* to come bustling up and ask us sternly, "What is your positive purpose?" If so, we shall cordially urge Mr. Bliven[4] and his associates to find a nice tack and sit on it until they can think up some other purpose than pestering us. We shall, indeed, be glad to supply the tack, as our positive purpose, if that will satisfy them.

We are very well aware that the danger of freedom, including free speech, is that it gives leeway for speech against it; anybody who doesn't know that fact and accept it is not for freedom. Not long ago several writers signed a protest against censorship of a communistic-labor paper. They explained that they "believed in free speech as necessary in a democracy." A nice bit of hedging. We believe in it for its own sake, as necessary to us; therefore the communist-labor paper must be allowed to speak, even though it doesn't believe in free speech. When John Strachey* came over here we thought it was a bounderish trick to take advantage of free institutions to speak against them, but if he wants to be like that it must be tolerated. But there's no need to run after him and ask him to dinner.

Lately we read another book by John Rustgard,* *The Problem of Poverty*, which had a good deal of common sense in it, mostly first-hand observations of the fact that no "system" can make people universally industrious, prudent and thrifty; with the reasonable corollary that those who do manifest such qualities are entitled to the benefit accruing. But then Mr. Rustgard came to the strange conclusion that labor unions should be abolished—a strange non-sequitur. Unionizing is a measure of prudence, and though unions are subject to error in policy and are sometimes exploited by grafters and racketeers, their legal suppression means the flat suppression of freedom. And the peculiarity of freedom is that there is no way of keeping it for yourself after you have deprived others of it. You may retain privilege, but not freedom; and your privilege will always be on sufferance.

Freedom is dangerous. Possibly crawling on all fours might be safer than standing upright. But we like the view better up there.

Notes

1. Paterson had reviewed Fergusson's work in *"Books,"* January 19, 1936, and noticed it again in "Turns," February 16, 1936. These mentions were highly favorable, but in her review she joked about Fergusson's portrayal of modern males when confronted by women: men don't, she said, "know whether to climb a tree, reach for a gun, or wait to be eaten. Mr. Fergusson wastes no space on the predicament of the woman, who is not carnivorous and would rather not be shot, and can't imagine what the man is doing up a tree."
2. Paterson quotes Poem IX in A. E. Housman (1859–1936), *Last Poems* (1922).
3. This publication cannot be identified.
4. Bruce Bliven (1889–1977) was editor in chief of *The New Republic* (1930–1953).

14

Whose Agent Is He?

Paterson was one of the few writers who went to literary "teas" and actually wanted tea, not alcohol,[1] *but she was perpetually at odds with Prohibition. So were most of the people she encountered. The difference was her attitude toward the whole category of victimless crimes. Unlike the majority of Americans, she believed that all "laws based on what people ought to feel, but don't, are nothing new, and conspicuously unsuccessful."*[2] *If Prohibition was bad, so were the laws against victimless crimes in general. One example was the law against soliciting for prostitution. Well-publicized investigations showed that the law was corruptly enforced, in many ways, but the real problem was the law. Even "decent people," she thought, were "driven to accept corruption in the administration of law in general rather than submit to the presumptuous tyranny of the laws themselves. They are compelled to dodge about in the gaps between the crooks and the reformers."*[3]

With all the indignation that has been expressed over the convictions, by paid perjury and framed evidence, of girls charged with soliciting on the streets of New York, the protests have significantly and rather sickeningly avoided touching the real issue. Nobody has cared or dared to face the fact that the law under which such convictions were obtained—and the New York law is typical of most American State laws on the subject—is a source of corruption because it is inequitable by intention. In itself it is a kind of blackmail, being a legalization of privilege, of the double standard.

The definition of the crime or misdemeanor of "soliciting" betrays the determination of those who put it on the statute books and keep it there, to secure a masculine advantage. In earlier times no trouble was taken to disguise the purpose. The inequality of the sexes was not only assumed but stated. Women were frankly penalized in innumerable ways. Often enough it was predicated that they had no standing whatever in law. Only as property were they entitled to legal recognition, and then not for their own benefit but for that of the men of their family, fathers or husbands. On the other hand, some extra responsibility attached to the men of the family. This theory could not maintain itself in a political system based on axiomatic human rights and equality. After hundreds of years of gradual change most of the disabilities of women have been lifted. Even this particular law had to be redrafted in new terms to retain the one here involved.

But in its present form it is rather more obnoxious than before, since it adds hypocrisy to injustice. Men of decent instincts avoid thinking of it. When forced to do so, they save their feelings, if not their self-respect, by denunciation of the mere incidents of its operation. They don't care to stand up in court beside Chile Mapocha Acuna.[4] But that is where they belong, as long as they approve the law.

For if the law is not meant to suppress venal sex relations, then it has no object whatever. Its only possible purpose is to prevent making sex an article of commerce.

Serious reasons, both social and emotional—call them moral and religious, if you prefer—can be adduced against prostitution. Whether or not legislation is an effective means of stopping it is another question, still open to debate. The most stringent laws have failed in the past, under economic pressure. If there is less commercialized vice in the United States than there was, say, thirty years ago, it would seem to be chiefly because the opportunities for women to earn a living in other ways than that of selling themselves have been correspondingly increased.

But a venal sex transaction is an act which requires two principals to commit. There are other crimes of this dual nature, such as bribery, in which the guilt of both parties is obviously equal. Also it is a legal maxim that whoever pays for the commission of a crime assumes full guilt: "Who does it by another does it himself." By these fundamental principles of law the man would be a little more guilty than the woman, having paid for and then participated in the act. To dodge this basic axiom, the law in question was carefully and consciously drawn. The girls are not charged with illicit sex relations, in which some man would necessarily be involved. They are accused of "soliciting." It is thus made a crime—in the present instance, specifically, a misdemeanor—to suggest to another person, a man, that he commit with them an act which is not in itself a crime. Could a more contemptible chicanery be imagined for the purpose of exculpating the man? How are the legislators and magistrates and lawyers engaged in enforcing such a statute, and the worthy citizens who lend it tacit support, any better than the nasty little informer who gives paid testimony?

It may be argued that it is a misdemeanor for a man to "solicit," that is, to accost a woman on the street with improper proposals; and therefore there is no lack of equity. This is another quibble. It is a misdemeanor for any person to annoy any other person, on the street or elsewhere, for no good reason. If one should address a stranger and follow him and persist in talking about the weather, the law would afford protection on request. It is a disorderly act. If any man cares to complain of the undesired attentions of a strange woman he must be heard.

But when the man has followed her, without compulsion, to a room, and further indicated his willingness by some overt sign, such as removing his coat, before the police can break in, after which the woman only is arrested, the travesty of justice is palpable.

With such a law, the employment of an *agent provocateur* inevitably follows. He is pernicious, but he is a symptom; an effect, not a cause. Whose agent is he? The phrase itself reveals a higher responsibility. In short, if prostitution is a crime, and two persons are shown to have intended to commit this crime, then the law has a fair pretext. As it stands, it is devoid of the slightest shred of equity. Puritan laws against sexual immorality have been much jeered at. Certainly it is arguable that they were both harsh and futile. They may have been mistaken, and they might cause resentment, rebellion, and of course law-breaking. But they do not poison the sources of justice. They don't contravene equity. The issue is drawn on principle, and opinions may be honestly held on either side.

The present law against soliciting is vitiated by the same humbug on the part of respectable people which taints the prohibition law. The sale of liquor is a crime, but not the purchase. The only conceivable object of prohibition is to prevent drinking. It is based on the belief that drinking is wrong. The buyer is the one who intends to drink. But even if he actually does drink the liquor, still he is not guilty under the law, while the vendor is.

In the case of the convicted girls, men are only silencing their own uneasy conscience by an outcry against the police and the decoy. This is nothing new; it is the immemorial way in which respectable people seek to avoid responsibility for an iniquity by which they profit. Before the Civil War slave owners professed to despise slave dealers and overseers, who were in fact their agents, executing their orders. At the same time they defended the institution of slavery, and demanded that the law as embodied in the Constitution be respected.[5] Justice commands respect; it does not need to ask for it.

Good men and true[6] who are willing to defend the law against soliciting, as it stands, ought not to repudiate Chile Mapocha Acuna; they are all members of the same club.

The Nation, *February 11, 1931, 153–54. Reprinted by permission of* The Nation.

Notes

1. "Sometimes there is no tea at literary teas, and we have to raise a distressful row to get it—and don't we just" ("Turns," April 12, 1936).
2. "Turns," November 16, 1930.
3. "Turns," July 3, 1932.
4. Acuna (c. 1899–?), professional police informant and frame-up artist, was the star witness in a highly publicized investigation of police and judicial shakedowns of women accused of solicitation.
5. As Paterson emphasized in GM (136), the Constitution never mentions slavery by name. Here she is presumably referring to Article I, Section 9, concerning the "importation of . . . persons," and Article IV, Section 2, concerning persons "held to service or labour."
6. People chosen for juries were often called "good men and true."

15

Monkey-gland Economics[1]

Unlike many people who became libertarians or conservatives after disillusionment with socialism, communism, or the New Deal, Paterson never granted credence to any of the economic "solutions" that have periodically swept the country. She survived Free Silver, the Single Tax, the New Economic Era, Technocracy, the Soviet of Engineers, the Blue Eagle, the Townsend Plan, the Planned Economy, and the Mixed Economy. "America," she said, "has always been prolific of economic fantasies."[2] *She was not about to fall for the Mature Economy.*

Excepting pure despotism, it is customary for a government to offer the public some plea of imperative national necessity for inordinate taxation. As men could not be worse off in anarchy[3] or brute savagery than with a government which strips them to the bone, obviously there is a rational limit to the *proper* expense of government. And even politicians do not quite like to admit that they are making a tax grab solely for their own pockets, or to win the next election. But the validity of the pretext given for government spending always varies by inverse ratio to the unchecked power of government to take what it pleases regardless of injury to the taxpayer. The theory of the Mature Economy is the latest excuse offered in a period of dizzy increase of the political power, of taxes, borrowing and spending.

Mr. Terborgh[4] undertakes to demolish this theory, though it is no easy task to boil down the economic jargon to a definite meaning, and quite impossible to refute a string of words that mean nothing whatever. What could be extracted from such a phrase as "a society geared to a high peakload of capital goods production"? (The phrase belongs to Dr. Alvin H. Hansen,[5] and he can have it.) A high peakload is a tautology, since the peakload is the highest load; and you just don't gear to a peakload anyhow; try it. It is nothing but a mixed metaphor. But Mr. Terborgh gives the statement of the theory from its proponent's verbatim in order to be fair. It may be best to make a briefer résumé in English.

An economy then would be fully "mature" if it ever got to the point beyond which there could be no further increase of productive capital assets. That would mean there would be no further investment of net savings in the economy. This condition must be understood clearly. It does not refer to the savings of an individual who may invest in previously existent capital assets, seasoned securities; but to a possible net surplus of savings in the economy, accumulated when or after there could be no further use for venture capital, because there would be no field for new enterprise at all, no undeveloped territory, inventions, or anything. And before reaching full or absolute "maturity," the *rate* of increase of total capital assets might be expected to slow down. It is assumed that total capital wouldn't increase faster and faster or even at a steady rate until it came to a sudden stop instanter. Then from the moment it did begin to slow down, of course the rate of entirely new investment, venture capital from savings, must decline commensurately.

But when savings go into venture capital, the process generally requires new buildings, new machinery and so forth, by which part of such savings invested becomes new income as wages and salaries of workers who do the building or make the machinery. Therefore a declining rate of venture capital investment means a direct decline in jobs, an increasing unemployment with no hope of a future upturn.

To take up the slack of such unemployment, the Mature Economists contend, it is necessary or desirable for the government to grab by taxation that margin of net surplus savings for which no venture capital investment is open, and spend the money. It is also asserted or implied that the American economy is *already* on the down curve toward "maturity"; therefore such savings ought to be expropriated from now on. It is not explained why the citizens couldn't just as well spend their own savings on themselves for consumption goods. They need a lot of stuff right now, including food, clothes, motor cars, houses, and maybe a vacation in the loony bin to think things over. Mr. Terborgh notes these oddities of present application.

But most of Mr. Terborgh's effort is directed toward showing the basic fallacy of the whole theory by facts and logic. Of course there is a catch in it, which dodges all conditions of proof. No economy has ever yet become "mature." In the past many economies have certainly declined to the verge of extinction under government control, taxation, and spending; but never because a *free* economy *could not* have found use for venture capital. Then how is it to be known when a decline would actually indicate imminent "maturity"? There is no way, since previous declines could not show any clue, to match up. The theory therefore by its nature simply cannot fit any facts of previous record. All genuine scientific prediction has to rest on facts of record in the past, the thing which has already happened, in a known sequence. A system of mathematics that came out wrong when applied to yesterday's data couldn't very well be correct in relation to future operations.

The fallacy in the assumption of an investment standstill in the future is that new industrial investment arises from technological progress, discoveries and inventions which, being discoveries and inventions, are by their nature utterly and forever unpredictable. They are precisely the incalculable element in economics. A calculation based on the incalculable goes one better than unscrewing the inscrutable. That factor has always made a monkey of the gloomy forecaster of the total future. There were self-appointed prophets who didn't see how there could be any new capital development after the canals and railroads and steam engine. Mr. Terborgh sums up these premature economists neatly: "Because they cannot see what is coming, they assume that nothing is coming."

But in conclusion Mr. Terborgh turns on himself, by saying that there must be "economic statesmanship, both public and private to create under the altered social, political and economic conditions of today an environment hospitable to enterprise." Might as well point to a slab of concrete and suggest that one must create *under it* an environment hospitable to raising vegetables. It can't be done. The concrete would have to be removed. The social, political and economic conditions at any time are just what constitute the environment of enterprise. They will have to be "altered" back again, to permit enterprise, or else. That can be done, but it means that the necessity must be recognized.

Because of Mr. Terborgh's conclusion, this book presents a tough problem in itself, being an example of a prevailing practice by which relevant facts and rational argument are suddenly brought to a flat non-sequitur. Do not such attempts at an impossible compromise tend to more danger or harm than the errors they set out to combat? History indicates that even clear refutations of foolish theories don't take much effect, being negative. What finally disposes of a fallacy is a positive and correct theory in the same field, provable in application, which simply displaces previous error and leaves it to be forgotten. Fallacies flourish in the absence of exact knowledge; and the processes of production need to be understood thoroughly, on positive axioms and principles.

Mr. Terborgh comments on the rapid spread of the notion of Economic Maturity, and seems to imply that it is altogether new. It isn't. It is a revamped version of the Marxist Communist theory of the relation of industrial capitalism to undeveloped colonial areas and the presumed final exhaustion of the latter. That is why it has got around so fast in the channels of Communist propaganda. It serves the Communist purpose perfectly for the time being.

American Affairs, *July 1945, 159–60. Content reproduced with permission from The Conference Board, Inc.*

Notes

1. It isn't known whether Paterson or the journal editor supplied the title, which is not in her usual style. It refers to an operation in which tissue from monkey testicles was grafted onto human testicles, with the aim of reversing the aging process.
2. "Turns," February 13, 1938.
3. Paterson, who had objected vigorously when her friend John Chamberlain* called her a "philosophical anarchist" ("Turns," August 6, 1939), named a chapter of GM "The Fallacy of Anarchism."
4. George Terborgh (1897–1989), influential economist and author of *The Bogey of Economic Maturity* (1945), which Paterson is reviewing.
5. Alvin Harvey Hansen (1887–1975), Harvard economist, was a chief American promoter of Keynesian economics.

16

The Elusive Law of Wages

In an era in which economic discussion was dominated by the reputed "interests" of big business and organized labor, Paterson was most interested in the usefulness and virtue of free markets: "An industrial society cannot continue to exist except as a free society, from which it takes its being. There is no alternative. Never mind 'building an industrial society'; secure a free society and it will be industrial; extinguish freedom and industry will vanish with it. And that's that."[1]

Mr. Rucker[2] tackles a tough question, which is the wage factor in a dynamic economy. With a production system arising from the division of labor, there is necessarily a subsequent division of the product. Wages are one part of such division. But how is it or should it be made, in what proportion?

Now here is a paradox of economic history, which Mr. Rucker notes to begin with. In Europe, all kinds of regulations have always been imposed on economic relations, fixing prices, hours, wages, limiting jobs or entry into specific occupations, limiting output and exchanges—every darned thing. Never was there a wholly free market. And the general intention was to make such things what it was conceived they *ought* to be. (The just price, the just wage, or whatever.) Meanwhile the workingman seldom got more than a bare living, if he could keep out of slavery or serfdom.

Then the United States came into being, with nothing but contract law to cover wages, prices, industry and trade. It was, at last, the Free Market. "Unprotected" American labor was open to exploitation. Exploitation means hiring a man and paying him wages for productive labor. Apparently it is a horrible thing to do. And they did it. A man with a job and a man who wanted work settled it between them. Wages were adjusted by the market, which incidentally had to absorb a large influx of immigrant labor and equate expanding industry with the pull of frontier land, throughout good times and hard times and all sorts of local variables. That meant innumerable changes in wages, sometimes up, sometimes down. Nothing was pegged. Yet American labor presently commanded the highest pay ever known, with an unprecedented standard of living and opportunity to rise from the ranks.

Mr. Rucker suggests that if any constants can be found in this whole process, they must represent scientific laws in industry. And he finds that statistical study does show such constants, by averages, in given periods.

One constant is that, taking the whole output of manufactures, labor gets a fairly constant percentage or ratio of what is called "Value Added by Manufacture." This is so no matter how the total annual income of labor or total of employment or average annual wage varied during the same period. But the total annual income of labor likewise bears a fairly constant ratio to the total volume of goods. So does the average annual wage correspond to the rate of productivity. And the number of jobs, or ratio of employment to unemployment, bears a relation to the ratio of firms making a profit to those making no profit. Finally, industrial payrolls and farm income correspond constantly.

Certainly if these statistical correspondences or relations are so, they cannot be altogether without significance. And they are a study, not of what ought to be, but of what *is*.

Broken down, of course, they are not so simple; inverse ratios also appear. If the prices of farm products are low, relative to the prices of manufactured goods, that means low *volume* of manufactures, though there may be simultaneously high wage *rates*, along with a low *average annual income* for labor, and high unemployment. Labor might be getting a dollar an hour, with wheat at seventy-five cents a bushel, for instance; but in that case there would be heavy unemployment in industry, or those employed would not have many hours employment in the week or year. These interactions cannot all be stated briefly. But Mr. Rucker thinks that any kind of enforced price fixing, rigid prices—whether imposed by government regulation or unions or whatever—must cause the injurious discrepancy of prices. This seems pretty obviously true.

In brief, Mr. Rucker says labor really *is* paid according to production volume and the rate of productivity, and that apparently it can get neither more nor less, in total or in average. But interference with the Free Market can and does reduce both the volume of production and the rate of productivity; and it can't do anything else. Such interference cannot raise production or the rate of productivity; consequently it cannot increase the total annual wage or the average annual wage. It must decrease them. That also seems pretty demonstrably true. Here we have a statement of what is so in the nature of things, not of what ought to be.

"Labor's road to plenty" then is the Free Market, no political regulation beyond contract law—and perhaps no unions? Mr. Rucker finds that unions do not actually obtain higher wages for labor, taking all the industry which is unionized. (But if unions were suppressed by law, there could be no Free Market either; because the right of contract gives men the right to form unions. This also is so in the nature of things—what is, not what ought to be.) However, Mr. Rucker does not suggest at all that unions should be suppressed. He suggests that labor and management must come to an understanding of the fact, which his statistics indicate, that it is actually *impossible* for either to *benefit* at the *expense* of the other.

Then they could adjust wages to production—by an hourly base rate, and some further distribution "proportionate to productivity." Probably some such arrangement is needed in industry. Mr. Rucker points out that the real use of the hourly wage rate makes it indispensable to fix differentials for work of different value (skilled or unskilled). But taken by itself the hourly wage rate has an element of rigidity in relation to production; and piecework rates alone certainly used to be liable to the speed-up and subsequent piece-rate cutting. It may well be that the introduction of a combined method of wage payment, by which the wage earner could be sure increased production would mean increased pay *for him* (he doesn't care what it is on an average for industry as a whole!), might be an enormous advance in the production system.

But one would like to know, if labor really does, by a natural law of industry, necessarily get a constant ratio of value added, what went wrong in the worst early years of the English industrial revolution? Was the rate of productivity really so low it would not yield a decent living wage or decent hours for labor? Or what other factor came in?

Mr. Rucker's enquiry is rather limited for such a subject. The catch in statistical averages is that they are necessarily found within a given field; and one must know what *creates* or *constitutes* the field, before one can know if they indicate any law other than the mathematical law that averages can be found in any field. One must know all possible interferences, and whether they are avoidable or controllable. For example, Mr. Rucker thinks that labor and management must understand that their interest is really the same, not opposed interests, and act upon that knowledge by agreement. I think it is true that their interests are the same. But the existence of labor unions may not be caused by the *interest* of labor, but by its physical position as dislocated mass,[3] and that is another question altogether, a factor which would prevent labor acting upon its interest by intelligent volition. It is not in a man's interest to fall out of a window, but he does if he loses his balance just the same. I suggest that the real problem is the absence of political structure at present—without that, there can be no contract law, no free market, and in due course no industry or labor. That is the "field"; the *political* structure.

Then there is another drawback to statistical averages, which is rather hard to explain briefly. If you got the average height of a bunch of school children, the one thing you wouldn't find among those children would be any one child who was actually that height. The "average height" is a height no child is. Now, Mr. Rucker finds an average ratio of division of value added, an average percentage which goes for wages out of the *total* population. He posits then that this ratio or percentage would serve as a guide for any *one* business to go by, in paying wages. Or perhaps for any one branch of industry—I don't know. But would it? I can't see how. The free market *per se* consists of persons making exchanges, whether of goods, or of wages and labor, each asking the most he can get, and offering the least the other party will take, in competition with other bids. *Average* wages and prices, and fairly even wages and prices in like things, do *result* from that; but it is the competition which makes them. And some firms go broke because they can't meet the market. The possibilities are too complex to follow through all the way, but somehow it strikes me as being less simple than Mr. Rucker makes it, because he takes the *result* of one process—the competitive bidding, asked and offered, process of the free market—and suggests using it to *begin* with, which would initiate a quite different process. Averages are like that.

Haven't some big businesses occasionally run *for a while* at an actual deficit, a loss, and still pulled through? In that case, it seems to me there are extremely troublesome complications possible with a wage sliding down and down while other firms may be running at a profit. What would the workmen do? It looks like a dissolving view.

American Affairs, *July 1945, 160–62. Content Reproduced with permission from The Conference Board, Inc.*

Notes

1. "Turns," May 17, 1942.
2. Allen Willis Rucker (1897–1964), author of *Labor's Road to Plenty* (1945), which Paterson is reviewing.
3. An application of the "engineering" ideas of GM: the mass of citizens without real property is a shifting base, or no base at all, for the structure of government; they are, as it were, detached from permanent interests.

17

The Man with One Idea

Paterson weighed capitalism in her balance and pronounced it the only justifiable form of economic life. Individual capitalists, however, must be judged on their own merits. In assessing Henry Ford, she blissfully ignored his contributions to industrial progress, slighted his courage as a risk taker, and sneered at his attempts to preserve the relics of America's past. For her, none of that counted when compared with his role as a cultural illiterate, a feckless do-good, and a tyrannical meddler in his employees' lives.

Tragedies that provide almost continuous laughter are rather rare. Yet this book,[1] on the whole, justifies its title; though opened at random it will evoke a smile, and several episodes are as uproariously comic as the broader farce scenes of *Penguin Island*. And nowhere has the author striven for comic effect. On the contrary, he has exercised commendable restraint, realizing that it would be impossible to invent Henry Ford and injudicious to touch him up. The tragedy, as well as the humor, is in the immense disproportion between the man and the events which produced him.

Mr. Leonard[2] confesses that he was moved to begin this study of Henry Ford by burning moral indignation. He saw Ford as the "evil genius of twentieth-century America, a first cause" of all that is cheap and ugly in our era, from "rusty tin cans" to the hypocrisy of prohibition and the worship of standardized ignorance. He was horrified by the inhuman processes of speeded-up mass production in the great factories; and by the Ford by-product of petty tyranny over private lives through the system of espionage and arbitrary interference, inevitably producing sullen, cowed resentment.[3]

As Mr. Leonard gathered his material and began to compose it, the emphasis shifted. At the last he found himself pitying the man Henry Ford, deciding that Ford was no worse than other captains of industry, perhaps not so bad as some. "His motives were often benign. . . .

He really wanted to use his unprecedented wealth to help humanity, point out the various errors of which it was guilty. . . ." Yet Ford's altruistic endeavors merely exposed him to the onslaught of "cranks, fanatics, even criminals." He became a national and then an international joke. As a secondary consequence he grew embittered, and once at least he sought revenge for his disappointment—when he was defeated for the Senate.[4] Again the result was pure farce. Finally and tragically, he was passed by the procession he had led so long. He lost his place at the head of the long industrial assembly line; and the line goes on. And still he does not know what it was all about, any more than the fabled fly on the wheel.

Mr. Leonard gives the bare facts of Ford's early life briefly, regarding amplification as an unfruitful task. Ford was born in 1863 on a farm near Dearborn, Michigan. His father was an Irish immigrant, his mother of Pennsylvania Dutch stock. Like all boys, he tinkered with mechanical contraptions. Drifting naturally to Detroit, he found intermittent employment in its machine shops. When out of work he retreated to the paternal farm. He built the first Ford in 1893, drove it for three years, then sold it for $200 and built some more, one at a time, privately. At forty he had saved no money, and had resigned from his one important job as chief engineer with the Detroit Automobile Company. He had acquired a wife and son; "he made an unfortunate personal impression and had few friends." Nevertheless, in 1903 he managed to collect, "in driblets," the $28,000 capital for the Ford Motor Company. The money was put up by the Dodge brothers, the savings of their machine shop; by a coal-dealer named Malcolmson, and others unknown to fame. Ford contributed his one idea, to make a cheap car for the large public. He stuck to that like glue, breaking successively with his backers and associates, and buying up a majority of the company's stock. Within five years he had the control. Within ten years he was a billionaire.

Mr. Leonard thinks it was the unproductiveness of war that stirred Ford to his first large effort toward benefiting humanity. But he had achieved his only original objective. He had nowhere to go from there. He could make his car a little cheaper, perhaps; but otherwise he dared not entertain any thought of change, because that would have entailed abandoning the great idea. The money came pouring in, and what was he to do with it? One day the door to his office was left open for a few minutes, and the eloquent and undoubtedly well-meaning Madame Rosika Schwimmer entered. Ford embarked on the Peace Ship, in one sense his first flivver.[5]

The chapter on the Peace Ship is brilliant selective rewriting. Every detail is incredible and precious. The loading of Noah's ark must have been tame compared to the scene of the sailing of the *Oscar II.* A mob of curious idlers had gathered at the dock. Reporters fought their way through. Stowaways were forcibly ejected at intervals. "The proportion of actual lunatics was probably small," Mr. Leonard summarizes judicially, "but the general impression was that of a revival in a psychopathic ward." The ship's saloons were decorated with olive branches and stuffed doves. Various enthusiasts made speeches over the rail. Berton Braley,* one of the special correspondents, was getting married in a space hastily cleared of baggage. Dr. Pease,* the anti-tobacco crusader, was among those present. William Jennings Bryan* came aboard, was presented with a squirrel in a small wire cage, and carried it under his arm until the ship sailed. Other squirrels were released. Judge Ben Lindsey* exclaimed: "Oh, God, why am I here?" And after the ship had actually started, in a deafening uproar of cheers, whistles, and peace hymns, Urban Ledoux, "Mr. Zero," dived off the dock and swam after it. He was rescued and brought back to shore.[6]

So was Ford, though not until he had reached Norway. His friend and adviser, Dean Marquis,* went along expressly to get him back.

The Peace Ship was Ford's most spectacular blunder. But every time he has gone off his own lot he has come to grief in some absurd way. He really might have been President, Mr. Leonard thinks, if he had had the slightest notion of what the President is, what powers and duties attach to the position. Mr. Leonard gives Calvin Coolidge the credit of side-tracking Ford from the route to the White House with the bait of Muscle Shoals;[7] which of course was not in the President's control, though Ford supposed it must be. Perhaps he imagined that the President ran the country in the same sense that he ran his factory. But Ford defeated himself for the Senatorship, when he ran in 1918. He had talked a little too much, in the first flush of enthusiasm at finding himself a national figure. The things he said needed only to be quoted. And he had rashly got himself involved in a libel suit with the Chicago *Tribune.*[8] That was almost as funny as the Peace Ship. His counsel could not keep Ford off the stand. Thus he was forced to reveal that he did not know the difference between Benedict Arnold and Arnold Bennett*; that he thought the American Revolution had occurred in 1812; and that he "could read, slowly," but not well enough to risk reading a paragraph aloud in court.

Since then Ford's career has been a slow diminuendo. His Wayside Inn, with its collection of relics of the pre-motor age, Mr. Leonard finds pathetically significant. It is Ford's retreat from reality, from the desolation of the industrial centers.[9] And so his biographer sums up Ford as "a man in some ways friendly, simple, kindly," possessed of "a billion dollars—more or less—which he had come into partly by accident, partly by ruthlessness, partly by a strange sort of non-rational intelligence," an incalculable fortune he was anxious to spend for the benevolent purpose that "all men should have the happiness that comes from living correctly." Hence the anti-cigarette and prohibition propaganda, the inquisition of private spies into the private lives of employees, and even the impracticable projects linked up with Muscle Shoals.

Henry Ford's idea of the Good Life, Mr. Leonard concludes, was formed by his rural or small-town environment, which had preserved the tradition of the frontier. "Ford had grown up under the influence of this point of view, and had absorbed it into his very soul. . . . The leisurely, non-productive pleasures are not in favor where the memory of the frontier still lingers. Nor is anything else which does not contribute to the gathering of things, more things." In prescribing a life devoid of variety, delight, or intellectual stimulus, narrowed down to work and sleep and paced by clockwork, Henry Ford, Mr. Leonard believes, was absurdly and illogically trying to perpetuate the small town. I regret that I cannot follow Mr. Leonard on this point. I can only suppose that he never lived on the frontier. His own picture of Ford's early life, drifting, tinkering, idling, suggests precisely the opposite of the regulated routine of the ideal Ford factory workers. No, a small mind is a small mind anywhere. Barring his narrowly specialized organizing ability, Ford is remarkably like Philip II of Spain, or the last Czar of Russia. The unfortunate Czar had no brains whatever. So it is idle to speculate whether or not he meant well. He really didn't mean anything. But while I disagree with Mr. Leonard on this particular deduction, I heartily recommend his book for its general sanity, excellent writing, and rich entertainment value.

The Nation, *April 13, 1932, 435–36. Reprinted by permission of* The Nation.

Notes

1. The book is *The Tragedy of Henry Ford* (1932), which Paterson is reviewing, by Joshua Norton Leonard (see note 2). *Penguin Island* (below) is a satirical novel by Anatole France.*
2. Jonathan Norton Leonard (1903–1975), author of *The Tragedy of Henry Ford* and books on many other subjects.

3. Ford's Sociological Department and Service Department made intrusive investigations of workers' lives.
4. Ford was the Michigan Democratic Party's candidate for the Senate in 1918.
5. A flivver was a Model T Ford or other cheap car. The Peace Ship was the *Oscar II,* an ocean liner that Ford chartered (1915) to sail to Europe to produce a negotiated settlement of World War I. Rosika Schwimmer (1877–1948) was a Hungarian feminist and pacifist and persuader of Henry Ford.
6. Bryan favored peace but did not journey on the peace ship. The squirrels signified other people's opinions of the voyagers' nuttiness. The self-denominated Mr. Zero was an insane person or a publicity seeker, or both.
7. A place on the Tennessee River in northern Alabama where President Wilson started construction of a dam and munitions factories during World War I. After the war, Henry Ford tried to buy the site and make it the nucleus of a giant industrial complex, but there was opposition in Congress and Ford finally relinquished the idea.
8. Ford sued the *Tribune* for calling him "an ignorant idealist" and "an anarchistic enemy of the nation." When the case was tried in 1919, the jury, apparently convinced that the second charge was false but the first was true, awarded Ford six cents in damages.
9. In 1924, Ford restored the early-eighteenth-century Wayside Inn, in South Sudbury, Massachusetts. In 1929 he dedicated the world's largest museum of industry and invention, the Henry Ford Museum and its associated Greenfield Village, in Dearborn, Michigan. Leonard's book, which is less a biography than a series of episodes worked up largely for satirical purposes, mentions the Wayside Inn but fails to mention the Village and Museum.

18

What Do They Do All Day?

This account of the ways in which Paterson made herself a writer unwelcome to the New York Herald Tribune *and an advisor unwelcome to many conservatives and nascent libertarians was written for* National Review. *William F. Buckley, Jr.,* the publisher and editor of* National Review, *was enthusiastic about the article but insisted that the name of one of its targets, Jasper Crane,* be omitted. There was no reason, Buckley thought, to attack him personally. Paterson could just call him a du Pont executive. Paterson rejected Buckley's proposal, and until now the article has remained unpublished.*

The article is enough to show, if there were no other evidence, that Paterson could be a difficult person. It also shows that she knew she was difficult. But the essay is about more than her own disposition. It dramatizes vivid episodes in the long history of conflict and resentment between conservative and libertarian intellectuals, on the one hand, and the businesspeople whose rights they have tried to defend, on the other. Few conservative or libertarian writers have been pleased with the attitude of capitalists toward advocates of capitalism. As Paterson's essay indicates, the relationship may be least happy when the capitalists are officials of large organizations, more accustomed to dealing with other officials of large organizations than with scrappy writers such as Isabel Paterson.

On its merits, such a mild little book as *The Uncommon Man,*[1] by Crawford H. Greenewalt,* would rate about a paragraph of notice in the same vein, and that mainly because of the position of its author. Mr. Greenewalt is president of E. I. du Pont de Nemours & Company (colloquially known as du Ponts, *tout court*), which on a combined scale of values, including commercial integrity, size, duration and historic importance, is tops among American industrial corporations.[2] The record promises something more than might be expected from, say, a successful manufacturer of pretzels. Actually, the pretzel-bender would have to deliver considerably more than the present exhibit in order to get into print. But its provenance does lend this book a peculiar interest. Read in the context of contemporary events, it fixed my attention by what it does not contain. Also I had personal reasons, which will appear later.

The book is composed of a series of lectures, "sponsored by the Graduate School of Business, Columbia University," with a Preface by the Dean of the School, Courtney C. Brown.* Unless you enjoy skidding in a panful of melted butter, you may be inclined to by-pass the Preface, yet it is not devoid of significance. Just bear it in mind.

The Dean informs us that "while preparing these lectures, Mr. Greenewalt was occupied not only with the management of a large company but with another literary venture which I am told is a definitive study of the life and habits of the hummingbird." And Mr. Greenewalt mentions, as an occupational hazard of executives, "being suspended between the frying-pan and the fire." Small wonder that he didn't quite get around to his titular subject. Suspended between the Preface and a dizzy spell, I find it difficult to get *anywhere*. The effect of Academic (or C-Minus) Prose lingers for hours. I should fancy that was Mr. Greenewalt's trouble, except that I don't see how he could have read the Preface before writing the book. Must have been the hummingbird.

Be that as it may, the subject is weirdly elusive. At the outset (Page 1), he bogs down with "common men who were inspired to uncommon levels of achievement."[3] Flagpole sitters? No: "when multiplied by millions, this is America, these her uncommon men." Surely even flagpole sitters multiplied (heaven forbid) by millions must cease to be uncommon. Mr. Greenewalt was inspired to a contradiction in terms. To clinch it, he "does not deprecate the unusually gifted individual," naming at random Franklin, Eli Whitney* and Lincoln, "but such as these do not make a nation."

As a matter of fact, they do. I say so. Though I hate to contradict Mr. Greenewalt, because inevitably he does that himself at the next corner. And he is apt to throw in a phrase that caroms off to meet still another contradiction. Thus on Page 57, doubtless haunted by that uneasy feeling of having forgotten to put out the cat, he spares "a special word" for "the truly uncommon man, no synthetic genius, no composite leader, some lone individual" (naming Henry Ford, Einstein and Kreisler),[4] "it is he who is the indispensable man." Very well, blindfold yourself, turn around twice, and pin the title on the proper person. —Henry Ford! Wrong.

Now you may peek into the Preface, seventh paragraph: "This is no simple analysis, nor should one expect all of the prescriptions to enlist total acceptance. It is a virtue of this forthright excursion into management psychology, economics and social organization that in its preparation the author has without intent demonstrated the qualities of The Uncommon Man. He has personified his own prescription." Got it?—Mr. Greenewalt! Correct.

When Mr. Greenewalt gets down to cases, he means "the individual in the corporation," and draws on his own experience. He denies that corporations tend to impose "excessive conformity" on their employees. They can't afford to; they need personal initiative. And it is good news that he finds it "offensive" to grade people by "psychological testing bureaus." Du Pont executives are not cast to type; and they have no recognizable symbols of status, such as hierarchic motor cars or approved tailoring. Mr. Greenewalt testifies that one of the company's executives sports a baseball cap while driving a Corvette roadster, instead of a Buick. (Well, I don't know, I'd keep an eye on that feller. I allow that nothing can be done about the executive who bores the pants off his associates by bragging of the performance of his Opel.[5])

Mr. Greenewalt himself doesn't even own a gray flannel suit.[6] And he plays the clarinet. You can imagine what a board meeting would sound like if all the directors were required to play the clarinet. At this point, or near-by, Mr. Greenewalt puts the question: "How much, or, better, how little conformity should be tolerated?" Never mind the syntax; I guess one clarinet player is enough. Then he can be president; and you won't hear any more snide music criticism around the head office. Listen, I know as well as you do, or better—(if the character who is heckling me has a saxophone, throw him out; he belongs in the stockholders meeting, not the board-room)—I was going to say, but definitely, a saxophone is too much. Mr. Greenewalt is cautious: "Let us conform as little as is necessary to good manners, pleasant relationships, and the highest use of individual talent." Or, as the mate said to the captain: "All I want is *cee*-vility, and damn little of that."

Now I hope everything is perfectly clear, except one item I have to go back and pick up. If I ramble it is not altogether my fault; I am trying to follow Mr. Greenewalt's curves. He says: "the modern corporation is a slice of society in microcosm." It isn't, no matter how you slice it. When Mr. Greenewalt is not compounding a contradiction, he refreshes himself by mixing a metaphor. Someone ought to tell him what he is president of; and I will in a minute. But what he obviously needs is a good secretary of the old-fashioned (non-graduate) school.[7]

When I was a girl, and employed by bankers who owned a few small corporations on the side, my bosses lent me to their lawyer (R. B. Bennett, K. C.)[8] in an emergency. Forthwith R. B. offered to hire me away from them. He said his regular secretary didn't take his dictation accurately, whereas I did. I replied that he was mistaken, reminding him that his girl had been a court reporter and couldn't break the habit of transcribing verbatim; whereas I straightened out his sentences from my shorthand notes. At that R. B. upped his ante; he proposed to have me articled as a law student in his office. Mr. Greenewalt says he doesn't yell at his secretary, but then she lets him appear in public with his verbal slip showing. Once I made R. B. so mad I thought he'd have a stroke, but as soon as he recovered he renewed his offer. He said I had a legal mind. Whatever its potential, at the age I was then, I had nothing on my mind but a pompadour. The invitation to the bar simply appalled me. Without my aid or encouragement, R. B. became Premier of Canada, a baron in the English peerage, and a member of the Privy Council, in brilliant succession; while I became a writer. Possibly that was my mistake. Between the Dean and Mr. Greenewalt, the prospect for writers looks dim. Still, it looks dimmish for executives too, according to Mr. Greenewalt.... The above digression is not irrelevant, incompetent, or immaterial. I was leading up to the statement that private corporations are legal constructs designed primarily to limit personal liability in capital risk ventures. Conversely, the specific limitation, in series, permits the hook-up for the long circuit of energy to form a production system, by extending action in time and space beyond the lifetime and scope of one man.[9] It is as necessary to modern high-energy production as the engineers' lay-out for the plant, or the mechanical sequence. If the erroneous notion prevails that a corporation is "society in microcosm," corporations will be expected to do numerous things that are none of their business; and Mr. Greenewalt himself says that they are already gummed up with "paternalism."

Mr. Greenewalt resents the "stereotype" (which he attributes to popular fiction) of the business man as uncouth, incult[10] and unscrupulous; and still worse, lacking in glamor. And he believes that in consequence of such undeserved obloquy, the business man is unjustly penalized; all he gets is money and the income tax snatches most of it. He comments wistfully that the government does not deprive Marilyn Monroe of a percentage of her glamor.—Excuse me; Miss Monroe supplies the glamor herself; she is paid in money, and the income tax nicks her as severely as it does a corporation president. Is it possible that numerous elderly men whose public faces cause one to turn the page hastily are suffering from the delusion that the camera invests them with glamor, the same as Marilyn Monroe?

Mr. Greenewalt's conclusion seems to bear out this hypothesis. He says "the business man is a victim of his poor press."

In a back-handed way, he is at least fifty per cent right. The press is peculiarly a capitalist institution; publishing is business enterprise; and the periodical press depends directly on business advertisements for financial support. If the business man has a poor press (in any sense of the adjective), how come so? Certainly it is *his* press.

During the nineteen thirties, I had a job on a New York newspaper, when Communism broke out like hives among the "intellectuals" and the scions and toadies of the rich. A program of mass murder, torture, looting and absolute slavery gave them a great kick. (It does not appeal to me.) Communism was high fashion. The Rockefellers hired a painter who was a prominent Communist to decorate Rockefeller Center, and he featured a portrait of Lenin. The son of a Morgan partner turned a none-too-bright Red.[11] Sweet girl graduates of Vassar enthusiastically joined the Mattress Workers Union for the Cause. To be fashionable it was not necessary to carry a Party card; fellow-travellers were quite chic—and they had their reward, in cushy jobs and flattering publicity.[12]

The fact that Communists "infiltrated the press" has been proved beyond dispute by various autobiographical "confessions," and before a Senate Investigating Committee by first-hand testimony of ex-Communists, further confirmed by unwilling witnesses taking the Fifth Amendment.[13] The Senate Committee Report was buried in a brief notice on Page 32 of the paper I used to work for: no flowers. Anyone who fondly believes that all the Communists have been fumigated out of the press would buy the Brooklyn Bridge from a traditional bunco-steerer in full regalia of checked suit and buffalo-horn moustaches.

I was *not* a Communist. I am against organized corruption and planned murder. One woman, the ex-wife of a leading Communist in New York, warned me that if I persisted in writing the truth about Communism, I would be "immobilized," barred from promotion and ultimately I would be out of a job. . . . I have never seen in the confessions of ex-Communists an account of the Communist method of attacking an anti-Communist writer; but I know it at first-hand. Slander is spread assiduously (Communists love that assignment). Personal influence is used. Shoals of derogatory letters are written to the editor, apparently from respectable sources. Certainly the newspaper I worked for withstood a heavy barrage of that sort of thing, from within and without, for years; I have no doubt that I should have fared worse on any other newspaper.

Of course promotion *was* blocked. The syndicate editor of the paper, Harry Staton,[14] wanted to take me on as a syndicated columnist. I said: "You won't be allowed to." He said: "Why not?" I said: "You'll see." After a month or so, he said: "I *know* I can sell a column by you, but I can't get the green light for it here." Harry looked like and was a hard-boiled egg; and he ran the syndicate profitably. I said only: "I told you so." When the truth dawned on him later, his comment was unsuitable for publication. One person who knew the score said to me: "Why do you never speak of those things?" mentioning a certain incident. I said, "If I did, some fool would accuse me of having a persecution complex. That's the Party Line, and all the fools repeat it without even knowing where they heard it." Presently I was obliged to refer to the incident, and my editor[15] replied promptly: "Oh, you have a persecution complex." I think the brute stupidity one encountered was the most sickening aspect of the period. When millions of Russians were dying of famine, American correspondents in Russia didn't know it! They were happy sending official handouts as "news."[16] Once I met Mary Heaton Vorse* and said: "What do you think of those starving millions?" She said: "I don't know; I wasn't there." And she grinned. I shall never forget that grin.

A very well-informed person asked me: "Do you know what you are up against?" I said: "Yes, I know, you mean the Communists; that wouldn't matter if you can tell me how I am to get past the (deleted) 'conservatives,' the middle-of-the-roaders, the one-worlders,[17] the stooges and do-goods."

I didn't get past them. I was demoted from the daily book review and my place was filled by a recruit from the *Nation*.[18]

However, I had a book to write,[19] and I wrote it Sundays and holidays and sometimes double-shift, working around the clock. The book was a study of political economy as engineering, including the action of the law as governing the relation of forces. As it required a description of how a high-energy production system works, it showed also why Communism cannot produce even subsistence, and meets the deficit by starving slave labor and raiding free economies.

My publisher thought the book important and both of us recognized that its best chance was for a long, slow sale. So we had a "gentleman's agreement" that he would keep the book in print. The agreement was not kept, possibly for lack of gentlemen.

But before publication, even before the publisher's pre-season catalogue had been made up, he received a postcard from "Tass," the Soviet official "news" agency, *asking for a review copy of my book.* Who tipped off "Tass"? This sample of brassy impudence was almost matched by an editor of the *New Republic,* who wrote to *me* asking for a copy.[20]

After publication, I received a lot of commendatory letters from business men; but as far as I know, none of them wrote to the editor of the newspaper. This was during the war; and there was one grotesque item, a letter *from a Wall Street* address, accusing me of "near treason" because I denounced the revolting, shameful alliance with Russia.[21] Treason to Russia, I presume.... The friendly letters were really helpful.

Some business men not only wrote but called on me; and one was a top-rank du Pont executive, Mr. Jasper Crane, a very courteous gentleman. His object was to line up effective opposition to Communism. I don't think he ever wrote to my editor. I was over-worked, underpaid and exhausted, but I gave him what assistance I could.... He intended to raise a fund to donate sets of selected books, mine among them, to libraries and colleges.

I daresay he thought me ungrateful. Writing was my job. I said I wished business men would at least think like business men and use business methods. Business consists of production and exchange, not giving things away. In the modern world, to get ideas in circulation, they must be sold, in the medium of print. Distribution is the function of the market.

On this issue I am afraid we never arrived at mutual understanding. He was more or less aware of the infestation of the press by Communists. Once he asked me, what should business men do. I said bluntly: "Pull your advertising." He was shocked: "Oh, we couldn't do that." For my part, I know no sound reason why business men should finance a conspiracy to cut their own throats, unless they feel that they deserve the treatment.... Once I asked another business man why he advertised in a certain magazine, in view of its content. He said that to place or with-hold advertising according to the ideas and values expressed by a periodical would be "censorship by the dollar." This notion is idiotic.

A free press exists by virtue of the continuous choice of everyone concerned: the enterpriser who risks capital; the editors who select the text; the readers who buy it; *and* the business men whose advertising enables it to make a profit. In placing advertising someone *must* make a choice; and business men cannot escape responsibility by shirking it. Any moronic teen-ager who wants a steady supply of "comics" has "influence" with the press, and the business man pays for him without blinking. The business man also pays for the carbon monoxide school of journalistic pundits who argue that we must be kind to Kruschchev* and make much of Mikoyan.[22] It is by default of his moral obligation that the business man has reduced himself to nullity in relation to the press.

And by his nullity he *shuts out of the market* the writers who would be on his side.

The perfect example of the business man's attitude to the press occurred during Mikoyan's visit—perfect in its imbecile confusion. After Mikoyan had been escorted around to case the joint at several banks (one known as the Rockefeller bank), he was given a dinner at the Economic Club.[23] A misguided reporter tried to cover this exclusive social affair. The Club bouncer took care of *that* reporter. . . . I don't know what the Economic Club is for, beyond entertaining visiting thugs; but its membership includes Bill Robinson,* president of Coca Cola, former business manager of the *Herald-Tribune*, and close friend of President Eisenhower. Also Mr. James Linen,* publisher of *Time* magazine. (Might one hint that Mr. Henry P. [sic] Luce* should send his Linen to the laundry?)

I must say, and would emphasize, that no du Pont executives have joined in these vultures' love feasts. But Mr. Greenewalt's plaint was made on behalf of big business men. Before he undertakes their defence, he might take a long, close, thoughtful look at them, as now on exhibit. It strikes me that we have gone back to the Thirties, with big business men leading the procession. I suggest further that he should ponder the comment of a steelworker on strike, as reported in the N. Y. *Times*.—"When Kozlov* came here (to Pittsburgh) who fawned on that guy? Not us 'proletariat.' Management even took him through the Homestead plant. The Chancellor of Pitt[24] threw him a garden party. I got the feeling that the Communist big bosses and our big bosses want the same thing!"

When that steelworker reads that the only people Kruschchev asked to meet, insisted on meeting, were the American capitalists, I don't think it will be easy to argue him out of his previous feeling.

To resume my narrative, some time after I declined to be given away, I read with astonishment a Letter to a Stockholder, or "open letter" written by Mr. Walter S. Carpenter, jr.,* then president of du Ponts. The stockholder had said that big executive salaries were excessive and should be reduced. Mr. Carpenter replied that twenty-five years earlier his take-home pay was $60,000 a year, out of a nominal salary of $78,570; and that it had gone down to $48,000 out of a nominal $175,000. Reckoning currency depreciation, his pay had been cut in half. I don't know if that pacified the stockholder; it gave me the creeps. I wrote to Mr. Carpenter: "The large executive salaries were made possible primarily by the antecedent political institutions, in which enterprise could be carried on. Those salaries would have been justified if the men who drew them had understood and maintained the over-all conditions—if they had known their business and done the *whole* job for which they were paid.... That is what your pay envelope is telling you. If you don't understand you will get a much sharper notification in much less than another twenty-five years . . . or your successor will, if he also tries to get by with doing only half a job . . . Your salary has been cut because you haven't earned it."[25]

Mr. Carpenter said plaintively to Mr. Crane: "Why does she say this to me?" Mr. Crane replied: "Because it is true." (Mr. Crane told me this himself, in the presence of a third person.)

So now Mr. Carpenter's successor, Mr. Greenewalt, is complaining that *his* take-home pay is only $30,000 out of $330,000 nominal salary. In real value, he gets about half as much as his predecessor.

And apparently neither of them gave a thought to where the diverted flow of energy goes, what it *does*. They are channels of destructive forces, breaks in the dyke. Mr. Greenewalt seems to be bothered only by his diminished pay, and by the question, if this goes on, who will want the job after him if it doesn't pay more. Is he sure that there will be any such job, after him? What is going on is the confiscation of wealth at an accelerating rate; don't forget the inheritance taxes. Mr. Greenewalt reads Roman history. He might study particularly the end of the Republic, which was marked by wholesale expropriation and *proscription of great families*, the *gens*, if they happened to belong to a losing faction. Now we have an ominous sign; lately the national chairman of the Republican Party practically read big business men out of the party. Many business men are accustomed to contribute to both of our major political parties. That is to say, they treat political parties as a racket to be bought off. In so doing, they make the party a racket. So now they have no party.

To continue my narrative, in due course I was fired from my newspaper job, on three weeks notice. A former Washington correspondent of the *Daily Worker*[26] had been taken on as a featured writer. (That newspaper [the *Herald Tribune*] has always been slightly schizophrenic since the days of Horace Greeley*; I suppose just then it was making an effort to be consistent.)

About that time Mr. Crane collected backing for a magazine, intended to expound the principles of free enterprise.[27] Again I made myself *persona non grata* by objecting that it was not set up as a business enterprise. There are always plenty of people ready to sit down beside a hunk of capital, like Tierra del Fuegians gnawing at a defunct stranded whale; but I don't think that is a cogent example of free enterprise. (If at this point the reader sympathizes with Mr. Crane, that's all right with me. He is a very nice man. So are they all, most amiable men. And their feelings are hurt. Will Cuppy* once asked me reproachfully, didn't I want to be America's sweetheart? The answer—I'll bet you've guessed it—is No. That is not my job.)

Being "immobilized," I was thankful for a much-needed rest, until I was again startled by reading in the news an interview with a new president of du Ponts: Mr. Greenewalt. He was distressed because his infant grandchild had been indicted under the Anti-Trust laws, as a stockholder in a corporation.[28] Mr. Greenewalt was quoted as saying that nevertheless he was in favor of the Anti-Trust laws; indeed, he had always thought they should be in the Constitution. Presumably he felt that his grandchild should be exempt from a bad law, and then it would be good enough. (The Anti-Trust laws are bad law because they do not and *cannot* designate what *action* they are to forbid and punish.)

Well, I knew it was hopeless, but I had a mind to complete the record. I wrote to Mr. Greenewalt and asked him for a job, on the ground that there ought to be *someone* in Wilmington[29] who would know what the Constitution *is.* It is not a code of civil or criminal law applying to persons. It is a fundamental law framing a charter of our Federal government, allotting and delimiting the separate powers of the three branches, and reserving all powers not specified to the States or the citizens; with the Bill of Rights binding the Government strictly. That's all.

Seriously, I thought that while big business employs rafts of specialists in research for waterproof bags suitable for us to put our heads in (if we have no other use for our heads) it might be advisable for them to learn the pre-requisites of our civilization, and what is happening to it. For instance, our Constitution stands on the premise of Natural Law; that is, not only the physical laws of nature, but moral law in the universe as the valid authority and norm for jurisprudence, the test of positive law. In the past century we have almost lost that premise. Now the idea of Natural Law is at least two thousand years old, but it has never been adequately defined or proved to be truly existent in the nature of things; and I think it could be. So I thought it should be a subject of research for men whose existence depends on it. I was acquainted with several persons—one of course was Dr. Clarence Manion,* and another was an executive of U. S. Steel—I believed to be qualified to *think* on that subject; and I supposed there might be others of the du Pont connection. Roughly sketched, I believed it might be possible for a highly intelligent society to emerge, as happened in the American Revolutionary era, by the discussion of ideas by men of speculative intellect and experience.[30] Especially there might be a revival of genuine political thought, not pork-barrel and ward-heeler "politics," but large impersonal issues, and principles applicable in practice. As a practical matter, observe the shift of economic forces in this country during the past thirty years, the change of direction of heavy transport, more and more of it moving north-south instead of east-west, which must certainly alter the political balance as well. . . . However, I did not go into this in detail. I asked for a job.

I am afraid Mr. Greenewalt was annoyed. He said the interview to which I referred was "garbled." He was of the opinion that Natural Law should be relegated to academic studies. He wrote: "Your devastating commentary on my intelligence leads me to think that anything I might say might be considered no more than a concrete demonstration of your original supposition."[31] —In short, no job; Mr. Crane concurring.

It was only fair to Mr. Greenewalt to point out that if he thought the matter over, he must perceive that obviously I had supposed him to be intelligent. What I had said was that he, and business men generally, were ignorant of the most important factor affecting their business. I trust this cleared up the misunderstanding; but I have no concrete evidence whether it did or not, as I was out of range. (I don't think he meant concrete; the word is unnecessary in his sentence.)

I am nearing the end of the story. . . . When Mikoyan was here being entertained so chummily, I wrote to Mr. Greenewalt asking why did not big business men protest. The readiness of some of them to consort with a murder gang, and the silence of the rest, was evoking bitter contempt. That is a lasting and most dangerous sentiment to its object. I was not "picking on" the du Pont organization; to the contrary, I believed they were the most likely to protest in the name of decency. If they did, it would give a lead to others. If they would not, one could have little expectation that the executives of any other corporation would recognize the moral issue. And I am glad to note that one of the du Pont family *has* set his name to a strong protest against the Kruschchev parade of insolence.

However, I had no reply from Mr. Greenewalt. He has now got an Assistant to the President, who answered instead that he would "present the material to Mr. Greenewalt as soon as convenient." Evidently it isn't convenient. But I like the Court Circular tone of being "presented."[32]

In his book, Mr. Greenewalt recalls "with some embarrassment a visit by a young lady who was preparing a college thesis on management duties. The first thing she asked me was what did I do all day." He was unable to answer. I will hazard a guess that what he was doing at the moment was put over on him as conducive to good "public relations."... Possibly the college girl will graduate into a government bureau in Washington, and then she will send out directives telling business executives what to do all day.

As a last resort, it occurred to me to enquire about the relation of big business men to the press from the other side. I was rather anxious over the chance that if business men did exercise an influence on the press, they might demand, not only glamor, but the literary style of the Dean of the Graduate School of Business; and then our last state would be worse than our first.[33]

So I enlisted the skills of a representative of the press to evaluate—won't someone please *stop* me! I mean to say, I asked a first-class newspaperman, Ted Hall,* to read the Dean's preface, and translate it for me. Ted is on the *Newark News*. New Jersey swarms with business executives and labor leaders and politicians and scientific gents and academic luminaries, not to mention assorted eggheads who call on the editor because they want to see their names in the paper the same as everyone else. On due occasion it is Ted's job to garble their messages into English if possible. It is his misfortunate that he really can write. Concentrating his faculties, he read every word of the preface, though it rocked him back on his heels when he came to this sentence: "Stimulation of uncommon effort and suppression of pressures toward conformity requires a conscious and continuing effort to maximize both personal freedom and incentives." Then Ted extended the book toward me at arm's length, an eloquent gesture. "If you can figure that out," he said, "you've cracked the code."

August? 1959–September 1959.

Notes

1. Crawford H. Greenewalt, *The Uncommon Man: The Individual in the Organization* (New York: McGraw-Hill, 1959). On the circumstances of Paterson's writing about this book, and of her writing not being published, see WD 351–53.
2. Under the general heading of "integrity" Paterson may have placed the support given by leading members of the du Pont company to the campaign to repeal Prohibition and then to the attempt by 1928 Democratic presidential candidate Al Smith* and others to defeat the New Deal. See George Wolkskill, *The Revolt of the Conservatives: A History of the American Liberty League, 1934–1940* (Boston: Houghton Mifflin, 1962).
3. Here, as in a handful of other places in this essay, Paterson changes Greenewalt's text as she quotes it, though without altering its meaning. Usually she does so by omitting unnecessary words. Occasionally she adds a word such as "the." In this case, however, she makes a mistake in her reading of the final word. The original phrasing is: "common men who, whatever their motives, whatever their goals, were inspired to uncommon levels of accomplishment" (page 1).
4. Fritz Kreisler (1875–1962): Austrian American violinist. "The truly uncommon man . . . lone individual": phrases quoted from pages 56–58 of Greenewalt's book.
5. The motorists are discussed by their colleague Greenewalt (53).
6. *The Man in the Gray Flannel Suit* (1955), a novel by Sloan Wilson (1920–2003), popularized this stereotype of the corporate businessman.
7. In 1910, Paterson had been such a secretary to her first newspaper boss, the publisher of the *Spokane Inland Herald.*
8. Richard Bedford Bennett, K. C. (King's Counsel), later 1st Viscount Bennett (1870–1947), employed Paterson in his law office in Calgary, Alberta. He served as prime minister of Canada (1930–1935) and in 1941 received a title in the British peerage.
9. An application of the theory elaborated in GM. The long circuit is the system of economic exchange that allows people to buy and sell the products of human energy across barriers of time and space. Here Paterson suggests that the series of hook-ups between producers and consumers is enabled, in part, by the legal devices that allow for limited-liability corporations.
10. Uncultivated.
11. The "Red" was Corliss Lamont,* the son of Thomas W. Lamont,* a leading figure in the J. P. Morgan* banking company. He supported Marxist causes and defended communist governments from Stalin to Castro. The murals were executed for Rockefeller Center in New York by noted Mexican painter Diego Rivera (1886–1957), a communist. They were destroyed because they exalted Soviet communism and violently attacked capitalism.
12. "Therefore when thou doest thine alms, do not sound a trumpet before thee, as the hypocrites do in the synagogues and in the streets, that they may have glory of men. Verily I say unto you, they have their reward" (Matthew 6:2).
13. Presumably a reference to hearings by the Senate Internal Security Subcommittee—called the McCarran Committee—in 1955–1956, highlighted by the testimony of Winston Burdett (1913–1993), then of CBS, about his role as a Soviet spy and the involvement of other journalists with communism.

14. Staton (c. 1880–1959) was manager of the *Herald Tribune* syndicate (1924–1947).
15. Irita [Eye-REET-a] Van Doren (1891–1966). Van Doren was the mistress of Wendell Willkie,* Republican presidential nominee in 1940, and the *Herald Tribune* was a traditionally Republican newspaper. For discussion of Van Doren's relationship with Paterson, see WD 245–46, 315–23.
16. Walter Duranty (1884–1957), Moscow bureau chief of the *New York Times* and winner of the Pulitzer Prize, is now notorious for having done this. He and other friends of the communist regime denied the existence of the great famine in the Soviet Union. Paterson had no doubts on the subject: "The Russian government, for political expediency, and with no debate allowed, 'relieved' the famine-stricken peasants of what food they had." About such deniers as British socialists Sidney and Beatrice Webb (1859–1947, 1858–1943) she noted that "there is, unfortunately, a peculiar cold cruelty, or perhaps insensibility is a better word, about the statistical mind, which enables the Webbs to regard a million peasants starved to death as merely a row of figures on paper" ("Turns," January 5, 1936; March 29, 1936).
17. "One world" was a phrase that came from Paterson's neighborhood. In 1943, Wendell Willkie (see note 15, above) published a book entitled *One World*, arguing that when World War II was over the United States must continue to cooperate with the Soviet Union. A crucial person to this publication was Tom Bevans (1912–2003), son-in-law of Paterson's editor Irita Van Doren and, with Bevans' wife, the current illustrator of Paterson's column. Interviewed in 1994, Bevans told Stephen Cox: "I got a lot of credit for naming that book and bringing it into Simon and Schuster. He [Willkie] had done a piece for the newspapers with Joe Barnes [Joseph Barnes (1907–1970), a far-left writer for the *Herald Tribune*] and we were sitting around in the living room discussing whether it would make a book, and I took the idea down to Simon and Schuster. I originally suggested *One World or None*."
18. *The Nation* was notoriously leftwing. Paterson apparently refers to Lewis Gannett,* author of the *Herald Tribune*'s daily review column "Books and Things," who worked for *The Nation* before joining the *Herald Tribune* as a daily book reviewer in 1930. In 1939, he was voted best book reviewer by the American Writers Congress, governing body of the League of American Writers, a front group of the Communist Party. In a letter to Burton Rascoe's* wife Hazel, written at the end of August or the beginning of September 1931, Paterson said, "[F]rom the middle of September I shan't be doing reviews for the daily any more; got to go back to the Sunday [*Herald Tribune 'Books'*] exclusively. . . . Lewis Gannett will do the daily every day." But Paterson would do daily reviews, for a time, later on (see Paterson to Burton Rascoe, July 1936, below).
19. *The God of the Machine.*
20. The request from TASS (March 24, 1943) is in the Paterson Papers.
21. On this letter (from Schroeder Boulton), see "Turns," August 2, 1942, page 52, above, and note 17, page 54.
22. In January 1959 Soviet First Deputy Premier Anastas Mikoyan (1895–1978) paid a goodwill visit to the United States. Paterson spelled Khrushchev's name as Kruschchev.

23. A club for executives in New York City, in which public policy issues are discussed.
24. The University of Pittsburgh.
25. According to the du Pont company, "during the Great Depression, Carpenter pushed the company's leaders to accept and adapt to increased government regulation of corporate affairs, although he was overruled by the du Ponts" (http://www2.dupont.com/Phoenix_Heritage/en_US/1940_b_detail.html).
26. The *Daily Worker* was the Communist newspaper. The correspondent has not been identified. Paterson's last column for the *Herald Tribune* is dated January 30, 1949.
27. This magazine was founded as *The Freeman* (1950).
28. Prompted by the "garbled interview" of Greenewalt, mentioned below, Paterson appears to be thinking of a federal antitrust suit brought against the du Pont corporation and du Pont family members holding stock in certain other entities controlled by it. The people legally accused of conspiracy for voting as a bloc, thereby restraining trade, included fifty-nine child defendants, some as young as eight months. Greenewalt had married into the du Pont family; his children (apparently, he had no grandchildren at the time) were among the defendants (*Chicago Tribune*, November 20, 1952). He asked whether his descendants would "all be haled into court as criminals, so long as there's a drop of du Pont blood in their veins?" The du Pont corporation was harassed for many years by antitrust suits, but Greenewalt persistently declared his support of antitrust laws. "The Sherman Antitrust Act," he said, "is a blessing. It would have been in the Bill of Rights if the founders could have foreseen that this would be an industrial nation" (*Washington Post*, March 30, 1952).
29. The du Pont company had its headquarters in Wilmington, Delaware.
30. "H. M. Parshley* writes that he has read somewhere that 'there never was an Age of Reason; just a reasonable person now and then.' Yes, but sometimes there were as many as four or five at once; that is what was called the Age of Reason" ("Turns," March 11, 1934).
31. C. H. Greenewalt to Paterson, May 16, 1952. Paterson omits the original "somewhat" preceding "devastating."
32. W. G. Weisbrod to Paterson, March 5, 1959. Paterson quotes the operative words of the original. The Court Circular is an official report of events in the lives of the British royal family.
33. In Matthew 12:43–45 and Luke 11:24–26, Jesus says that when an evil spirit has been expelled from a person he may return with many more evil spirits, and "the last state of that man is worse than the first."

19

Adventures in Biology and Bunk

During the 1920s there was a craze for explanations of history and society based on race and genetics. "Nordics" were credited with the responsibility for true civilization, and families such as the "Jukeses" were used to exemplify genetic incompetence. Paterson opposed this intellectual craze, as she opposed all others.

John Langdon-Davies would be the last person to expect that *The New Age of Faith* (Viking Press) might sway public opinion to any great extent.[1] He says explicitly that people believe what they want to believe, and choose their reasons afterward, twisting the facts to fit whichever theory flatters them most. No matter; it is vastly refreshing to come across such a witty and unsentimental exposure of current fallacies concerning genetics, "racial superiorities," and the human aspects of biology generally.

Mr. Langdon-Davies is a working scientist, not a popular publicist.[2] He has no panacea to offer for whatever is wrong with the world, and holds out no hope of any scientific Utopia. To him, intellectual integrity is the highest good. But he has enough of unregenerate human nature in him to enjoy making mincemeat of the smug sophistries of A. E. Wiggam, Lothrop Stoddard, and Madison Grant.[3] And he meets them on their own ground, giving the results of modern research in the language of the layman, and quoting chapter and verse for his authorities. His logic is brutally lucid. As a scientific slugger, one would have to go back to [Thomas] Huxley* to find his equal; though it would be too much to expect again the classic perfection of Huxley's style; for Huxley was a literary genius who happened to be also a rationalist, in the most exact sense of the word—a combination of Spartan sinews and Athenian elegance. Langdon-Davies writes clearly because he thinks clearly, but he does not cultivate the graces for their own sake.

He is particularly amused and exasperated by the manner in which the stern doctrine of evolution has been distorted to pamper patriotic conceit. Rather unkindly, he reminds us that "the survival of the fittest" means only that those who survive are thereby proved to be fit. In short, the survivors survive. He denies in toto Madison Grant's elaborate fiction of "the passing of the Great Race" (which Grant borrowed from the Germanized Englishman, Houston Stewart Chamberlain,* without credit). But even if there had been a specific "Nordic race," if it passed, that settles it; Darwin cannot help it. It must have been unfit—biologically inferior! As for racial difficulties in general, Mr. Langdon-Davies points out to the alarmed Lothrop Stoddard that the various "racial indexes," such as cephalic measurement, height, color of eye and skin, and texture of hair, are indeed so various, so thoroughly distributed and mismatched among the nations of the earth, that they only prove there is no such thing as a pure race. Psychological race characteristics are even more confusing, he shows with cynical clarity, as no genuinely scientific data exists upon this subject, inasmuch as we have no means of gauging the effect of environment and education upon any individual, much less upon the mass of the populace. Talent only manifests itself by opportunity; Praxiteles* himself could not have been a sculptor without marble, nor, in fact, without the whole civilization of Greece behind him.

But it is with A. E. Wiggam and his trained germ-plasm that Mr. Langdon-Davies has the most fun. Upon Mr. Wiggam's pet exhibits, the Jukeses and the Edwardses, he executes the high justice, the middle and the low.

Mr. Wiggam's reading of the Edwards family history is fairly familiar. Three hundred years ago Richard Edwards married Elizabeth Tuthill, somewhere in New England. From this happy union sprang no less than twelve college presidents, 265 college graduates, sixty-five college professors, sixty physicians, 100 clergymen, seventy-five army officers, sixty "prominent authors," 100 lawyers, thirty judges, eighty public officials, three congressmen, two United States senators, and one vice president. Elizabeth gets all the credit for this, from Mr. Wiggam, since Richard had another wife, whose offspring evidently had to work for a living and never rose above obscurity. Hence Mr. Wiggam deduces that one should be very careful about choosing one's grandmother, as there is nothing like heredity.

Mr. Langdon-Davies concedes that it is indeed the authentic hay sandwich, but that Elizabeth Tuthill has not received full justice from

Mr. Wiggam. Mr. Wiggam records that she possessed "great beauty, a strong will, extreme intellectual vigor and a mental grasp akin to rapacity." He omitted to mention that she was divorced for "adultery and other notorious immoralities," being "afflicted with an extraordinary deficiency in moral sense"; and furthermore, that "one of her sisters murdered her own son and a brother murdered her own sister"—feats which make the terrible Jukeses look respectable by comparison. To me it has always been fairly obvious that Jonathan Edwards* himself was a criminal lunatic, of sadistic inclinations—what other description would fit a man who gloated over the thought of "infant damnation" and the everlasting torments of Hell? Thus endeth the first lesson in eugenics.

A briefer but equally cogent treatise upon "biology and the advancement of man," which confines itself exclusively to the interlocking questions of heredity and environment, is *Prometheus*, by H. S. Jennings.[4] This is one of the "Today and Tomorrow" series of scientific and philosophical monographs published by Duttons. It is impossible to do justice to these stimulating volumes in a mere review; but as they do not repeat but supplement each other, no reader who recognizes "the moral obligation to be intelligent"[5] can afford to miss either.

McNaught's Monthly, *December 1925, 188–89.*

Notes

1. John Langdon-Davies (1897–1971), whose book *The New Age of Faith* (1925) Paterson is reviewing, was a South African English journalist and independent advocate of leftwing causes.
2. Paterson clearly thought that Langdon-Davies exemplified the scientific attitude. Nevertheless, he was not a scientist but a popularizer of science.
3. Madison Grant (1865–1937) was an American attorney, environmentalist, and theorist of "Nordic" racial superiority whose book *The Passing of the Great Race* (1916) was mildly popular. Albert Edward Wiggam (1871–1957), a widely read American journalist, was one of many authors who discussed the Juke or Jukes family, thought to embody genetic inferiority over several generations. The Edwards family was his example of genetic success. Theodore Lothrop Stoddard (1883–1950) was an American historian and author of *The Rising Tide of Color Against White World-Supremacy* (1920).
4. Herbert Spencer Jennings (1868–1947) was an American geneticist especially noted for his work on evolutionary processes. *Prometheus* was published in 1925.
5. The title of an essay by John Erskine (1879–1951), inspirer of the Great Books movement.

20

The Riddle of Chief Justice Taney in the Dred Scott Decision

In 1857, the Supreme Court ruled, in an opinion written by Chief Justice Roger B. Taney, that Dred Scott,* a man attempting to be freed from slavery, had no standing to sue for freedom. The basis of this decision was Taney's idea that African Americans were not and could not be citizens, because the Constitution was not intended to provide for that possibility.*

Paterson had been interested in the case for a long time. She considered the decision completely wrong, although she strongly advocated the principle of judicial review embodied in the Supreme Court. In her view, constitutional government was designed as a self-limiting system, requiring a Court that could review and invalidate unconstitutional legislation. Only in this way could individual liberty be protected. In early 1936, she defended judicial review against attacks provoked by Supreme Court decisions invalidating New Deal economic legislation, attacks that presaged Franklin Roosevelt's unsuccessful "court packing" scheme a year later. She noticed that the same people who were asking what right the Court had "to tell Congress and the Senate what laws they must enact" depended on the Court to invalidate laws infringing the Bill of Rights. She also observed that the principle of judicial review was enshrined in the Federalist *Papers (*Federalist *No. 78). When opponents of the Court brought up the Dred Scott decision, they were announcing what everyone knew, that "the Supreme Court is not infallible." But they were missing "the interesting point about the Dred Scott case," which was "the specific basis of the decision. That point was that Dred Scott, as a slave, 'could bring no suit in the United States Court.' He was not entitled to a hearing, had no standing whatever before the law. The case was 'dismissed for want of jurisdiction.' The Court, in fact, took itself out of the picture"—which was just what its modern critics wanted it to do.*[1]

In 1949, Paterson approached the topic from another angle, asking how Justice Taney, a younger contemporary of the Founders, could so radically have mistaken their constitutional principles. Her review of the history of the Dred Scott case emphasizes its placement in an era in which property qualifications for voting were yielding to universal manhood suffrage. Simultaneously, many people who wanted to abolish slavery were demanding that freed slaves be deported "back" to Africa. But if African Americans were recognized as citizens, they could not be deported, and they must be allowed to vote. Paterson believed that in a desperate attempt to escape from this logic, Taney distorted the Founders' plain conceptions of individual rights. Her own position was that "race, color, or previous condition of servitude" should be considered irrelevant to suffrage: "The correct qualifications lie in local residence and allegiance and real property."[2]

Ninety years have elapsed since the Supreme Court of the United States disposed of the appeal on the case of Scott vs. Sanford,[3] by a pronouncement known ever since as the Dred Scott decision. To be exact, the date was March 6, 1857, two days after the inaugural of James Buchanan as president, a sequence by no means accidental. The platform approved of the people by Buchanan's election had declared for the preservation of the Union under the Constitution as the "paramount issue," and to that end promised "non-interference by Congress with slavery in state and territory or in the District of Columbia." The Dred Scott case might have been adjudged months earlier, but moderate men considered the postponement wise, to avoid making it a campaign issue.

It was, indeed, eight years since the plea of the Negro Dred Scott had first been entered in any court. Briefly, the case was this: Dred Scott was born in slavery in Virginia, sold as a slave in Missouri, and taken thence by his new owner to Illinois (a free state), and subsequently to Fort Snelling in the Northwest Territories. Later Dred Scott returned to Missouri with his master. Years afterward, he brought suit in St. Louis, in the Missouri state courts, for his liberty, claiming that his residence in Illinois had freed him by virtue of the state constitution; and further, that his residence in Wisconsin Territory gave him freedom by virtue of the Missouri Compromise,[4] which was in effect during his sojourn, though since abrogated.

The legal shifts and changes during those eight years would be tedious to recite, and are hard to follow except by a lawyer. One assumes that a lawyer would thread the maze with facility, though I have been asked by a well known "liberal" member of the bar, in a candid moment: "What *was* the Dred Scott decision?" He really did not know; yet he had just referred to it as a symbol or slogan. It is a classic in that line.

Perhaps if the celebrated case were not thus obscure to the average man, the phrase would not serve so well. Stripped of the sustaining arguments, the actual decision was sadly lacking in dramatic quality. It was simply that the Court had no jurisdiction.

So tame a conclusion hardly has the ring of battle. But the Dred Scott decision certainly was a subject of embittered debate during Buchanan's administration, while the Civil War was brewing. Surely it had something to do with splitting the old political parties and throwing the next election to the candidate of the new Republican party, in which the abolitionist element was influential.

This is the more curious in that the sentiment of the Court was the same as that expressed in the Democratic platform. Its earnest desire was to "settle a controversy" which had "long and seriously agitated the country." So said one justice (Catron*); while another (Wayne*) said a judicial decision was required to secure "harmony." It is an interesting sidelight that the first intention of the justices who concurred in the decision was to avoid mentioning either the Missouri Compromise or the contention of the defense which denied the right of a Negro to sue in the Federal courts. There were other technical grounds sufficient for dismissal on "no jurisdiction." But two of the justices, McLean* and Curtis,* meant to dissent and they let their colleagues know that they would bring both the dangerous topics into their judicial opinions. So Chief Justice Taney thought it incumbent upon him to expound his reasons fully and make it final.

He spent two weeks of arduous labor on the task.[5] It is only fair to believe that his object was to compose disputation, not to inflame it.

Buchanan hoped for repose. Alexander H. Stephens,* so soon to become vice president of the Confederacy, thought that a decision must end "the political question as to the power of the people in their Territorial legislatures. It will be, in effect, a *res adjudicata*."[6] And Lincoln in the Fremont campaign,[7] had said that the Supreme Court was the proper tribunal to settle such points, and that when it did so the Republicans would abide by what the Court held to be the law, challenging the Democrats to do the same. (These comments are taken from *Abraham Lincoln* by Albert J. Beveridge.) It seemed that everyone yearned for peace and quiet, and counted upon obtaining those happy conditions from a Supreme Court decision in the Dred

Scott case. They got their decision; and the controversy burst forth with redoubled fury.

Naturally the first blast was directed against Chief Justice Taney, especially for the arguments which he had designed to copper-rivet his conclusion. These were that the Missouri Compromise had never been valid (the import being that the Federal government had no constitutional power to forbid slavery in a territory); and further, that no Negro, of slave ancestry, could ever be a citizen of a state or of the nation. The "practical" politicians were most concerned over the status of the Territories. Abolitionists were most exasperated by the denial of any chance of citizenship to Negroes. So the Dred Scott decision became a raging campaign issue for the next four years.

The Civil War reversed Taney's judgment by force of arms; the Thirteenth and Fourteenth Amendments wiped out chattel slavery and recognized the citizenship of the ex-slaves; and Taney's reputation has been deemed *res adjudicata* for all time. He stands morally condemned as the man who misused the highest office of justice to condemn the Negro race to perpetual bondage in a nation dedicated to liberty. His decision was generally interpreted as saying that a Negro had no human rights and should never be free.

Now however wrong Taney was, that is not what he said; and there is a riddle in his position or intention which has never been cleared up.

It is not proposed here to evade the popular verdict by discovering in Taney qualities irrelevant to the charge. Whitewashing notorious historical characters or "humanizing" great men by their foibles may be an entertaining pastime, but it has no other value. Maybe Torquemada* was kind to his mother; but it is quite beside the point on which he is rightly detested. It is equally immaterial to Washington's merits that in his later years he had false teeth. But the mystery about Taney concerns the very action which gave him his unenviable place in history. Taney himself would not unravel it while he was alive; yet most mysteriously, he expected posterity to vindicate him, as he wrote in a private letter: "I have an abiding confidence that this act of my judicial life will stand the test of time and the sober judgment of the country."

His previous career and personal life should have some significance in relation to his crucial decision; but they do not add up neatly either. I will take the main items from Beveridge: Roger Brooke Taney belonged to one of the old Catholic families of Maryland and was devout in his religion. He was well educated, well-read and widely informed, with a sound legal training. As a young man he became a leader of the Maryland bar; and during middle life he held cabinet positions in the Federal government. In politics he was an adherent and adviser of Andrew Jackson; and Jackson as president appointed Taney to succeed John Marshall* as Chief Justice in 1836. During the ensuing twenty years, he won the respect of the nation and the affection of his associates. Like Washington, he was said to hold a fiery temperament under firm control; his demeanor was calm, courteous, and considerate.

And he might have avoided the thankless Dred Scott case by retiring from the bench. He was eighty years of age, in feeble health, and saddened by the recent loss of his wife, and of a dearly loved daughter. Probably a sense of duty prompted him to make his great mistake.

Again, there is a basic contradiction in the several reasons he gave to support his ruling. In deciding that the Missouri Compromise had been unconstitutional, he seemed a "strict constructionist," determined to limit the Federal powers to the closest interpretation of the document. He may have been strong on "states' rights," though that is not quite the same thing. But when he said that the Constitution excluded Negroes from citizenship, he read into it a proviso neither expressed nor implied by its wording, and a power encroaching on the primary attribute of the states by virtue of which they had federated—the attribute of original citizenship.

Taney's contention was lamentably weak, being nothing but inference from antecedent and external circumstances. He cited the fact that slavery did exist in the Colonies; and said that Negroes were then regarded as "beings of an inferior order . . . so far inferior that they had no rights which a white man was bound to respect," and that "this opinion was at that time fixed and universal in civilized portions of the white race. It was regarded as an axiom in morals as well as in politics, which no one thought of disputing, or supposed to be open to dispute." Hence (he said) the axiom of the Declaration of Independence, that all men are endowed by their Creator with inalienable rights, was not meant or understood when written as including Negroes. He said the Founders used "the ordinary language of the day," and could not have meant "all men" when they said "all men," because if they did, their conduct as slaveholders was inconsistent with their words.

Taney's position was absurd. The special habit of mind of the Founders was that they were great generalizers, abstract thinkers, reasoning logically from principles to ascertain how men should conduct their lives and frame their institutions, rather than following precedent or confusing the local with the universal. To them, an ancient wrong was all the worse for its antiquity. Theirs was the Age of Reason in opposition to precedent.

As an educated man, Taney must have known that sentiment against slavery had risen noticeably throughout the "civilized world" during the eighteenth century, following Locke.* Various writers, clerics and public men had expressed anti-slavery opinions; such an easy worldling as Horace Walpole* took for granted that it was wrong and hoped it might pass away. Feeling against slavery had even got into romantic fiction. The only plea offered in extenuation was the trouble and cost of abolishing it. Above all, it is impossible to suppose that Taney was not acquainted with Mansfield's decision,[8] the famous ruling that English law gave no warrant for slavery, so that a slave who set foot upon the soil of England thereby became free. Mansfield's decision was immediately recognized as a legal landmark; and it was made in 1772, before the American Revolution began or the Declaration of Independence was written. Incidentally, in Jefferson's first draft of the Declaration there was a phrase, deleted from the accepted text (perhaps by someone with a nicer sense of irony than Jefferson), stating as a grievance that England had imposed the slave trade on the Colonies! If no one thought slavery an injustice to the Negroes, it is hard to see why Jefferson should complain of it.

If Taney had read the Constitution with no end of his own in view, he could have seen in its expressed terms how the Founders reconciled *for the time being* and hoped to square *in the long run* the inconsistency of their professions and practice, their public and private affairs. Though the Constitution as adopted did not abolish slavery, neither did it admit the word "slave." The references which would include the slaves designate them as "persons held to service"—persons, not property—classifying them with apprentices and indentured servants. The one clause relating solely to slavery, but still not using the word, was that which allowed the power and indicated the intention of the Federal government to stop the importation of slaves after 1808—which was done when the time came.

After Federation, the expectation that general emancipation would proceed gradually and peacefully seemed in course of realization. One after another the Northern states became free states; ultimately Virginia was to come within one legislative vote of passing an emancipation act;[9] and there was always some private manumission by slave owners to indicate that "all men" was understood to mean all men.

Is any confirmation of Taney's argument to be found in the informal opinions of the Founders and their contemporaries? On the whole, they run to the contrary; yet they do not supply any positive political conclusion either.

Washington wrote in a private letter that he didn't like to think of the subject of slavery, meaning that it was embarrassing and painful; but he had resolved never to buy or sell a slave. When he broke the resolution a few times in the matter of buying, he was apologetic. Finally, he emancipated his slaves in his will, which took effect.

Jefferson should yield more illumination, since he was more of a theorist than Washington. But Jefferson's various statements seem to leave confusion worse confounded. He called slavery despotism. He said it depraved the masters as much as the slaves; and "violated the liberties" which are "the gift of God." He acknowledged the very inconsistency which Taney said the Founders could not have committed. And Jefferson said flatly that "whatever their [the Negroes'][10] degree of talent, it is no measure of their rights." That is plain enough, anyhow; and it refutes Taney authoritatively.

But Jefferson never made any direct move nor advocated any immediate measure for emancipation. His will provided for the emancipation of no more than five of his slaves (and he owned above two hundred). As he died insolvent, even those five would not have been freed but for the personal donation of his executors. His other slaves were sold to satisfy his debts. It was like Washington that his intention was carried out; and perhaps like Jefferson that his eloquent reflections on the injustice of slavery did his slaves no good.

Yet Jefferson's cogitations recurred repeatedly to one proposal—that was the deportation of the slaves.[11] Certainly if there were no Negroes in the country there would be no problem of Negro slavery. It is not apparent when he adopted this notion, but he had it in mind as early as 1797, for he wrote then: "Whither shall the colored emigrants go? . . . If something is not done, and done soon, we shall be the murderers of our own children." He feared the possibility of a slave insurrection, such as had so lately occurred in the French West Indies.[12] It didn't happen; but in 1817 he still advocated deportation. "I am ready and desirous to make any sacrifice which shall ensure their gradual but complete retirement from the States and . . . establish them elsewhere in freedom and safety. But I have not perceived the growth of this disposition in the rising generation, of which I once had sanguine hopes. . . . I leave it, therefore, to time, and not at all without hope that the day will come."

By 1824 he thought it impossible to "retire" all the Negroes. There were already a million and a half of them, and cost of the project looked prohibitive. Still he did not think that "getting rid of them is forever impossible." His modified suggestion was that from a date to be fixed, the "afterborn" (children of slave parents) should be free, and should be deported as they grew up. The older slave generation would then die out in time. Jefferson does not seem to have considered the feelings of the slave parents losing their children. He said: "I have never yet been able to conceive any other practicable plan." So it would seem that he took for granted that any plan to abolish slavery must require the deportation of the Negroes.

With all this, one cannot avoid the supposition that Taney was disingenuous in his arguments. He was born in 1776[13]; he was cradled in the Revolution. He was twenty-four before Washington died; Jefferson and John Adams survived until Taney was fifty. That is to say, he spent his formative years among men who made or remembered the Revolution and the intellectual atmosphere of the Revolutionary period. He must have been familiar with the scheme of deportation. As early as 1786 the English started a colony in Sierra Leone to take care of ex-slaves; and the America Colonization Society began the settlement of freed slaves in Liberia about 1821. What is more, John Marshall, Taney's predecessor as Chief Justice, was active in supporting the Liberian project.

As a young man, Taney himself inherited some slaves from his father, and he emancipated them promptly, excepting two or three aged ones who were past work, whom he supported for the rest of their lives. Obviously, then, Taney did not believe that Negroes as such should properly be slaves.

Nor did the Dred Scott decision say so. It simply left the power of emancipation in the States and with the slave owners individually, where it was before. Then what difference did it make?

The answer to that is the key to Taney's decision, the reading of the riddle. If the Dred Scott decision stood, what must be its general and permanent effect? The novel feature of it was the ruling that Negroes could never be citizens of the United States. But there is no inherent or inevitable reason why a non-citizen, an alien, may not be free, own property, and enjoy the equal protection of the law in his person. Large numbers of aliens have resided comfortably in the United States for indefinite periods with no manifest disadvantage or harm. In what respect does the status of an alien *necessarily* differ from that of a citizen?

In just one thing: the alien cannot claim the right to remain in the country. *He must be always deportable.*

During the Revolutionary period there was an important idea, widely discussed and tentatively held, which Taney did not mention, though it bears on the subject of slavery. That was the secular theory of the "perfectibility" of man. One must presume that Taney never subscribed to it himself, for it is contrary to Catholic doctrine; but he could hardly have been ignorant of it. (The nineteenth century translated it into the term "progress.") Precisely by that notion the Founders could undertake their resolute fight for their own liberty, pledging "their lives, their property and their sacred honor," in spite of being the direct inheritors and owners of slaves. "Perfectibility" must involve a process in time. The founding of the United States was looked on to some extent as an experiment or test case to be tried out consciously.

Belonging to a genuinely scientific era, the Founders supposed it must be within the range of the mind to ascertain how political organization worked, and by that knowledge to form a government for free men. They had over two thousand years of history to draw on for data, if only of errors to be avoided. With that perspective, it was evident that between the civilization in which they had been bred, however imperfect it might be, and the primitive culture from which the African slaves had recently been taken by force, there was a gap of ages. If the theory of perfectibility were universally true, possibly the gap could be closed by education and environment; the time might be shortened, perhaps reduced to a few generations as against millennia; but at the very least some time was required. The change would not be effected instantaneously by emancipation. On the contrary, it seemed as if emancipation must confront the States in which the Negro population was numerous with an equally grave question, to which the supposed answer was obviously disastrous. Self government is not automatic; yet if the slaves were to become free men and citizens, must they not also have the vote? If not, why not?

Chief Justice Taney burked theories, facts, and sentiments to serve his hidden purpose. He transposed the conditions of two periods, both well within his knowledge.

The dangerous reaction, the intellectual defense of slavery on the grounds of the innate inferiority of the Negro race, and the emergence of a minority of Southerners determined to maintain slavery permanently, was a rather late development as positive doctrine. It came after the first quarter of the nineteenth century. The modern "economic interpretation of history" tends to trace this reaction to nothing but zooming cotton profits.[14] It is idle to debate that opinion, for if it were true it would be idle to debate any course of human action. By such interpretation the American Revolution could not have occurred—not with the pre-Revolutionary slave-owner interest so strong. George Washington could not have existed, and it would be impossible to invent him. Jefferson would be inconceivable.

On the other hand, the defensive explanation that the changed attitude of the South in regard to slavery was due mainly to resentment of Abolitionist denunciations is glaringly inadequate. It bears no proportion to the vital importance of the principles at stake, the critical danger of conflict, and the character and mental level of the best men of the South. Certainly it is not adequate to the material interests affected. Injured sensibilities are not negligible; but economic factors have physical weight and force. The error of the "economic interpreters" is that they do not see the most obvious fact about the material things they say are determinant, the laws governing physical weight and force—which is that the incidence depends upon direction, turning on pivot points; and the pivot points are established from an intellectual position, an idea. An erroneous position sets a wrong direction. The lack of any idea or direction spells disequilibrium, random motion, and destruction.[15]

Then if the movement toward full freedom was slowed down, and the direction shifted, what was the error—whether a wrong idea or the absence of any idea to govern the physical elements?

Trying to get around this question instead of reasoning it through to a correct answer, Taney landed in the most perilous position imaginable. No doubt he was a more learned jurist than Jefferson, and that was his undoing. Believing, like Jefferson, that Negro slavery in the United States involved some peculiar danger that could be averted only by eliminating the Negroes, he saw also that they could be shipped out as "property" as long as they were slaves; but if they were freed first, how could they be compelled to go if they were not willing? Perhaps Jefferson had an uneasy apprehension of the difficulty when he said that "if a slave can have a country in the world, it must be any other in preference to that in which he is born to live and labor for another." But the context implies that he was thinking only of the doubtful loyalty of the slaves. Taney obviously saw the real point. A citizen cannot be deported. *And an alien has no claim to vote.*

Such was his legal "solution." But in order to exclude the native-born American Negro from citizenship, he left no rational or natural basis of citizenship for anyone. If it is not a birthright, from what source can it be derived? Citizenship by naturalization is a grant validated by the native right in the grantor; it is impossible to confer what one has not got oneself. And without original or natural rights anywhere, constitutions and laws can be nothing but verbal statements of temporary dominant forces (as Justice Holmes was to say they were half a century later—"force is the ultima ratio").[16] If Taney meant that, he miscalculated the dominant forces. But he did not mean that; he said that the Court was not to be "a mere reflex of the popular opinion of the day."[17] He thought he was taking the long view.

Here one can but conjecture: if he saw that he was undercutting the reality of natural rights, he may have persuaded himself that the special case could not arise again after the Negroes were cleared out.

The bribe of the righteous is usually a supposed good to be secured by a little twisting of principle, of course only this once. It is easy to understand why Taney did not explain his purpose, when the controversy was already so complex and heated. He thought he had insured an indefinite lease of time for deportation, during which it would make no difference if the Negroes were freed. He may even have believed that he had removed the substantial obstacle to emancipation.

For indeed the opposition to emancipation, the inertia or reaction of the South, most marked in the tendency to silence discussion,[18] had increased commensurately with the movement of the whole country toward democracy, that is, toward unqualified suffrage and the assumption that the "will" of the majority is the equivalent of a moral principle. "The propertyless masses were beginning to enter politics. Between 1812 and 1821 six Western states entered the Union with constitutions providing for universal white manhood suffrage or a close approximation; and between 1810 and 1821 four of the older states substantially dropped property qualifications for voters. . . . Between 1828 and 1848 the vote trebled, although the population did not quite double."[19]

The great difficulty was the matter of the vote. And though the Dred Scott decision did not settle it, neither did the Civil War. It is not yet settled, nor ever will be until the function of the vote is understood—as it never has been.

In every branch of science, the major hindrance to the advance of knowledge is the human propensity to fix upon some superficial or accidental aspect of a combination and take it for an integral, causative element. The phrase "race problem" is a false fixation of this kind. There are no race problems; what are called such are strictly political problems. The two general questions are: what is the true function of government? and by what instrumentality can it be performed?

The axiom of the inalienable rights of the individual says that government rightly is only the agent of the citizen (as John Jay* defined it);[20] and its sole purpose is to preserve individual liberty. Thus hereditary monarchy and aristocracy, as well as sheer tyranny, are debarred. It must be a republic, "a government of laws and not of men," with the necessary offices filled by representatives.

Voting seems to be the indicated method of choosing representatives; and in an election, the majority must be decisive.

Yet there is no moral reason why the will of the majority should prevail; else slavery, for example, would be right if a majority imposed it on a minority. This is an extremely disconcerting truth which the Founders did not blink. The Constitution, a strict limitation of the scope of government, must restrict majority action closely. But a constitution cannot be foolproof. It can always be destroyed, and most easily by the voters. And it is destroyed, it is inoperative, whenever the *scope* of government is so extended that "anything goes" on a majority vote; it is no matter, then, if the hollow forms of the legislative, executive and judiciary remain.

The modern democratic presumption is that the vote itself is a "right." This is a confusion of terms. Rights are abstractions. But they are exercised concretely in action. Voting is an action intended to authorize some material effect, though it is physically a discontinuous action, a signal, not a direct impulsion. On the signal, physical forces are released or checked, not by the voter directly, but by other persons. If the material effect does occur, and is to be controlled, kept to its specific purpose, by the voter, he must be in some real physical relation to his agent. What is the real physical relation, if any, of the voter to government? It must be that of any principal to his agent.

He is the source of supply. The material effect is the levying and spending of tax money. The supplier is in control as long as it is possible for him to cut the supply, that is, to resist undue exactions or misapplications of the funds, and no longer. Further, action can be controlled only from a physical base of resistance. Land is the only base. The action of voting, giving the signal, is justified by the right of the voter only if he can control the result of his action.[21] Nobody can have a right to perform any action when he cannot answer and pay for the consequences. He must be materially qualified to do so. The true qualification for the vote is real property; and the voter must qualify himself. If he does not choose to do so, his abstract right is unimpaired, since he is still free to qualify himself whenever he chooses. But when one man must pay taxes and another may vote to elect the officials who levy and spend them, the supplier has no control, and the function of the vote is nullified. Government then becomes an agency of extortion. Thenceforward the producer, the taxpayer, is under a disguised and partial system of slavery, forced "to live and labor for another."

By the democratic premise of unqualified "manhood" suffrage with its concomitant assumption of a "right" of majority over-riding the true primary right of the individual, the free white Southerners were logically boxed. In that position, it was more than likely that if they freed the slaves they must also in effect change places with them. They were naturally reluctant to take such a chance. To evade it, the desperate argued that a Negro was not quite a human being, a man. The ordinary man, at a loss for reasons, merely hoped for delay enough to last his time. Taney as a jurist fell back on expediency by a legal device which in his philosophy he may have deemed justified by human imperfection. But neither desperation, delay, nor device availed. They never do. Only a correct solution will answer a problem.

With the Civil War and Reconstruction, that which the Southerners feared exceedingly came upon them.[22] If it be retorted that they got what they deserved, the whole modern world falls under the judgment, having incurred the same disaster by the same error. It was Taney's worst luck that he had a majority with him; and he has it to this day, in a world enslaved.

"The Riddle of Chief Justice Taney in the Dred Scott Decision" originally appeared in The Georgia Review, *3.2 (Summer 1949) 192–203,*

Notes

1. "Turns," January 26, 1936; February 23, 1936.
2. GM 159.
3. Often spelled "Sandford."
4. The congressional enactment of 1820, forbidding slavery in territories north of parallel 36° 30' and permitting it in those to the south of that parallel.
5. The chief justice's opinion is about 26,000 words long.

6. A nineteenth-century synonym for "res judicata": a matter already judged.
7. John C. Fremont (1813–1890) was the Republican nominee for president in 1856.
8. William Murray, 1st Earl of Mansfield (1705–1793), chief justice of the King's Bench; his judgment in Somersett's Case (1772) was that slavery was so "odious" that it could be authorized only by positive law, and such law did not exist in England.
9. Paterson seems to be thinking of a famous controversy in Virginia (1831–1832) regarding various possible forms of emancipation. There was a series of votes in the legislature, none of them as close as Paterson indicates.
10. Paterson's [brackets].
11. Paterson's attitude toward Jefferson—a subject that, she said, "can never lose interest"—was complicated: he was "a great genius," but he "came within a hair's breadth of being caught in the fatal 'mechanistic' political philosophy which Europe was adopting—the philosophy of the present day planners, the absolutists and collectivists and totalitarian state advocates. Because he was born and bred in the New World, and because he was also a man of extraordinary sensibility, responsive to his free environment, he split the shell of the doctrinaire, but bits of it stuck to him—he couldn't help trying occasionally to work out everything in a sort of mathematical order, for instance his educational schemes; and in a pinch, he would resort to the political power as the absolute, when he had it in his own hands, though he would protest instantly when others put it over on him" ("Turns," December 20, 1942). Paterson also deplored Jefferson's impractical life. Standing in his bedroom at Monticello, she maintained to the guides that "He died a bankrupt!" (Muriel Hall, interview, 1994).
12. Especially the revolution in Haiti, which began in 1791.
13. Paterson's mistake for 1777. Taney was twenty-two when Washington died and forty-nine when Adams and Jefferson died.
14. "The economic interpretation of even a commercial venture is nonsense"—in the sense that it omits human choice and individual goals and values from the explanation ("Turns," November 26, 1939).
15. This passage, which is fitted to the "engineering" explanations of GM, is a compressed version of several of Paterson's ideas. The point is that economic goods (and by extension, economic "factors") do not move themselves; they take their direction from human decisions. Human minds decide where and how to move them. The same tiny amount of cranial energy used in deciding to route a freight car to San Francisco can also route it to New York. If no conscious decision is made, the material "factors" will move, if at all, in random and destructive ways. The politics involved in such decisions, or lack of decisions, governs the material factors, not the other way around.
16. Oliver Wendell Holmes, Jr. (1841–1935; associate justice of the Supreme Court, 1902–1932) to John Pollock, February 1, 1920: "Force, mitigated so far as may be by good manners, is the *ultima ratio*, and between two groups that want to make inconsistent kinds of world I see no remedy except force." "Ultima ratio" should be understood as "final argument."
17. Taney's words in the decision were "the mere reflex of the popular opinion or passion of the day."

18. In 1835, for example, attempts by abolitionists to send antislavery literature into the South by means of the US mails were met with destruction of mail and violent intimidation of suspected sympathizers with abolition.
19. Richard Hofstadter,* *The American Political Tradition.* [Paterson's note.] Paterson is quoting Chapter 3 of Hofstadter's book (1948). The original passage begins, "However, the people, the propertyless masses, were beginning, at first quietly and almost unobtrusively, to enter politics."
20. Perhaps a mistake for James Madison, Jay's collaborator on the *Federalist* Papers. "The federal and State governments are in fact but different agents and trustees of the people" (Madison, *Federalist* No. 46). But perhaps Paterson is thinking of Jay's opinion as chief justice of the United States in the case of Chisholm vs. Georgia (1793), in which he referred to government officials as "agents of the people." (See Walter Stahr, *John Jay: Founding Father* [New York: Hambledon and London, 2005] 295.)
21. In this passage, Paterson repeats the imagery of GM, and its theory that the vote needs to be linked not just to property but to real property, however small—because, Paterson thinks, only power distributed across immovable "bases" can provide enough "resistance" to the centralizing power of government. Her brief statement about action and control is related to the idea that voters cannot direct the course of government in detail but can, by exercising their "mass veto," arrest its action (GM 23, 123–26, 159–62).
22. An echo of Job 3:25—"the thing which I greatly feared is come upon me"—and Mark 4:41: "And they feared exceedingly, and said one to another, What manner of man is this[?]"

21

Has the World Grown Smaller?

The world, we are told, has grown smaller. Airplanes, radio, television, and other marvels of modern science have practically annihilated time and space for the human race. It takes only three days for a plane to circle the globe, and less than three minutes for television to show what is happening on the other side of this solid earth. Therefore, the popular argument says, we must bring our ideas up to date accordingly. We must get rid of obsolete theories and institutions, such as the individual liberty of Americans and the national sovereignty of the United States. These statements are put forward as obvious and indisputable.

Recently, I met a distinguished scientist, an American citizen with a European background and international honors. He had been abroad for several years and had just returned. "The world has grown smaller," he said. "We must think in terms of the facts of today. One can cross the Atlantic in twenty-four hours."

"Can you?" I asked.

The scientist stopped in his tracks, obstructing traffic slightly, though the sidewalk had not grown either larger or smaller. "Why," he exclaimed, looking a bit dazed, "when I came to America first, over forty years ago, it took me only twelve days, from Paris to New York, on a slow boat. I was young and poor and couldn't afford a fast liner. But this time it took me two and a half months to get back."

Columbus crossed the Atlantic in less time than that.

Those are the facts. Let us think in those terms, and see what they really signify. In point of fact, I cannot get to China now, though Marco Polo got there in the thirteenth century. I cannot go around the world at all, though Magellan's crew did so early in the sixteenth century. As lately as 1885 an American, George Kennan,* visited Siberia to interview the political prisoners there, exiled by the Czar up to the number of two and three hundred every year; the convict colonies numbered thousands of persons, more or less closely guarded though there were frequent escapes. Kennan wrote a book on what he had seen there, in ample detail, which aroused deep indignation in the free countries. But nobody from outside could now get anywhere near the Soviet prison camps in Siberia, from which nobody escapes, and in which millions of captives are dying of slave labor, hunger, and exposure. And apparently nobody cares. There and elsewhere in our "small world" innumerable people are either being driven like cattle, at a foot pace, where they do not want to go; or herded like cattle behind barbed wire fences where they do not wish to stay, turned back by bayonets when they try to break out, perishing in misery, unable to get anywhere at all. But one cannot see this by television. No television would be permitted to transmit the appalling sight. Information on the subject leaks out uncertainly, in driblets, generally taking longer to reach the public than the news from China carried by Marco Polo.

It is indeed true that forty years ago, or as lately as 1913, anyone from a civilized nation could go practically anywhere at will, comfortably, speedily, and as safely as he could stroll down Main Street. That is no longer the case. The truth is that those who talk in such terms as if they were now true are "living in the past." They refer to conditions which have ceased to exist.

Whatever has been happening during the last forty years surely should be recognized, studied, and thoroughly understood if we are to think in terms of the facts, and draw rational conclusions from the past and present as a guide to the future.

There are primary facts with which rational thought must begin, as the human race began, in order to trace the processes by which we ever got anywhere. They are the natural conditions of existence. There are only four general ways by which human beings can exist on this earth—four types of economy, or means of obtaining subsistence. Naturally the economies could and did progress from crude to skilled stages of development; also they can exist contemporaneously, becoming somewhat mixed and reacting on one another. But they are not difficult to distinguish in essentials.

(1) The savage society, or "snatch economy," of wandering hunters who live by the bounty of nature, on what they can kill or pick up.
(2) The pastoral nomad society, wandering herdsmen who live in the main off their tame animals.
(3) The agricultural society, in which men have learned to get most of their living from cultivated crops.

(4) The industrial economy, ranging all the way from handicrafts to high-speed, high-energy motor machine production; and requiring a general exchange system.

Americans hold this truth to be self-evident, that all men are created with an inalienable right to life, liberty, and the pursuit of happiness—the choice of what we will do. Liberty consists in the natural right of the individual to exercise his natural faculties in the natural world. In the various economies described, which are the only possible forms, the extent to which a man can use and benefit by his liberty is easily seen.

The savage can move about at his own risk as far and fast as his muscle power will carry him on such food as he can find.

The pastoral nomad can go wherever there is pasture for his beasts, moving as fast as they can walk and graze. But his economy, though it keeps him mobile, cannot develop into the industrial phase.

The primitive farmer must remain on the land he cultivates. He has begun *fixed base production*, which in its earlier stages tends to immobilize him. But the fixed base is the prerequisite of the use of mechanical tools for *production*. With property in land, metal work and the application of harnessed energy begin.

The industrial economy, operating from the fixed base and still including farming and animal husbandry, combines all the advantages of the three more primitive economies, and raises from them a new power. It is the only economy capable of extending man's range of movement and accelerating his velocity. It increases the variety of materials for use, and choice of activities, until man is free of the whole surface of the globe, and even of the air. Only the industrial economy can generate surplus energy, store it up, direct and control it, so as to afford human beings the full exercise of their natural liberty. With industry, man is *mobilized* far beyond his original condition.

All motion is expenditure of energy, which must be constantly restored if the given activity is to be continued. Thus an economy is an energy circuit, maintained by the persons it supports. This is equally true of the most primitive and the most advanced societies. It is a factual description, not a metaphor. A savage family constitutes the smallest human energy circuit, picking up maintenance from the bounty of nature, and rearing children as replacement. In our modern industrial economy, the materials used in the energy circuit, and the related actions, are infinitely more complex and extensive, but it has the same primary, basic requirement. *At least as much energy must be brought into the circuit constantly as is expended from it.* Failing this continuous maintenance and replacement, it will break down, and the human beings in it must die, for it is their physical means of subsistence.

For unknown ages it would seem that man remained in the savage society, which will support only a scanty population at bare subsistence level. The pastoral nomad society, though presumably less ancient, is also of unknown antiquity, and likewise has a specific limit of population and cultural comfort. Then during at least six thousand years of pre-machine civilization, a small margin of surplus production was achieved which went into exchange and required the invention of money. With these advances, man was again mobilized; they made travel possible without carrying provisions. The range of movement was greatly extended.

But the maximum velocity still seemed to be fixed by purely natural limits. It was restricted to the speed, endurance, and availability of muscle power—human or animal. In the Roman Empire, after the great main roads were built through Europe and the Near East, the imperial post sped between Rome and the ends of the Empire as fast as relays of riders or slave-driven galleys could cover the distance. But these express methods comprised only a negligible percentage of conveyance. The average rate of speed of transports and communications—freight and travellers—by land was the rate of an ox-cart. Commercial shipping certainly was no faster. In the Acts of the Apostles, we may read how it took all winter for St. Paul to reach Rome from Jerusalem, in the custody of Roman soldiers, sailing on a mixed freight and passenger ship. It is a high estimate to assume that the average rate of speed of the energy circuit of the period was three miles an hour.

Cro-Magnon Man might have got about as rapidly, and perhaps as far if he had wished. But he could not carry the freight. The freight and the improved way of life were surplus energy, out of handicraft production. So much had been gained.

Napoleon's couriers could make no better time than the messengers of Augustus Caesar. Nor did goods move faster by land in 1800 than they did two thousand years earlier. But they did move faster by water, and in greater quantity. That was a further gain. Yet Napoleon could not supply the army of four hundred thousand soldiers he marched to Moscow; that was why three-fourths of them did not return. In the transport of the period, supply for such an army over such a distance was impossible. And velocity in an army had rather diminished than increased; it is doubtful if Napoleon's regiments could move as fast as Genghis Khan, or even a Roman legion.

But in the Great War not yet ended, the United States supplied four or five million men all around the world, by rapid transport, organized with instantaneous communication.

In hundreds of thousands of years, the range had fluctuated while the maximum velocity remained fixed. In six thousand years the range was extended by a new means, surplus production from fixed bases; but the margin of surplus also seemed to be fixed within the limits of handicraft production, so velocity was limited to muscle-power motion.

Then in one hundred and fifty years, or since about 1800, production accelerated by a geometric ratio, until the average rate of speed of transport and communication rose to about thirty miles an hour with a correspondent increase in tonnage (at a rough and probably low estimate) for the United States. The standard of living rose equally, and so did the population. It is probable that there are about as many Indians now living on the North American continent as when Columbus arrived, but there are also a hundred and sixty million of the newcomers! The increase in surplus energy is fantastic; it rose from zero to something like four h. p. per capita. During the same period the population of Europe tripled and the recurrent famines of that area practically ceased.

The thing that happened was a large scale *conversion of mass into energy*. The splitting of the atom is only the ultimate expression of that process.

Two thousand years ago the Greeks were on the verge of inventing motor power, but they stopped short. Why did that weary time elapse before science got under way again? Why did the margin of surplus energy remain so low for ten thousand years, and then rise to the power of the dynamo in less than two hundred years? There must have been some peculiar problem to be solved, outside of the mechanics of actual production.

There was. The problem which had to be solved before production could get under way was the problem of government.

Savages have no formal government, no separate organization for that purpose. They do not need it, having only portable property; and they cannot support it, having no surplus energy.

Pastoral nomads have only personal government by a tribal chief, who can be deposed without violence if he is incompetent. He has no means of ruling by force, for the reason that there is not enough surplus energy to support an executive organization separately, and also, *pressure cannot be accumulated against a mobile object*—that is, a member of the tribe.

Formal government with executive force comes into existence with fixed base production. It arises from the necessity of maintaining title to immovable property, land and buildings and the like, in the absence of the owner, so that the individual may enjoy the mobility which surplus production affords. Such government is also capable of executing criminal law in order to cut the sequence of reprisals, or blood feuds. When government performs these proper functions, law is not a restriction of liberty. It is, in fact, a means of extending the exercise of natural liberty; it offsets time and distance in the system of exchange. It obviates the natural limitation of primitive fixed base production, the immobilization of the producer within a small area.

But since pressure can be accumulated against fixed objects, or men engaged in fixed base production, it is necessary for the producer to have an adequate method of keeping government to its proper function. Otherwise government immediately becomes tyranny. So it was and so it remained for thousands of years. Throughout the whole of "civilized" history up to about 1800, government claimed authority to bind men to the soil, to prescribe and limit their work, to prevent exchange of goods, and to put them to forced labor—in brief, to stop productive enterprise. Thus it nullified the great intrinsic advantage of fixed base production.

A slave no longer has even his own natural energy at his own disposal. In the ancient despotisms, where every man's property and person were subject to seizure by the king, nobody could accumulate capital and put it into production with certainty of getting the benefit himself. Under feudalism, the serf and tenant had no mobility; nor could they get the good of improvements on the land, which is possible with individual ownership, by freehold. The individual had no standing. He must get permission to work, license to trade; men were stopped on the roads, goods taxed at every city gate and provincial border. Liberty was not recognized as a natural right; no one dared to assert it. The language of permission speaks only of "liberties" or "freedoms" in the plural, which is to say, grants from authority to do some particular thing, to reside in one small area, or to move a few miles. Government was such a chain and a burden that it made men long for the original freedom of the savage.

In such conditions, only small local energy circuits can be organized, with a trickle of trade from a tiny surplus. It was impossible to form a high-energy circuit operating over an extended area. As recently as 1707, or before the union of England and Scotland, England alone was "the most populous area within Europe in which trade was not obstructed by artificial barriers."[1] In England also the individual was least restricted by government in his choice of occupation, least taxed, safest from arbitrary arrest or confiscation, and no longer bound to the soil. That comparatively greater freedom made the British Empire.

Yet even England imposed restrictions on colonial industry and trade. The United States was obliged to break away. It expanded over the continent with unexampled velocity. The free citizens were actually free at last, not only nominally but with the necessary institutions for the fullest exercise of freedom: freehold land, contract law, and limited government. Liberty creates its own physical means of expression. The existence and influence of the United States tended to diminish restrictions everywhere. With Great Britain and the United States as the two major powers, the great world energy circuit was formed, having such volume and speed that the transcendent power was at last expressed in the airplane and in radio communication. For a brief period, the whole world was practically open; only Russia and Turkey hindered travelers by requiring passports, and they found it difficult to refuse them. Freedom is power. Any nation in which the citizens are actually free can liberate the whole world, not by conquest, but by the flow of energy overcoming the inertia of government control elsewhere. The less free countries have not the power to resist even by force of arms, for the high-energy circuit can pay for the world-wide protection of its own nationals and trade out of its vast surplus.

But a "world government" under which no one is free would still have no energy circuit; internal restrictions would prevent it. And the unfortunate inhabitants of the globe would have no recourse against such universal oppression.

Trade is the power line of the long circuit of energy. At any period, a map showing the trade routes with figures of the speed and volume of traffic would give the index of surplus energy and optimum population.

Now take such figures of today. The rational deduction is terrifying. Such a depleted energy circuit cannot possibly support the previously existent population. It is not supporting them. They are perishing, dying down to the lower optimum.

For even the volume of goods transported now is by no means the actual volume of trade. Military supplies are not trade. No materials expropriated by government, whether in taxes or in kind, are in the energy circuit; they are not exchanged, they are merely consumed or destroyed. Even if they are given away in "relief," and consumed by civilians, nothing comes back from them for maintenance and further production. They are a depletion of the energy circuit. Also the travel of government officials, unlike travel for trade, is merely a depletion returning nothing. And such government shipments and travel constitute a large part of the use of transport today.

Regrettably, the exponents of "free trade" do not stipulate a really free trade. It is not free trade when a private business in one country deals with government controlled or government bonused or government owned goods from another country. Free trade would have to be trade between free economies. Government intervention within a nation cuts the energy circuit; so that there is no equivalence in such exchanges. When goods are exported at a cost in human lives, from a slave economy—as Russia exported wheat forcibly taken from the starving farm population during the 1930's—it is not free trade to receive such commodities. It is slave trade.

There are two means by which the long circuit of energy may be destroyed, though both are actions of government. One is by government restrictions on the producer, expropriation or forced labor. The other is depletion by taxes. Up to a certain point, such expense will be shown in a shortage of goods, in diminished production. Below that point, when there is no longer any surplus, the expense appears in the death rate.

What then has happened during the past forty years? An enormous increase in government, in both positive restrictions on the individual and on property use, and increased taxes; and a converse decline in speed and volume of transport and of communication for the individual, which signifies that the energy circuit has broken down to such an extent that it cannot support the existing population. And the increase of government has not brought peace; rather it has made peace impossible. The surplus population must now be exterminated—by government. By war, famine, pestilence and mass "liquidation."

Those are the facts.

It is easily possible to calculate approximately how long an economy takes to run down and stop after government control has been imposed on it. As with a rising energy level, so with a decline; the coefficient is the average rate of speed of transport and communication, taken at the time the controls are imposed. It can take some time to run down by consuming capital assets. Russian production sank below subsistence level with the Bolshevik revolution; it has existed ever since on borrowed means and with a deficit in lives—prisoners worked to death. The British debacle dates from various piecemeal impositions of the political power which do not give one exact date; the actions include the Lloyd George budget of 1909 with its confiscatory death duties and subsequent currency depreciation and seizure of investment securities. The significant imposition in the United Sates began in 1929 with the extension of government into finance and "relief." The Roman Empire took three hundred years to collapse from depletion, after the political power had become absolute in the emperor so that citizens could not resist increasing taxation and forced labor.

If the average rate of speed in the Roman economy was three miles an hour, and the modern rate is thirty miles an hour, the equation is as follows:

3 miles per hour—300 years
30 miles per hour—30 years

The argument for such increase of government has always been that the increased complexity of an industrial economy requires more government. The plain, unalterable, physical fact is that high energy, high velocity, and great volume of production require proportionately less government. The long circuit must be unimpeded. It was formed during the period in which government diminished; it has collapsed as government has increased. The world is perishing from too much government.[2]

"Has the World Grown Smaller?" originally appeared in The Georgia Review, *2.2 (Summer 1948) 177–85 © 1948 by The University of Georgia. Published by permission of* The Georgia Review.

Notes

1. Source unknown.
2. The last sentence appears to be a subtly reproving echo of Ayn Rand. Near the conclusion of *The Fountainhead* (1943), Rand's hero, Howard Roark, delivers a courtroom speech in which he says that "the world is perishing from an orgy of self-sacrifice."

22

A Man of Destiny

Paterson challenged anyone to "rewrite the Declaration of Independence without reference to a divine source of human rights. It cannot be done; the axiom is missing."[1] *She held that the human world cannot be explained in the absence of a God who gave the universe its structure and infused it with his energy, a God who provided human beings with their nature and dignity. She was therefore especially interested in* Human Destiny, *a work by a distinguished scientist that presented a theistic account of evolution and a defense of individual freedom.*

It was said of Edmund Burke* that if one had met him, unknown, taking shelter from the rain under a shed, one would have thought: "This is an extraordinary man."[2] . . . In the office where I worked, another woman whose desk stood nearer the door enquired: "Do you mind telling me who was your caller, the man who just went out?" I told her, and added: "Why did you ask?" She had never before put such a question. She said: "I was sure he was somebody."

That was Pierre Lecomte du Nouy.* To describe such a man is all the more difficult. Details do not convey the impression of active intellect, intense vitality and unaffected charm, which were borne out by the diversity of his talents and accomplishments. His life is equally impossible to summarize. The one who knew him best, his wife, has told the story as briefly as it can be done (*The Road to "Human Destiny,"* by Mary Lecomte du Nouy, Longmas Green, $5.00), exquisitely economical in three hundred odd pages, a portrait in silver point. Given only the space of a review, what can be said? A friend declared that "he was twenty men rolled into one." Nevertheless, he exhibited a rare consistency, and in the end a clear pattern emerges. Even his two ambitions were interwoven; he wished to make a lasting contribution to human progress, and to realize a great love, and his various and brilliant gifts were brought together to serve both purposes.

A thorough Frenchman, born in Paris, and bred in a milieu of the arts, letters and learned professions, at eighteen he was a cowboy in Texas. Had he lived in the seventeenth century, surely he would have left his name on the map of North America as one of the famous French explorers. As it was, he went home and at twenty-two graduated from the Sorbonne, a licentiate in law. He then became secretary to Aristide Briand.* Among his early friends were Guy de Maupassant,* Buffalo Bill* and Maurice Maeterlinck!* He wrote fiction and plays, he made a hit as an actor, and declined to follow it up. It was too easy. From boyhood he showed remarkable mechanical aptitude; obviously he could have made his fortune in machine industry. Instead, he used his talent to devise precision instruments for scientific research. He was an omnivorous reader; he was "serious" in the French sense of the word; he was a social favorite for his gaiety; the visible world delighted him; and he could live as a recluse for the sake of his work. He married (*en secondes noces*[3]) an American girl, brought up mainly in Paris, who had not the slightest interest in science before she met Pierre Lecomte du Nouy. After their marriage, she became his laboratory assistant, translated his books, and proofread his technical articles.

Well, you see, it's not much use. Once I had an interview with the late Dr. Millikan,* and we spoke of du Nouy. Dr. Millikan testified in the highest terms to du Nouy's standing as a scientist. But what really seemed to strike Millikan was du Nouy's perfect fluency in the American idiom, and the fact that he had written a best seller on a scientific subject.

The first World War started du Nouy on his scientific career, direct from the front line, where he fought with his regiment, the "Blue Devils." Visiting a military hospital, he met Carrel*; and Carrel requested that du Nouy be assigned as a research assistant to aid in systematizing the Carrel-Dakin technique.[4] Immediately after the war, du Nouy made his settled choice of science as a whole-time pursuit. Declining a definite offer of stardom in the movies, he preferred the glamor of the Rockefeller Institute[5] and the fascinating question of surface tension of liquids. Concerning that subject, this reviewer knows less than a mosquito larva, which, I have been informed, is able to hang head down by its tail from the surface tension of the water. Pierre du Nouy would not have been annoyed by such a digression; he would have been amused. And it is not irrelevant, for his passionate preoccupation with science was always pointed to a *living* universe. Thus the phenomena of surface tension led him to study molecular action, which is the threshold where the difference becomes manifest between the inorganic and the organic.

All his scientific investigations ran *contra mundi*,[6] clean contrary to the orthodoxy in science, which postulated a universe bound by the materialistic determinism of pure chance, and atheistic by necessity. Such indeed was the bleak climate of opinion enveloping the society in which he was reared, tempered only by lingering tradition and gentle manners. In his youth he accepted the materialistic view more or less passively—until he became a scientist, and his penetrating intelligence gradually converted him to an unshakable conviction that God exists and *acts* in a rational universe. His wit and humor helped him. The spectacle of scientists employing their minds to prove to other minds that there can be no such thing as a mind to recognize a proof, appealed to him as both comic and tragic, the ultimate paradox.

His faith in a rational order was justified in strange ways against heavy odds. Though the Rockefeller Institute was reluctant to lose him, private considerations obliged him to return to France. There he was attached to the Pasteur Institute for nine years, until the position became untenable. Later he failed narrowly of election to the Collège de France. The cause of these reverses was simple. Scientific determinism has long been in course of transmutation into a political creed, the dogma of Communism. Too many scientists had gone to "the Left." Pierre du Nouy was marked as "a dangerous man"; he was an individualist. He must be stopped. (Here is an illuminating instance of the uses of endowed institutions and bureaucratic patronage.)

Briefly depressed, du Nouy quickly turned ill fortune into an opportunity. For several years he had been meditating a book which should give a new interpretation of the processes and meaning of evolution. Now he had time for it. By cutting him off from research, he remarked, his opponents "have succeeded in making me say what I think."

He headed straight for America and the West, where the very air revived his spirits "like champagne." In a cabin on the edge of the Grand Canyon he wrote the first draft of the original version of his book, three volumes in French, which subsequently was to be rewritten and condensed to one volume in English as *Human Destiny*. He took the manuscript back to France to finish it.

The rest of the story includes the desperate years of the second World War, the terror and heartbreak of France under German occupation, the Resistance, deadly danger and cold hunger, and all the while the book getting itself written—"a gleam in the darkness." In 1942, du Nouy and his wife contrived to escape to the United States. He had only five years left, but he lived to see *Human Destiny* in print, in both French and English, and a world-wide success. I am glad of that.

There is perennial incomprehension of what makes a "timely" book. Genuinely timely ideas are *new* ideas, counter to the fashion which has had its run. *Human Destiny* had a public unconsciously *waiting for it.* I was waiting for it consciously myself. When I was young I read Darwin's *Origin of Species.* I mean I actually read it. In spite of the tedious prose, it held my attention; and I was amazed at the conclusion, inasmuch as the chain of evidence had broken in two sharply just before the last link. The argument is that in the organic order species originate from elementary types by variations (the variations are not accounted for, but are at least conceivable), and then by the survival of the variations best adapted to the environment. Adapted is the keyword.

But in fact the human species *does not* do anything of the kind; it survives by adapting the environment to human desires and needs. Please note that our bare needs don't comprise a strong enough motive for survival. We must desire something above and beyond animal existence, brute necessity. And the material technology of survival for humanity requires for its use at least elementary recognition of moral law.

So it was about time some scientist should observe the most conspicuous attribute of his own species. As a specimen, Charles Darwin himself is worthy of classification. Why did he spend three happy years being seasick on the *Beagle* and tramping from end to end of South America collecting bothersome specimens in vast quantities to make his cabin more uncomfortable, and then spend laborious years examining shells in the hope of discovering something about the universe which would be no help whatever to him in respect of his survival, and which unhappily has been so misconstrued as to put the rest of us in imminent peril of extinction? Apparently one reason he was dubious about design was the shape of his nose. Whenever he was almost ready to admit design in the universe, he backed off with the reflection that no rational scheme of things would have given him such a nose, nobody would have designed it.

Scientists are a very peculiar species indeed. It is even possible that they are human. I hope to go into that on some future occasion. Meanwhile, it always gives me pleasure to remember Alexander Agassiz.* He, Alexander, to the bitter end didn't subscribe to Darwin's theory. And he went to Africa and observed giraffes. Darwin had theorized that giraffes got their long necks by way of adaptation to browsing off tall trees. All the giraffes Alexander Agassiz observed—all, without exception—were browsing from low shrubs.

As I said before, we get along somehow, scientists included, by adapting the facts to our own wishes. At least, we have so far; I hope we haven't run out our string, now that the scientists have gratified their wish for atom bombs. Their projects to adapt us to the bomb aren't attractive. "Every social order derives its sanctions from the prevailing conception of the cosmic order." This flash of intuitive genius and perfect phrasing must be credited to Admiral Ben Moreell.* Communism derives from the imagined cosmic order of mechanistic determinism. The result is civilization in ruins. Many scientists nevertheless cling to mechanistic determinism as a description of the macrocosm, but they add to it the microcosm of atomic physics, which is ruled by pure chance. These are not offered as alternatives, but as two aspects of the universe, although the scientists themselves say there is no connection between them, and yet one is supposed to be the substance of the other. After destruction, chaos. In short, modern science gives us no cosmos whatever. What social order can derive from that? Nothing from nothing.[7]

What du Nouy was driving at was a conception of the universe *as an instrument of value.* And that is the one thing we know about it for certain, by direct experience of the part of it which we inhabit. It is also the one thing that scientists hitherto have positively refused to take into account. They say, in effect, they can't measure "value"; but they also imply that whatever they cannot measure doesn't exist, or cannot be admitted by science. Is that true? It is possible to build a motor car. Yet value and design enter into it, and it does not run of itself, but by purpose and direction. And that is what we know and all we know about mechanism.

Well, here is another book, *Science and Christian Belief,* by C. A. Coulson* (Chapel Hill, $2.50), which has been awarded the Pierre Lecomte du Nouy Prize for this year. I regret that I cannot quite see why. The argument runs, as nearly as I can make it out—Professor Coulson's statements have something of the fuzziness of the Eddington school[8]—that scientists really don't know what they are talking about anyhow; and we may validate religion by our emotions toward the universe, and by personal religious experience. Doubtless that will reassure those who feel so already; it will not answer the need of a cosmos. If it be objected that the human mind cannot hope to comprehend the universe completely, I must reply that *complete* understanding is not required, only a general and rational notion of an actual (not contradictory) universe, which modern science denies. I cannot but think that a better choice might have been *The Biology of the Spirit*, by Edmund W. Sinnott* (Viking, $3.50). Professor Sinnott, a biologist, has begun to suspect that the Second Law of Thermodynamics[9] may not be the first and last law of the universe. Life doesn't obey it. There is, he confesses, "a tendency toward organization." I suggest that there is a tendency to organization even in the inorganic order. I was just wondering when some scientist would notice that. A few more books looking in this direction, and we may begin to hope for a rational society.

"A Man of Destiny: Pierre Lecomte du Nouy," National Review, *January 4, 1956, 26–28. Reprinted by permission of* National Review.

Notes

1. GM 70.
2. As said by Samuel Johnson* in James Boswell's* *Life of Samuel Johnson.*
3. Spanish: in a second marriage.
4. An advanced method of treating wounds.
5. The Rockefeller Institute for Medical Research.
6. Latin; a common corruption of "contra mundum": against the world.
7. "Nothing will come of nothing": *King Lear,* Act 1, Scene 1.
8. Arthur Stanley Eddington (1882–1944), a famous English astrophysicist and popularizer of Einstein's theory of relativity, had published *Why I Believe in God* (1930).
9. The Second Law indicates that in a closed system entropy increases until equilibrium is reached and energy is equally dispersed, with nothing hotter or colder than anything else.

23

Learning to Read: Child's Play

Paterson believed that "almost any normal child could be an infant prodigy if it were given half a chance." But what can you expect? "What can the baby make of a world of adults that leave the radio blatting all day, subsist on a mental diet of alleged comic strips, and spend their time between wars cooking up more wars"? She took direct action to give the potential prodigies a chance. Her subjects, or beneficiaries, were the children of her friends. "Our friends . . . see us taking babies out of cribs and high-chairs when they yell, and giving them what they ask for as long as it is not high explosive or a lethal weapon or a bottle of cyanide. The onlookers don't grasp the fact that we believe in treating even an infant as a rational being, which it is. . . . It wants to know things, with almost pathetic eagerness, and looks to adults for information and intelligence. You may say the poor child makes a bad mistake there, but surely it is a natural error and not to be held against it."[1] *When it came to teaching children to read, Paterson was insistent that mistakes not be made—as she is in the following essay, which was a big hit with the readers of* National Review.

Since parents began to protest that their children were not being taught to read, write, spell, or master elementary arithmetic in the public schools, the response from the teaching profession has been overwhelming. The spate of verbiage poured forth, in counter-offensive and justification, by "educators" and "educationalists," is beyond computation without an electronic calculator.

I have not studied this edifying output at length. To be candid, much of it is written in a peculiar and hideous jargon (called "teacher talk" by one of its exponents) from which the human eye rebounds like a tennis ball. Possibly the dialect does double duty; aside from the content, it might be offered in evidence to show why teachers would hardly consider reading and writing desirable accomplishments. One teacher did vouch that the reason "why Johnny can't read" is that he, the teacher, didn't think it necessary. Fussy parents who remain dissatisfied with the veracious simplicity of that statement have a wide and various choice of other answers. That the answers do not agree precisely shouldn't be held against them. Irrelevance is the most effective aid to stupidity in an indefensible position. If the unconvinced complainers aren't wearied into acquiescence, they may be baffled beyond hope of ever getting to the point.

Thus it has been asserted that the public schools are no worse than they always were, which is to say that they never did teach Johnny to read. This appeal to tradition was documented by comparison of marked report cards for pupils past and present, although marks nowadays appear to be subjective flights of fancy. Lately I saw in a note from a child this arresting bit of news: "I got strate A's in spelling." I don't doubt it. But I am bound to admit that she is a highly gifted child. (Modern authorities on education say that the gifted or notably intelligent child is a grave problem in school.)

Another explanation is that a teacher is obliged to wait indefinitely for "reading readiness" in a child. By what token the readiness becomes manifest is not clear. Other teachers seem to intimate—they don't make an explicit offer—that if their salaries were jacked up they could, or would, really teach their pupils something. Or perhaps they mean that jacked-up salaries would hire better teachers; I cannot be positive which.

Some years ago teachers sternly admonished parents *not* to teach their children at home because that would conflict with the methods used in school. Home-taught children, able to read, would throw a school class into dire confusion. But recently I came upon an article by a teacher urging parents to teach their own children to read, with the provision that the said parents must consult the teacher. Presumably the teacher would impart to the parents the method by which the children failed to learn to read in school. I have before me an article which sets forth the "so-called word recognition method." This method requires "a bombardment of pictures labelled with words." But, the article asks, "what's to prevent Johnny from confusing B-A-L-L with F-A-L-L when the picture is missing?" Do not suggest idiotically that Johnny can tell B from F if he has learned the alphabet. Johnny has not learned the alphabet, and what's more, he isn't going to if his teacher can head him off. An assistant in the library of a famous university[2] informs me that students who do not know the alphabet matriculate there. I doubt if they stay the course; but what of it? Under bombardment, Johnny has been so "simulated to evaluate" and his "understanding has been deepened" so profoundly by "visualizing chicks and cows" and saying moo, moo and peep, peep, instead of "memorizing the spelling and parroting the pronunciation" of words, that it would be superfluous for him to attend a university.

Shocking Episode

If heedless parents should instruct their children secretly, I know what would happen. An unfortunate child was left in my care while her mother was in hospital. And the child had to stay at home for a week on account of a bad cold. Aged seven, she had spent a full year in school; and by some oversight she had picked up most of the alphabet. During that week I taught her to read. It was sheer indolence on my part; teaching her was the easiest way to keep her occupied. She liked learning. (So do most children; it is their nature to.) The episode is more shocking inasmuch as I had no textbook, and used some of Kipling's verse as reading matter, because it was at hand. Subsequently, at the end of the quarterly term, I happened to see the child's report card. Her teacher had written on it: "You will notice that Susie has now learned to read *by our method*." (My italics.) I'm sorry I don't know the method of that school by which a bright child takes a year to learn most of the alphabet. And I must add that the child's real name is not Susie. I don't want to bring the authentic Susies under suspicion at school.

The deplorable truth is that on chance occasions I have taught quite a few children to read, with no failures. Most culpably, the way I teach scarcely deserves to be called a method. Nobody could spend years acquiring it. And it is too late for me to reform. I began when I was ten years old, teaching three younger children to read. At that age I spent five or six weeks on the job, teaching an hour or so daily; however, writing and spelling lessons were included. My pupils had learned the alphabet previously. Nobody then knew enough to stop them; it was an era of dark ignorance. Nobody had heard of "reading readiness"; and I certainly did not crave to teach. My mother set me the task, and my juniors were ordered to learn. So I did and they did.

It wasn't painful; I was rather interested to discover that they did not all learn exactly alike, though I taught them alike. (That is all right because *they* do the learning, each in his or her own way from the same material.) The difference is in the two types of mind, one type which tends to memorize by graphic form and position, that is, by the eye-memory of an artist; and the other type which seems to incline more to ear-memory, by sounds; each of course reverses to recall *both* sounds and shapes. But you have to watch for the eye-memory in the beginning, or a young child may spell the word at the top of a spelling list when you have asked for the word at the bottom—because the child learned the spelling in the order from top to bottom, and is mentally recalling it in that order. All you need to do then is to point out the error, and the child will correct it. Eye-memory may be the slower in the beginning; on the other hand, after some correct practice, it may become extraordinarily quick; the artist's eye is indeed a seeing eye.

The sad aspect of this juvenile episode is that I didn't get a "thrill" out of it; whereas "progressive" teachers are "thrilled" if a child recognizes a word (though of course he can't spell it). If Johnny actually learned to read I fear a progressive teacher would be stricken with St. Vitus' dance.[3] Or would he be dismayed? My own insensibility I attribute to a wrong habit of mind. I expect children to learn. They also expect to learn. We are reasonably pleased by the accordant result; but it lacks the novelty, the *frisson*, of surprise.

Having given due notice that trouble will probably ensue if parents teach their children to read, I may as well proceed to tell them how to get into trouble with the least exertion, if they are bent upon it. First, we may answer the question, "why Johnny can't read," by general propositions.

1. If a child past mere infancy cannot read, there can be only two alternative reasons:
   Either it is incapable of learning to read,
   Or it has not been taught.
   This is a logical proposition.
2. Any child of normal intelligence (including sight and hearing) is capable of learning to read from the time it can speak in apposite, intelligible sentences.

This is demonstrable be experiment. But the assertion that the child is capable of learning to read is a rational induction from the given premise that it has already learned to talk. Because the intellectual process of reading is essentially the same as that of apposite speech, differing only in the specific opportunities of learning naturally open to an infant. In both instances it is a process of abstraction and intermediate notation by arbitrary signs indicating things, actions, relations, everything that language can communicate. In speech the signs are vocal sounds. In reading the signs are visible marks. The baby doesn't need formal lessons in order to learn speech, because in company of adults it hears the sounds and simultaneously sees objects, actions, etc., which they signify.

Babies: Intellectual Beings

Having learned speech, learning to read is literal child's play. The only difficulty is obviated by brief and simple formal instruction; which is necessary because otherwise the external features of the process are not wholly visible and audible. If one reads a book silently in the presence of a baby there is no clue whatever to the process involved. If one reads aloud, still the words are unlikely to signify anything in view to which the baby can refer or attach them; and there is no evidence that the words are derived from the book. At best, the child may get the impression that it is proper to hold a book while talking at random.

A baby is as nearly a pure intellectual being as possible. Its very first mental employment involves abstraction; with its vision not yet focused for detail, what it observes is the relative position of objects in space, an impersonal concept. When hungry or uncomfortable it cries, but it does not *think* of its own needs, neither in retrospect nor anticipation. It is engaged in contemplation, in learning something of the nature of the universe. And a baby's power of learning is so prodigious that if we did not take it for granted we should be in a constant state of amazement. The advantage of the adult consists largely in what he has gained from experience by means of that native power. That power of conscious knowledge does not belong to a creature which exists by adapting itself to its environment; it connotes a being who lives by adapting its environment to itself. (And that's where Darwin left himself and modern education out on a limb.)

Presumably the reason we do not fully appreciate the marvelous intellectual feats performed by babies is that we have forgotten the actual experience and truly we cannot imagine ourselves back into the condition of an infant. There is not even a fair analogy available. We cannot imagine ourselves as situated in a physical universe of which we have no knowledge whatever, no comparable experience by which to apprehend any part of it, no speech to ask questions, no physical means at first to move about freely—"no nothing," in the vernacular. *That* is starting from scratch. And that's what a baby does. Within a year it has usually got going on its own feet, utilized its mobility to investigate the qualities of things by its five senses, begun to observe conduct, and attained a basic knowledge of speech. A baby understands a good deal of speech before it can talk, because it hears clearly before it can articulate intelligibly. Also it becomes aware of time, of time elapsed rather than future time, at about the age of ten months; I don't know how and neither does anyone else.

Now if reading and writing were used for communication among adults only by means of a blackboard and reading aloud, with the alphabet permanently inscribed above, every child would learn to read as early as it learns to talk. (I trust that nobody who reads this will be over-persuaded to the extent of demanding that adults confine themselves to the blackboard method as described above. It is neither necessary nor convenient. But would that objection give pause to a progressive pedagogue? It never has; rather it seems to spur him on. I shudder at the prospect.)

Anyhow, the longer instruction in reading is deferred after the child can speak, the less "ready" the child will be, because the extreme rapidity with which a young child observes and memorizes tends to slow down and diminish. During the period when a child is memorizing something new every waking hour, twenty-six items, the letters of the alphabet (one of the greatest inventions of mankind) slipped into the young mind one by one, are as easy as pie. Yet those twenty-six signs, mostly denoted in sound by monosyllables, contain all the components of words, the elements of reading. I am not saying that it is imperative that a child should learn to read in its second year; I am saying that it is easily possible. Of course the child can still learn quickly for a good many years; but I should certainly advise that it be taught to read by the age of five, or earlier if you like, because early reading tends to facilitate correct spelling. Also rapid and correct readers usually have learned early.

Begin then by teaching the alphabet. It won't take very long, if you will be so kind as to refrain from distracting the child by blather about cows and chicks or saying this letter looks like something else and see the curly tail of that letter and B stands for blah-blah. With the complete alphabet in its usual order before the child, point to a letter, say "That is A" or B or C, etc.; and have the child repeat it. One letter may be enough for one lesson. (It would save time and effort if the alphabet were shown in four types, that is, printing and cursive each in both capitals and small letters, and in four lines, so that each letter can be identified in its four types at once. If you think the child won't understand their identity, you are mistaken. Odds on it has better brains than you have.) After several repetitions, ask the child to name the letter without your naming it first. Also recite the whole alphabet and have the child repeat it after you. That's *all*, until the child can name each letter at sight and recite the alphabet by heart.

Then go on to reading, and teach it in just the same way, naming a word, having the child spell it out, and giving the child the sounds of the letters in the word. As soon as a child has caught onto a few short words, tell it that long words are no harder to read than short ones, being made up of short sections. Don't push the child; but insist on correctness; do not allow the child to mumble, jumble, guess and give up. Guessing can be averted by proper timing; if a child can't remember, naturally it will hesitate; then you must name the letter or word before guessing begins.

Never be impatient. A child naturally accepts parental authority, and will do the best it can if it is not terrified or distracted. Don't grudge praise on just occasion.

Finally, the younger the child, the briefer the lesson should be. If you undertake to teach a child between two and three years old, five minutes is long enough to exact close attention, increasing to an hour or so by the age of seven. If the attention of an infant could be fixed for a considerable time, it would have no chance of survival in a world containing a multiplicity of objects which may impinge on it and which therefore must be observed at a glance. Two or three lessons may be given in a day if you choose. One a day will ensure a steady advance. If you will pay attention yourself you will see when the child is really unable to concentrate any longer; let that end the lesson. In compensation, the child has an astounding faculty of learning in a flash.

Trouble Ahead

Very well, the result will be that Johnny can read, and you and he will both be in for plenty of trouble. At school Johnny will be given insipid rubbish to putter over, until he is bored to stupefaction. You'll have to maintain his interest in reading at home. It is unlikely that he will get any higher marks. The prevailing system of marks was contrived to "equalize" the children, not to record the facts.

What Johnny and his parents are up against is a nation-wide vested interest of professionals who draw six years pay for teaching a child rather less than it could learn in about the equivalent of a year's time in school. There is also a paid lobby to advocate that interest, and a lot of politicians anxious for votes. And there is officialdom in general, the fraternity of bureaucrats, always ready to spring to the aid of their kind. Finally, though of much slighter influence, there are publishers whose "backlog" of textbooks is important to them—and a deep gouge in the taxpayer. Johnny's illiteracy is a valuable property, not precisely for him, but for a great many other people, who have put themselves across as the recognized authorities on education. To meddle with their major asset is to invite unpredictable reprisals.

Here is a curious item which got into the public press. Mr. and Mrs. Charles Dameron of Silver Springs, Md., adopted an eight-months-old baby girl, named Dori. Mr. Dameron is a Washington city fireman. The Damerons own their home. They are both comparatively young, of pleasing appearance; and Dori looks happy, in a family photo. Dori has grown to be two and a half years old and the Damerons thought it would be nice for her to have a brother. They applied to Maryland's Montgomery Social Service League to adopt a boy baby. The Social Service League said no, they would not allow the Damerons to adopt another child. Why not? Well, little Dori had been "tested." *She could read.* The Damerons had taught her! Dori (not the Damerons, of course) was accorded a very high IQ because she could read—an accomplishment which any normal child could be taught by the same age. Miss Elizabeth Montgomery, of the Social Service League, said: "If we had another very bright child, we would place it in a home we considered had superior advantages."

Let that be a lesson to *you,* if you intend to teach your Johnny to read. And don't say I didn't warn you. Some official egghead will surely find or make occasion to insult you publicly, personally, and gratuitously—for bucking the system. Still, if you are determined, here's luck; and in the long run Johnny may thank you.

National Review, *November 30, 1957. Reprinted by permission of* National Review.

Notes

1. "Turns," June 8, 1947.
2. Presumably Princeton. When this essay was written, Paterson lived near the university (at Rocky Hill, New Jersey) and often used its library.
3. A neurological disorder characterized by jerking motions of the limbs.

24

What the Christmas Story Means

No human brain should be expected to cope with this situation, writing just before Christmas something that won't appear till the day is quite past, not to mention the New Year rushing at us simultaneously. How can one cope with the order of events, unless by writing in Oriental style from right to left and from the bottom of the page up? >>

No matter, and never mind anything we may have said to the contrary; Christmas is a grand idea anyhow. One thing that is wrong with modern literature is that people no longer read the Bible enough. If they did they would still find the greatest models of stories and style, not to mention the one tale, the Christmas story, which is beyond imagining or imitating. The child laid in the manger, for lack of room in the inn, the star in the east, the wise men with gifts of gold and frankincense and myrrh, the wondering shepherds watching their flocks in the fields by night—what literary genius could have brought such elements together? And the world of that time was also filled with war and oppression, when "there went out a decree that all the world should be taxed," and even the tyrants were in terror, and people asked: "What shall we do?"[1] It might well have seemed that the human world must perish of its own stupidity and crimes; what hope was there? Yet that was the beginning of better things than had ever been known before, and of a still higher hope, of a far greater destiny than man had theretofore dreamed.

In our more frivolous moments, we read any books of scientific speculation we come across, and have had a copy of *Physics and Philosophy*, by Sir James Jeans,* on the shelf for some time, which is even more instructive than the author intended. From the contemplation of atomic physics, the author finally arrived at a tentative opinion that this is "a universe which looks as though it might conceivably form a dwelling place for free men, and not a mere shelter for brutes." Why, now, that's certainly a great discovery; but did no one think of it before? Suppose we simply observe the actions of men; there is the rather remarkable fact that whenever they fail to think of themselves as human, and are persuaded to believe themselves merely "higher" animals, or some mysterious phenomenon of the behavior of atoms, they are unable to act like mere animals, much less like matter under natural law. On the contrary, they act rather like devils, and materially, like matter with no natural law at all.

Also, in their peaceful and truly human pursuits, how do they behave? Like atoms? It is extremely difficult to think of one atom calling itself Sir James Jeans, peering at other atoms (whose names we don't happen to know), and saying resignedly: "I can't quite figure out the way this thing behaves. The best I can do is to say it has a sort of Principle of Indeterminacy. The atom named Einstein is reported as saying he cannot understand what people mean when they talk about the freedom of the will. But some other atoms say they can understand it, and insist it is true. I hardly know what to make of atoms. They are downright queer."

In such case, we consider it advisable to think a while about the Star in the East, that went and stood over where the young child lay; and try to reduce that to the behavior of atoms. Of course you can say the story never happened at all, but if it did not, what we mean is, please explain how the atoms came to imagine it. There really is a discrepancy somewhere. Now supposing, in this present world of horror and slaughter, men should begin again to realize that they are naturally free, would not that be the way to emerge from the nightmare death-and-life[2] they have got into?

By no means do we intend or imply any derogation of science; on the contrary, we ask, what should be the "reality," the nature, of a creature which is capable of scientific thought? Is not such thought in itself a unique attribute, distinguishing man from the order of brutes or of inanimate matter? Then how is he to account for himself or to find the true rules for his own conduct either in brute instinct or in mechanical processes? Must not his proper conduct pertain rather to his own peculiar relation to the universe, which enables him to relate by meaning the Child and the Star and the wise men and the shepherds and the cruel despot—the furthest heavens, the earth, man, and good and evil?

Notes

1. Luke 2:1, 3:10–14.
2. Paterson echoes Coleridge in *The Rime of the Ancient Mariner*: "The Nightmare Life-in-Death was she, / Who thicks man's blood with cold."

Part II

Letters

25

Letters to 1940

To Lillian Fischer*

Lillian Fischer, model and later fashion editor, was a friend from New York party days in the 1920s. Paterson would always enjoy Lillian's sturdy differences from herself.

Undated [April 1, 1925]

My dear girl,

I don't know why it has taken me two weeks to get started answering your letter—except that I had a couple of extra review articles to do when it arrived, and when I got them done, I fell back exhausted. By extra, I mean, for outside publications—it meant reading a dozen novels hurriedly, and all that.[1] But on the whole, I think my real reason was plain indolence. I grow more and more indolent every day of the world. I have no other real ambition than to do nothing at all. When summer impends, I just want to sit under a tree and Exist. In winter, by a fireplace.

I must have left your letter at home. Don't remember what I meant to say, while I was reading it. —But how can you care for satire if you are not interested in politics?—or religion, or art, or love, it could just as well be. Man is a political animal by nature, same as he is naturally pious, amative, combative, creative. Politics is part of the human comedy. Satire covers it all.[2] Politics is indeed about fifty per cent of the human comedy; because it ties up with everything else. Where can you escape politics? Don't read the Gospels, if you aren't interested in politics—for all the action is conditioned by the political background—the troubles of the Roman governor having to play politics between the Imperial throne and the gang in Jerusalem; the high priest[3] worried about Christ's possible political significance when he became so popular with the crowd; the gerrymandering between Herod and Pilate, trying to shift unpleasant responsibilities from one to another. —Later you can't help seeing Paul must have been a very slick[4] wardman before he turned Apostle. He was lobbygow for the Zealot party, in fact—one of their best plug-uglies. He didn't forget his skill, either, when it came to jockeying Peter and the other *real* disciples out of their advantage of seniority and personal knowledge of the Messiah.[5] —Most of the great satire is largely concerned with politics—Swift wrote for no other purpose (than his party); Voltaire was a great political force; so was Heine.*[6] What is there left of Anatole France's* GREAT work if you cut out the politics? It takes the Bergeret series, the *Gods are Athirst, Penguin Island, The Revolt of the Angels*—a large order.

No, now, you really don't like satire at all. Why should you, if you simply don't? It is not a moral nor even a social obligation to do so. I'll be darned if I feel that I *have to* like or appreciate or understand anything whatever. I am unfortunately almost tone deaf, and quite impervious to music; I wish I could enjoy it, but indeed, I support my defect with great equanimity. For I can't help it. I am also almost totally devoid of the sentiment of piety and reverence—that is why I enjoy satire. But I actually prefer not to be pious or reverent. I suit myself, in that respect, just as I am.

My God, if I am not the laziest woman alive, never to have got up as far as 48th Street yet to pick up a copy of the book to send you—but I just haven't. I think I will next week.—I am so preoccupied with the next, I go nowhere, see no one, do nothing.[7] Oh, especially I do nothing; I don't even write the book, which is my excuse for not doing anything else. But it is around about half done, I guess. I don't know whether it's any good or not. I haven't the least idea. Some parts of it I thought were good when I wrote them.

This is the next day, and I brought down your letter. I cannot figure out if you are at this moment on the Riviera, or back in that dear Paris; no matter, the letter will be sent after you, I daresay. By the way, Lee sent a postcard from Havana last week; I do not know if Edna is there or not.[8] I suppose I shall not see Europe for years and years—now that I am too aged to be imprudent and just take what money I have and go. I wish you would marry one of your blasted millionaires—or something!—and take me to Europe as a lady companion, or just a companion. Never mind about Egbert.[9] He is worse than useless to a woman. If I had any news of him I would tell you, but I have neither seen nor heard of him all winter, probably because Lee has not given any parties (except a scratch affair Christmas). Lee's been away himself, as remarked above. But you really ought to forget about Egbert. Are you one of these unfortunate females who are only attracted by detrimentals? Try to get over it. Think of your mother—think of me—don't be selfish. Shed a little lustre on our sex, like Peggy Hopkins,* who became famous because it was believed she actually got a little cash. I am endeavoring to propagate a new code of honor for women—so that it shall be an insult if a man doesn't hand over the money first and forthwith. The men fixed it up, you know, so that women were supposed to be insulted if money was offered. It is time we had our innings in[10] deciding what is to be the accepted bunk.

Did I tell you to read *The Constant Nymph*? You can get a copy of the English edition, I dessay.[11] It is the cleverest novel of the 1925 season, and quite charming too. Besides, if you wish to know what a genius—any genius—is like inside and irrevocably, it will show you. Perhaps then you will have sense enough to forget the very name of Egbert. Understand, I have nothing against him except that he has no money, never will have any, is a musician, and a philanderer, and a squalling, overgrown infant. I have only met him two or three times, but those items are obvious.

You will be horrified to learn that I have no more new spring clothes than a rabbit; don't know if I shall have any! I would like a suit with a short jacket, and underdress; but that would call for hat, shoes, everything; a passion for completeness makes me do without everything. If I can't have what I want, I do not even intend to want what I can have. The spring styles are very pretty, though. I can't get together money enough before June—and then it will be summer!

If I could remember what I may have told you of my meagre gaieties—I think I have been to the theatre four or five times this winter, and to as many as three not very momentous parties. Last Monday I saw Bruce McRae* and Grace George* in *She Had to Know*;[12] a very light, thin, truly amusing little comedy. It barely runs two hours, and could be done in less, but with two such excellent actors, I hardly care what they play. I have always admired Grace George as an actress—though God knows she had need to be able to act, for she was never good-looking and has been an antique ever since my infancy. And I simply adore Bruce McRae. He too is getting on in years; probably wears a toupee and so forth; but I do not scrutinize him too closely; I simply venerate his relics, as it were; for he was the handsomest and most debonair creature that ever trod the American stage. Did you ever notice him?

The other theatrical event (an event because it was adorned with my presence) was *Processional.*[13] It is a burlesque of the whole American scene; though it's framed on a staple melodrama plot. It really has a touch of genius in it; but do not on any account endeavor to discover its merits by reading the text as a book. Don't even open the said book. It has been published. But the play only existed on the stage. It was wonderfully acted and stage managed. The most original American play I ever saw, on my word. Hunks of it were dull, mind you, but at moments it just blazed up till you had to admit it contained the spark of genius. What the hell ails this typewriter? You'd never suppose I had been typing for forty years,[14] man and boy, to look at the mess this machine is making for me.

Oh, gosh, this is a deplorable thing to call a letter. No news whatever—nor wit nor wisdom to make up the lack. I might as well have mailed you a dictionary and let you choose the words. No more, no more! I wish I were on the Riviera with herds of handsome attendant swains competing for the privilege of toting me around in Rolls-Royces and all that. Oh, yes, I do wish it! I am a mere mush of romanticism at heart—and the thought of flowers, and moonlight, and all that sort of rot—the fact is, do you think there is anything in the world so amusing as a well-staged flirtation, with the setting, accessories, and vis-a-vis of the right sort? No, there is not.

Hoping you are the same,
Affectionately,
Isabel Mary etc

To Garreta Busey*

At the beginning of the 1930s, Paterson was saddened by the deaths of several of her friends, among them a man with whom she was romantically involved. She had not yet achieved great literary success, and what she regarded as the political and intellectual failures of the nation vexed her severely. She was starting to feel the onset of age and ill health. Even her wit turned bitterly against her. Her buoyancy would return, with the success of her novel Never Ask the End, *her newfound ability to buy land and build a house, and other, more mysterious factors. But that took a while to happen.*

Undated [November? 1931]

Dear Garreta,

I wrote a long letter to you immediately, but it was so boring and egotistical I didn't send it. I must return to normalcy.[15] Actually I suppose I'm not so melancholic as I sound—not sunk all the time. It *has* been a pretty bad year, two years almost, with death and disaster; and quite calmly, I do not see why the hell anyone should live beyond middle age.—I asked Norman Lindsay* the other day, forgetting he is probably about fifty, "After fifty, would one be better dead?" He paused a moment, and then replied simply: "Yes." He's extremely entertaining, a really brilliant talker. Has a wife, which is always sort of a bore—I mean, all relations are. Cuppy* talked to her and said she seemed to him a good honest hausfrau,[16] and he liked her. She said to Cuppy that she liked fat men, the sort you could poke your finger into, like a plump chicken. And Lindsay is as thin as Burton Rascoe,* the same lively type that can't get fat. I suppose the poor woman has been trying to feed him up, put some meat on his bones, for twenty years, and that's all the good it does! Another tragedy.

You see, besides that my mother is sort of fluttering away peacefully, three people I knew well died within the year. Nat [Roberts],* and Alta May [Coleman],* and two months ago Fern Forrester*; they were very close friends of each other, Alta May's crowd, and about the same age, the early forties—isn't that rather strange? And a fourth of the group has just had a dreadful operation, for cancer.[17]

Also two other friends, though not such close friends, are quite ill; one is Herschel Brickell's* wife, and I fear she is dying[18]; another is merely having a nervous breakdown.

So, as you say, the ceiling seems to be falling, and one doesn't know which way to duck. No wonder you begin writing epic poems. I have mislaid your letter, and cannot recall the exact details of the opus, but liked the verses you sent.

You ask me, where do I meet such people? Where, I ask you, can one avoid them? Why did you go to Colorado? —Yes, the woman in the country was merely a landlady. I never saw her before and never want to again.[19]

There was a lunch last week for H. G. Wells.* I didn't hear much that he said, but enough. He has the weirdest voice—exactly like one of those rubber toys, a rubber piglet, that make a sighing squeak when stepped on by accident. And he looks as if any chair he sits in is too big for him. Sort of abjectly pompous. I think he's become an unspeakable bore in his writing.

Walter Lippmann* was at the lunch too. It has just occurred to me who he is. The Hired Boy. I mean Jonas, out of the Rollo Books.[20]

What shall I do to cure myself of this rabid intolerance of stuffed shirts and blah and wirepulling and officialdom? Really, life used to be much more tolerable out West, before the West became Rotarian.[21] It wasn't, in my infancy, you know. It is just the same as the East now, or probably worse, so I have no refuge. I bottle up my real thoughts until I nearly bust. But they really aren't important thoughts, nobody's thoughts are, and why can't I realize that fact and leave it go at that? Probably I am a bore too, so why be snooty?

If I had any sense, I'd devote the energy employed in misanthropic cursings, to my Book, The Book.[22] It is half done, as I must have told you over and over; and it gets harder every minute, because how do I know if I am keeping up the interest or not? Or—O God—if it ever had any interest? You never saw such a fiendish undertaking as I went and undertook. Every page has got to be—oh, every *comma* even has got to be vitally important—hell and damnation. You do not yet understand about novels, but they are intrinsically the same as poems; I don't know how come you miss seeing that. You know that a poem has an organic form, or it is no good—and the form of a poem[23] exists only if practically every word is right, doesn't it? That is, the form of a poem is not the story, nor even strictly speaking, the idea; it is the absolute fusing of everything. Or isn't it?

I have just got my people moved from sitting under a tree.[24] You realize that that was a very difficult part to write. Few things are harder to write than people sitting under a tree. It is worse than walking on a grassy hill. I hope you grasp the point, which is that sitting there, they are themselves, with all that that implies, especially the complication that they are together, and therefore in that relation something else. Do I make myself clear? I feel that I do. But the hardest part is yet to come; for they are about to eat dinner, and it is necessary for them to eat dinner in such a way that the reader may know all about their families—that one had an Aunt Eliza and that another's grandfather was a bounty jumper[25] in the Civil War, and so on. Well, those are minor details, really; it is the immediate family that makes the difficulty. That one's life was blighted by a mother, and another's by a father; and they all had brothers and sisters, an obscure and dreadful business, this being entangled with dozens of strangers who compose one's family.

Last week Lewis Gannett asked me, what does Virginia Woolf's* new novel mean?[26] I started to tell him, but he interrupted me impatiently:

"It's all hokum, isn't it?"—And yet I go on writing novels! Which will have to be reviewed. —I think the Woolf novel is a complete failure, essentially a mistake, she was trying to do the impossible; but hokum—!!! I would say it is a mess, even, anything you like but hokum.

I wish you would come to New York for any vacation you get this winter; but I suppose that is hard, because Christmas is a home festival. But could you manage it some time? —I will now write a page, or half a page, of The Book, six times, and throw it away each time, and go to bed.

Affectionately,
Pat

Paterson then wrote another page of her letter.

It would be nice of you to write occasionally. I *am* rather depressed, and rather apprehensive that I am becoming a dreadful bore. The machinery is out of gear, the social instinct. I daresay this letter will show you what I mean. It is tedious. I am not exactly melancholy, but slack. Like those women who sit around all day with their hair uncombed. I comb my hair, but to no purpose. The whole world seems to be in such a dreadful mess. I think there is a real revolution begun in England. Maybe after that is over—that is, if I should happen to be right about there being a revolution—we shall stagger to some sort of equilibrium. But meantime I wander off into fruitless and tiresome talk such as this very paragraph. And bore myself and everybody else. They do not think there is or will be any actual revolution. They think a lot of things which to me seem unrelated to any actuality whatever. Immediately there descends on me the horrible conviction that we are talking on parallel lines, which cannot be made to meet even in infinity. Besides, I have a loose tooth. It doesn't ache, but when one finds a tooth just loose, is it not time to go?—I remember ten years ago, no, eight, telling Stuart Sherman,* with sudden exasperation, that Europe would never pay the war debts. He said, politely surprised, why won't they? I could only say, since it was impossible to deliver an explanation that would have had to be as long as Gibbon's* *Decline and Fall, Because they won't.* Everything that I think lately has an equally interminable series of reasons behind it, which are apparently the product of my sole ratiocination. So I exist in solitude. By all definitions, I am insane, am I not? I used to talk to Alta May [Coleman], and she had learned to pay no attention—it was hard on her, of course—and that enabled me to feel that I wasn't alone.

When I try to think what is the matter with me—not with the world—I am appalled. Why is it necessary for me to talk? Why should I bother people? The nicest people, such as Alta May, do not talk—not in the way I do. They possess their souls in sweet patience, and have the lovely gift of mental privacy. They say pleasant superficial things, which can do no harm. They do not exhibit their ignorance. It was talk that drove you to Denver, wasn't it?

I am sorry I moved. I hate the new apartment beyond expression. I am homesick for that dirty old corner of 34th street, I was used to it.[27] I hated it too, but I was used to it. You know how you feel about Urbana.—I haven't told you any news, but there isn't much, and I'd better stop. Farewell, Epaminondas.[28]

Pat

To Burton Rascoe*

Undated [December 1931]

>> Now I do not think we shall have what I call revolution in this country, during our time. The effect of revolution in England will be to check it here, by reaction. What you say about the recent trend of capitalism, which is trying to take over the government, to get the government to run its affairs and save it from the effect of its own insanity of foreign loans[29] (the capitalists themselves really don't [know] which they are trying to do, or if it's both, or what; they are dithering with ignorance of what both their left and right hands are doing)—what you say is true. But they are not going to succeed in creating that machinery. It is smashing itself now, in its first efforts at hooking up. The net result is the *bankruptcy* (not revolution) we are undergoing. Bankruptcy accompanies revolution, but it can and does occur without revolution, producing only a partial return to the *status quo ante.* This country experienced bankruptcy in the nineties.[30] Part of the loss was borne by foreign bondholders. That part of the situation is now reversed. It is a much worse bankruptcy. But that is all it is, all it promises to be as yet. The bankers have discredited themselves, and failed to organize the machinery they meant to. They are shown up, and the "control" cannot operate because it is a receivership, which nobody is willing to accept. All that anyone will accept is the old political arrangement after liquidation—Borah* has taken the first step to force the liquidation.[31]

You have to raise a generation, two generations of people who actually desire revolution for its own sake, before revolution occurs. The forerunners, the Voltaires and Shaws,* are old men, dead, before the revolution comes. We have not gone through that process yet. There is no particular *kind* of new order that people *want*. You and I, who are in the main representative, do not want revolution; we really want "normalcy." Cut the losses, and go on. Voltaire knew what he wanted—a constitutional monarchy, in effect a republic with a permanent head. The republic came, minus the too-limited head (of Louis), but that was a detail; in effect, what Voltaire demanded came to pass. Shaw knew what he wanted, socialism. It is coming. What do we want? Just what we had, before the crash. Are the Communists here Voltaires, Shaws, Tolstois—men big enough to cast so long a shadow? None of them is. They are a group, they have no general sentiment behind them. They are the Nine Tailors of Tooley Street.[32]

It is very possible that I am miscalculating the time factor entirely, and that you are nearest right, because the tempo of economics has been greatly speeded up since a hundred years ago. But against this I reckon the psychological tempo, which does not alter much, because each generation sets in its mould. It runs by generations. We just don't *want* revolution, unless we were born wanting it. That is, we do not want a new order, we don't want to change our thoughts. If our thoughts have been moulded on the desire for a new order, then the revolution does not appear in the light of changing our thoughts; it seems like a realization of them. It never is, there's that joker; and the pre-revolution revolutionists mostly die of heartbreak after the event. But they welcomed its beginnings.

Heavens, that's enough to make you fall into a coma for a week—such a harangue. I was just raving on.[33]

There isn't much news. Book business very bad, but no publishers visibly collapsing yet.

>> I ain't seen nobody much lately, seems to me. Yes, I met Sinclair Lewis.* Never saw such a pathetic wreck. Burnt-out. Saw him at the wedding reception of Horace Liveright and Elise Bartlett, a fairly drunken party,[34] which I left early. Horace looks like a dried codfish too. But Lewis looked like a goner; I was profoundly sorry. For reasons unknown, and he being half drunk of course, he seemed to think I was somebody for whom he had esteem, and was very nice to me in a queer vague touching way. I don't know what he associated with my name.[35]—I must stop writing letters and get on with my book, so you

need not be too alarmed; I shall not ramble at such dismal length again, but the disorganization of my goods and chattels affected the old bean.[36] Cuppy* is calming down after his publication. For weeks he bubbled around anxiously like a father in the hospital waiting-room. Do write, and I will reply rationally next time.

Love,
Pat

To Burton Rascoe

Undated [December 1931]

Darling, there is nothing the matter with your stuff in the [*New York*] *Sun*. It is O. K.

>> Doubtless the sole reason you didn't get in a footnote was that you weren't on the spot! I mean, in Cuppy's* book.[37] He was merely meeting emergencies, and in such a stew anyhow trying to get the thing done—only two or three months late for the time the publishers asked for it, but he really worked on it day and night—I don't think he knew what he was doing finally, and when he felt someone ought to go in a footnote I got in—as well as in all prefaces and dedications—because there I was, and had to read his copy, his proofs, and so forth, and tell him what I knew about the hyena. I've been useful to him merely as a listening ear. I know that is very useful indeed, but anyone will do. I think I have got all the credit that was coming to me and probably immortality to boot. Really, I think that is the best book since *Jurgen*[38]—am I wrong? So you and I will be remembered. I cannot overpraise it, I ought to be sick of the damn thing, but it seems to me more gorgeous every time I read it, and I read it over and over. And that, after the hours haunted by Jake[39] sitting beside my desk with a look of agonized appeal, wondering if I'm going to laugh at this one! His first attempt at a preface I thought wasn't very good, and I was bound to admit it to him. He walked up and down the office suffering the pangs of death, also wishing that he could choke me. It was an operation without anaesthetics. If I hadn't feared that a poor preface might affect the fortunes of the book I'd never have had the courage to speak. —He got splendid reviews. Stallings* wrote a really admirable review, very enthusiastic and very much to the point. Of course this awful year, the sales won't make Cuppy rich—if it goes over five thousand it will be thought to do well, whereas any other year

it would be twenty. But Jake would have that kind of luck. Anyhow, I think he is made as to reputation, no longer merely considered one of my irrational prejudices. People who like it rave over it. —I wish you could have met Norman Lindsay.* He's going back soon. He thinks Cuppy's book is a masterpiece, and says his wife has been driven distracted by his recurrent outbursts of mirth, thinking it over. Lindsay is really a grand egg.

Did you ever get a letter from Earle Balch, asking you to do a book he had in mind?* Do let me know.[40]

I think publishers are financing *Gentle Reader*.[41] I don't know why. It looks to me like just another of those things. I forget which publishers. A lot of them.

I dunno what's up. I still think England will revolute after another year or so. I anticipate every horrible thing I can imagine, but no doubt won't have thought of what actually will happen. All I can think of to do personally is try to watch out if they're going to begin inflating the currency here in the United States. It's the last dam that holds so far. After that the deluge.[42] Perhaps after we see the last of Mr. Hoover we may begin to mend a little, but the bills must be paid, and at best that means immense taxes and skulduggery of every kind, and long enough hard times still ahead. If they'd dump the wheat and cotton, go through the inevitable bankruptcy which is now being prolonged, I believe it would be the best thing, but only as a major operation is best for appendicitis. Not much fun while it's going on. Anyhow, I don't really know what to think. Why are you so worried? Personally, I mean—for it is impossible, it would be inhuman, not to feel the general misfortune. I've been so blue for a year past, I'm almost used to it. Whole nights of sheer paralysis of blues. I drive myself to work, to get through it.

My book[43] progresses with the majestic speed of a glacier. Oh, it's about two thirds done. I write every page eighty four times. I ought to get it done this winter. I didn't know anyone could take writing so hard. I didn't know one could write with such infinite pains. (Though Cuppy did!) You see, the blasted thing is a sort of distillation. Like wringing out a saturated solution—which is a mixed metaphor. I do not yet know if it is any good or simply drivel. It combines all the known difficulties of every mode of writing fiction—the stream of consciousness, clear objectivity, narrative, a general impression, an intellectual[44] meaning, high-pressure emotion, continuous sharp focus and a range of twenty years and the width of continents and oceans. I mean it would if I could write it. What I have got on paper is probably nothing but an example of what is meant by one's mind wandering. I am now deeply involved in that portion of it which deals with youthful love, the blind chance of where the lightning hits and who, and how incalculable the results are in terms of lives.[45] This is an awful job, full of pitfalls of almost inevitable bad taste, and immense disproportions to bring into some relation.

You will probably have a good laugh when at long last you read the damn book. You'll wonder what two other books I told you about in my letters. And how I got these delusions. —Perhaps, like Ethel M. Dell,* I am inspired—with the same results.

Today I moved again.[46] Back to where I was, if you'll believe it. Plain lunacy, in its more advanced stages. I can't help it; I was homesick and hated the new place, and couldn't sleep, and it was noisy. I was used to the disadvantages of the old place, and had room enough anyhow. I've had nothing to eat all day. Must go and get a sandwich. Do write at length and tell me when you are coming back and so forth. And how is Hazel [Rascoe].* I wish you folks would come back.[47] That is, unless you're happy out there. You know I always love you, near or far.

Pat

To Burton Rascoe

Undated [June 1932]

Dear Burton—

I didn't get your note in time. Maybe I can work it in[48] another time anyhow.

You know I never can remember even about my own stuff whether it appeared last week, this week or next week[49]—but if the piece you had Thursday, which you mentioned, was about the department store book, I did read it, and thought it excellent. I always look in the *Sun*, every day, in case they've changed your day. —When I sent back that clipping, I was sitting at my desk working with my hands and talking to someone at the same time, clearing off the desk, which is the only reason I just slipped it in an envelope, same as the Joyce book, with no note.

You won't believe it and neither do I but I finished my damn novel[50] last night at four a. m. Probably I brought on the heat wave, by intense concentration for[51] the previous fourteen hours. It was singular that the heat came on exactly contrary to anything I've ever noticed; I mean it began getting hot in the evening, and got hotter through the night; whereas usually I get a cool breeze from the bay, up the river, about one o'clock.

I shan't be happy now till you've read the book. I hope to land you with it in a week or two, if you can face the prospect. Will it be a bad interruption to your own work? Tell me if this is the wrong time; I'll wait.

I had formed a conviction that the novel would *never* be finished. It seemed to be a permanent part of my life. And maybe I was right, for—you mustn't tell anyone this—I shall have to spend September brooding further over the last seven pages. They've been written only three times, whereas eight times is the minimum that would make it come the way I want it. Maybe no one else would know the difference, but I can't help it—that's the way it insisted on being written. It seemed as if the process resembled dipping up water from a spring, and it had to have a given time to settle, come clear. It has really been interesting, though I hope it never happens again. I had to copy it off now because July and August are otherwise occupied, and those few pages make sense, probably no one else would see why I had to go over them again—they say what I want but not to my entire satisfaction; I can just as well fuss over them at leisure; I've got to find out and make some decision about a publisher in the meantime.

I liked your review of *Beauty Lies Beyond Hell*,[52] too. I've had all I can stand of that Sears-Roebuck catalogue style,[53] peppered with exclamation points. Also the steam-heated highbrow novel, such as Kay Boyle's* *Year Before Last* and Claire Spencer's* *Quick and the Dead*, which last I think is fancy tripe. Though Christopher Morley* is giving it a rave for us.[54]

—About Fort,[55] I almost forgot to say, why would I mind if it amused you to take a surreptitious dig at any opinion of mine? Nothing you could write would annoy me at any time, about anything. You see, I have a great advantage over you there; I can be so much more exasperating than you, I have natural gifts in that direction, so I can make you mad, though rarely and unintentionally, in spite of your being essentially good-natured; whereas you can't make me mad though I am bad-tempered (I hope not fundamentally bad-natured but quick-tempered certainly).—You may not have spotted the occasional pointed remarks Cuppy* aimed at me in *How to Tell Your Friends from the Apes*! I don't mean mentions by name—but for instance, about eating some sort of bird to enable the eater to argue down an opponent—to which he adds: "This is an error. There are some people who cannot be argued down no matter what one eats." I shouted with joy when I read that, and accused him instantly—he admitted that of course he meant me. Getting back at me for not believing in Freud. Personally, I should think a devout Freudian could believe anything. I forgot to knife him in the back with that at your house, or I would have, while we were for once on the same side.

Love to Hazel[56] and the kids.

Pat

To Garreta Busey

Undated [February 1, 1933]

Dear Garreta—

Having this evening reached a new low for all time in my opinion of the intelligence of the human race, I will write to you as usual at such moments. I have not yet traced the connection, and perhaps it would be better not. We seem to be governed by some esoteric law in confiding things to one another—maybe the survival of the fittest? >> To me race suicide is a beautiful thought. In fact, I think it is the only hope—I mean complete race suicide. It would solve all the problems. Because I called on my vice president at the bank the other day, and he informed me that in his opinion the one remedy for the depression would be to issue new paper currency in the ratio of five to one, that is, giving everyone now possessed of one dollar in paper money five dollars in paper money. I asked what that would do for those who have not even one dollar, but he was rather vague on that point. He was convinced, however, that the proposed procedure would raise prices without making anything dearer—perfectly clear, isn't it? He thought the government should also take over all gold mines and pay the owners—I don't know what with—and "develop new gold mines." He held the opinion that there were plenty of gold mines lying around waiting to be developed! You think I made that up? You know that one can't. He said too that the five to one multiplication of paper money would raise the price of wheat, thus enabling each farmer to raise twice as much wheat and be prosperous. Well, I could go on forever like that, because it seemed he could too, but then I went away from the bank. Only I must add that I asked him, just what would it do for me, reducing the value of my salary to one fifth of what it now is; and he said my salary would be raised proportionately—you can see how that would be, can't you? I felt I had to get this off my chest. You can pass on my banker's ideas to your father; it may shed a flood of light on the banking situation for him.

I don't think there is anything new around the office. Nobody ever tells me anything, anyhow.[57] Not if I can help it. I have enough to brood about. . . . I went to a lunch where Noel Coward* was guest of honor; and am going to a reception for Willa Cather* tomorrow; and I was at a Guild dinner where Mrs. Franklin D. Roosevelt spoke.[58] I can't seem to add anything to those simple facts, unless that Mrs. R. is worse than her photographs. Yes, she is. I have never seen such a fullgrown nitwit. She looks worse too. I hear rumors that she and her mother-in-law have always been at feud over which shall run Franklin, and the mother-in-law won by reason of having all the money, so Mrs. F. devoted herself to good works. It must be a happy home.

I'm trying to get the first chapter of a new novel to go right.[59] It won't, of course. I can't understand why the more I learn about writing—if I do learn anything—the harder it becomes. Because somehow new and more harrowing difficulties arise; I mean, you set yourself trying to do things you hadn't even imagined before. All I'm trying to write now is the imponderables of conversation between the two kinds of people who cannot converse, who see everything from opposite poles. For instance, if it were a conversation between me and Mrs. Franklin D. Roosevelt. . . . Cuppy's* solution, talking incessantly himself at the top of his voice from 7 to 10, is all right; but seldom employed. So I have to write of the other times, when the mutual effort is made, resulting in nothing at all. Except, of course, subconscious hatred. . . . Anne Parrish told me the other day that her brother-in-law, Thomas F. [sic] Lamont,* was much pleased with a notice I gave him; I was obliged to tell her that if he didn't know I was giving him the raspberry, there was no need to enlighten him.[60]

I have had some very amusing fan mail, of all kinds. The book[61] continues to sell moderately. I hope it goes on long enough to amount to something. I think the most flattering letter was from George Shively,[62] who is really a man of intelligence and taste. He wrote innocently that he thought nobody but himself had noticed that the book was "nostalgic," but maybe it was his own particular age (40) had made him think constantly of his childhood and youth while reading it. I informed him that that was what it was written to do, so I was glad he got it—but so did everyone else! I met him at Doris Ulmann's*[63] yesterday and he confessed further that he had actually wept while reading it. I told him that was because he had felt so sorry for himself—precisely what I tried to put over—it made him feel how sad it was that he used to be young and wasn't any more and everything he ever knew had vanished, and there was nothing left for him to do but die. He acknowledged that was precisely the effect. It has a different effect on the younger readers, of course; makes 'em feel as if they were in love. But I wish everyone wouldn't go around telling everyone else "*You* won't understand; it's too highbrow for you." Do they positively want to ruin my sales? Are you doing this too? Even a book-seller wrote me enthusiastically that she wouldn't sell it to everybody, and she felt sure I would approve. Other people inform me kindly that they have just managed to borrow a copy and like it very much. I inform them coldly that I can't imagine why they suppose I give a damn whether or not they read it; I want someone to buy it.

I guess that will do for the moment.

Affectionately,
Pat

To Lillian Fischer

September 16, 1933

Dear Lillian—

I got back all right,[64] but for the first week—it's a week yesterday—I've been so busy I couldn't even write a letter; more than that, I haven't even had time to cash my paycheck! Of course it's really because I'm such a triflin' animal, and hate to work or hurry, so I dawdle until the last minute and then feel overworked and put upon; and the main trouble is that I simply can't get up in the morning.[65] Anyhow, I've got things cleared up now. I was awfully bored on the boat coming back, until the last two days; spent all my time in gloomy seclusion in my stateroom; then I met some cheerful people so I felt better at the last, and am altogether much the better for the trip as a whole. I was too tired and ill to be any earthly use in Paris, but if I hadn't gone, I'd have just expired in the heat of New York, so I feel I was right in going. With the summer over, I can survive through another year. And next summer I can be in the country.

Needless to say, I found my house[66] was completely wrong, through my own fatal errors in figuring the size of it. This filled me with suicidal gloom all week, until tonight, unable to brood over it another moment without going and jumping off the dock; so at eleven o'clock I called up the unfortunate contractor and asked him could nothing be done about it—couldn't he stretch it somehow? (I have felt for some time that what this country needs is a folding or India rubber house, which can be expanded at a moment's notice to the desired size, or pushed in again like a concertina! You know what one really wants is a small house with a lot of room in it, which will be no trouble to look after and will accommodate any number of people at intervals. It should have just as many rooms as are necessary at any given time, but not when you don't want them. It should never require repairs, and should be surrounded by a self-tending garden and lawn). The contractor said he too had felt bad about the house all week, since we looked at it together and both perceived that the big room was simply wrong. He said it could be fixed, but would cost so much. Anything *can* be done, he said, but there's always the cost to consider. I said, is that all? I don't *care*—I do not care if it ruins me completely, I do not care even if I never live in the house myself, I simply cannot go on living at all unless we can fix that house. I'll go mad if I don't get it right. Just for once in my life, I must have something come out right. He sympathized with me, because he felt the same way about the house; he hated to be building a house that isn't right. His whole life is spent in building houses that aren't right, because he has to build what people order. So he was very nice, and I assured him it was entirely my own fault, which it is; and I guess maybe we'll get it fixed up. . . . I said,[67] it's really awful to make such horrible mistakes in the important things—getting married or building a house. He said, it's worse with a house than getting married, because you can get rid of the guy easier than you can the house! Anyhow, I shall tell him just to fix it and when he thinks it's all right tell me and then I'll go up and see it some more. I feel better, knowing it can be done, I don't seem to care if it ruins me.

Of course, I am cuckoo, but I realized that some time ago, and all I can do is make allowances for it. The simple fact is that if I tried to live in that house, knowing and feeling that it is *wrong,* I'd be taken away in a straitjacket finally. I got into an apartment that felt wrong,[68] it really was wrong in fact, with the fireplace in the wrong place and so forth, and I had to move out again because I got so I couldn't sleep nights, couldn't even go to bed! I just sat up brooding, feeling as if I were in jail or a trap. And with the whole world out of joint the way it is, slipping sideways and falling on one's head, it would be too much to feel that my house is wrong too. So that's that; it's got to be fixed. I feel a thousand per cent better since deciding it *must* be fixed. It is not a pretentious house, and all I ask is that it shouldn't be noticeable in any way. And after all, even with the extra expense, it would be more sensible to get it right; then it would be a good investment of the whole sum, a salable house. If I died, or whatever, one could get the money out of it again. . . . You see how much I've had it on my mind all week; now I go on talking about it from sheer relief. I suppose it would be nice to have sense and not do those things in the first place, but that is too much to hope for. Life is mostly a series of errors—and the strange thing is that you can't see afterward why or how you ever *did* such a thing! Because in this case I really knew better all the time, I knew it ought to be different, only there was some incidental difficulty about the beams, so I said oh, never mind, and let it go wrong.

The worst thing about being the kind of chump I am is that when I've made my mistakes I know it; and I know when a thing is right. But too late. It gives me pleasure to look at you (though that isn't why I am fond of you), because you really do get the right clothes and wear them right; they're not only in fashion, they are right for you.

I held a lodge of sorrow[69] with Cuppy* the other evening, me talking about my house and he explaining to me a fatal error he had just made, which could not possibly be remedied. Both of us talked straight ahead on our several subjects, neither paying any attention to the other, until we were exhausted. Then he remarked that the argument seemed to be getting us nowhere.

I sent you the last volume of the Genji series,[70] and will get the other books you want immediately; I hadn't time to this week. I won't be busy next week; I had to go [to] the dentist twice this week too; I hope I have to go only once more and then be through until some fresh calamity occurs. Maybe there will be nothing more wrong with my teeth for a year or two.

I hope you're not working so hard; don't if you can help it. Be young and beautiful and happy as you deserve; this is the best of your life, and I like to think someone has good fortune. I haven't heard any news of any kind since I came back, nor been anywhere, so have nothing amusing to relate. I've begun again on my book,[71] and had better get on with it to pay for my house! Remember me to Frank;[72] he was so nice to me; and my best love to you.

Pat

To Burton Rascoe

Undated [late 1933?]

Dear Burton—

Sure I except you; but I swear I can hardly find anyone else who even suspects that something has happened. The general level of imbecility has struck a new low for all time, and it makes me sick to my stummick. You know what I think about Walter Lippmann* anyhow and always did.[73] Do you think that even just the two of us can't do a darned thing? I mean to say, sometimes even a single voice is heard—so I want to see that article of yours in print.

You know I'm actually for capitalism, I even accept all the implications; but this bastard oligarchic half-state-socialism[74] we're getting into looks to me like nothing but an everlasting mess; it won't help or "save" anybody in the end, it will just bring us *all* to the breadline. I doubt if they can actually make it work in any way, it will end in complete confusion; then we may go back to capitalism; I don't know—going back is always difficult, maybe impossible; I don't know; but I'm sure they won't get anything better. Even the best intentioned, honest "planners" like Stuart Chase* make their plans by leaving out people—substituting a sort of imaginary synthetic man—and in any event, it's the sanctimonious s. o. b.'s that get in power.[75] I suppose it would be nice if poverty and depressions and hardship were abolished, but honestly, don't[76] you think we've really had the best chance the world ever saw for the individual, and if it wouldn't work—I really think it worked pretty well—how in hell will they make any other system work better, since you'll have the same people in it? Man is as yet an unfinished article; he has to finish himself, by individual effort in the main; I dislike the attitude that the poor as a lump would "keep coal in their bath-tubs,"[77] it isn't true, but only because "the poor" are not all alike; and it's just as stupid to think of improving them all alike as to say "they" wouldn't "appreciate" better things. Some would and some wouldn't; plenty of the well-to-do might just as well be in the slums for all they really get out of their advantages. We're all pretty dumb; but my point is that all the worst troubles I've ever had couldn't have been cured by state action; some were private follies, some were natural disabilities; the poverty of my childhood was disagreeable, but I don't know what state action could have made my home happier; and all the chances and benefits I have enjoyed came from our system, our freedom—there are a few things the state can do, and ours really did them as effectively as they can be done, giving us security of our earnings (up till now) aside from our personal foolishness, and giving us a chance of education as far as it could reach, and then letting us more or less alone to try out this and that.[78]

I still think that's all a government can do *beneficially*; but it can oppress and injure without limit, and oppression and injury are no pleasanter if inflicted with alleged benevolent intentions. So I'm for the government we had, with capitalism and everything—I'd even much rather have a bloody old pirate like the elder Morgan* than a sanctimonious s.o.b. like Thomas W. Lamont.* I'd rather have Owney Madden than Walter Lippmann.[79] God damn all the saviors and do-goods; they always end by picking your pocket. And I'd rather we were all in the breadline than that the things they're trying on should work. We can get out of the breadline. In fact, I'm finally for the logical conclusion of what they're doing—complete national, private and public, bankruptcy, toward which I think we're headed by way of a currency inflation, rather than state socialism and everybody on the government payroll, turned into a herd of sheep. That's what I meant by saying there isn't a *man* left in the country; they all want to be "saved", have their noses wiped for them by Mussolini, or Roosevelt, or somebody. . . . I will say flatly, that I think a man may still be a man even if he's panhandling in the street, asking for handouts at kitchen doors, but not if he's in a government "camp." I'm for private charity rather than governmental aid; in fact, I think private charity is the only decent kind—one human being giving another a meal or a quarter. Wouldn't you rather come and ask me for a hand-out than the government? I'd sooner ask you, or any stranger in the street. I don't care how reactionary I sound, either.[80] And if I've got to starve to death, I don't care. Like Will Cuppy,* if this sort of thing is going on, then I don't want to. But as Hergesheimer* says, there *are* a few of us left; we can anyhow make a few derisive parting remarks. Do you think they can lick us? Hell, we've been busted before. . . . I hope to put some of this [in] my novel,[81] especially a few remarks on the kept intellectuals who have gently led the "right-thinking" people up to where they are now. But it probably won't work in; anyhow, I go right ahead writing the novel, perched as it were with my typewriter on the edge of the abyss—human beings *are* weird.

Pat

To Burton Rascoe

Paterson and her fellow literary critic Burton Rascoe wrote a series of letters to each other about the novelist and poet D. H. Lawrence. The correspondence may have been prompted by the publication of* Lorenzo in Taos *(1932), a book by Lawrence's friend Mabel Dodge Luhan (1879–1962). Paterson called it a "rich and nutty memoir" ("Turns," March 13, 1932) and had much to say about Lawrence with her friends. As she told Rascoe in a letter of late 1933 or early 1934, she was sympathetic toward Lawrence's early struggles with the English class system and toward his attempts to find a way of expressing "a very special talent. . . . If he was hysterical—I should say he was—at least he had reason enough; it was the hysteria of exhaustion, of nerves overstrained continuously, without one interval of rest, from the cradle to the grave." But she had her objections too, especially about Lawrence's mystical view of sex. Rascoe evidently asked her to record her opinions in detail; the following letter was a result.*

Undated [July 1933–January 1934]

Dear Burton—

Gosh, what a job—not that I mind trying, but the result is very likely to be fifty per cent nonsense, or more. You see, I don't deny that Lawrence had a special talent, though I am unable to estimate it critically because of my temperamental antipathy. And though the women who clustered around him were mostly nuts, of course you're right in saying that plenty of intelligent women (and men) liked his work, liked the man too. Apparently he inspired a good deal of real affection and what I might call disinterested appreciation, not hysterical enthusiasm.

A temperamental antipathy I suppose is something in the nature of things; any attempted explanation of it is merely naming a fact one way or another; it goes deeper than analysis can follow. Something laid before the foundations of the world.[82] I believe that you gave the most penetrating and just description of Lawrence, gave his classification in the human species, when you said he was a saint. I hate all saints, whether male or female. I dislike them just because; I can rationalize it, but it's simply dislike of the type. They go against the grain with me. They even make me feel sickish.

The saint, of course you realize or you wouldn't have detected that Lawrence was one, has none of the qualities which are popularly called "saintly." Those attributes, kindness, patience, gentleness, unselfishness, lack of egotism, are exactly the opposite of what a saint is. Persons having those qualities are never heard of outside their immediate circle, naturally. To get yourself canonized, even irregularly by some unorthodox sect, you have to get yourself noticed first—so a decidedly aggressive egotism is the first requisite of a saint. You notice Saint Francis making his first bid for sainthood by generously giving away *his father's* goods! And then by exhibitionism stripping himself naked. Now I don't mind a straightforward egotism, but I dislike the egotism that calls in God to justify it. That also, on my part, is just an emotional fact; I simply don't like it. Lawrence called in Nature as god to justify him—he was always speaking with the authority of some mysterious "dark flow" or whatever he was calling it for the day. Sex, sometimes. If people would do as he told them, the world would be all right, would be "healed"—would, in short be "saved"—the promise that every saint makes. In the teeth of the fact that his own life was a mess in every way. He could never imagine himself as being mistaken even for a moment. And of course it would be hard to check up on him because what he said never had any sense—it was pure emotionalism. (These statements of mine are getting rather vague and woozy). . . . It may be said that Lawrence was kind, generous, that he gave away money and did things for other people. One of his friends says he would be very angry if someone wouldn't accept money he offered, when it might be all the money he (Lawrence) had. That was exactly how he would do, with no regard for the other person's feelings or attitude.

Though I hate the phrase "inferiority complex," Lawrence had one, partly manifested in snobbery, partly in his incessant rowing with his wife and other women. He even used to beat her up to prove he was her "superior"—a more ridiculous mode of proof I can't imagine. Inferiority complexes bore me. A smidge of commonsense tells us that there is no single measure of intrinsic "superiority" or inferiority. We are all extraordinarily uneven in our aptitudes and qualities.

I can't look around me, even with my shortsighted vision, without perceiving a dozen people superior to me in manifest ways. A pretty girl is superior to me in that. My colored maid is superior to me in her gentle and pleasing manners—she has really nice manners. The contractor who is building my house is obviously my superior as a man who can organize, manage, get things done or do them with his own hands if necessary. The wop who lives across the road is my superior in that he can make a garden, and do lots of other absolutely indispensable things.[83] Probably he is superior in character, in the everyday virtues that enable a man to feed and raise a family and get a living for them. I should be very glad to have all those qualities—beauty, organizing ability, and so forth; but insofar as I haven't got them, I am glad someone has, and satisfied to respect those qualities where I see them, and not to keep screaming around trying to convince those people I'm just as good as they are. If I have any qualities of my own—I'm really not sure—I suppose they will show, and need not be screamed about either. So I just get sick of Lawrence's eternal yammering and pushing and running ahead—the way he couldn't even walk beside anyone on a path.

His "manliness." Oh, Lord! What on earth does that mean? Physiologically we are born male and female; but beside that, what is the measure of masculinity or femininity? I have no idea. Sexual capacity? well, you can't go around proving that to absolutely everybody. I presume I must be feminine because I *am* a woman—the adjective is a derivative of the fact. I don't see that I can do anything about it or need to insist upon it. I may wish to take on what is called men's work; if I succeed, then it becomes woman's work, because I'm doing it. . . . In short, I could never make any sense of Lawrence's insistence on "maleness" and "femaleness."

I do, of course, think vaguely of a man as a good *man* if he is capable in whatever he has to do—his job, his relations with his family, and so forth. Since children partly incapacitate a woman from earning a living for herself and the children, economic necessity makes it a man's job to support his family once he has started a family. He undertook that obligation; and equally, a woman has to look after her children. I suppose I'd think of her as a poor specimen of a woman if she shirked the obligation, after incurring it. But the meeting of responsibility is a human quality (or lack), not masculine or feminine. I just don't know how anyone can be more "manly" or "womanly" by trying. No effort or insistence will alter the physiological fact—unless by the method of Origen. . . .[84] Lawrence was always insisting that his "masculinity" should be "respected," by his wife and other women. What in hell did he mean? I hate gibberish.

You see I am expressing rather violently what I dislike in Lawrence. This would not invalidate what other people liked in him, but they'd have to express it, because my dislike gets in the way of my appreciating those other qualities of his, whatever they are. Possibly they found his emotionalism warming and stimulating. It doesn't do that for me; it makes me cold, it repels me. That is probably personal and idiosyncratic. I like a man to have more outward control. That's simple preference. I shouldn't like a woman of the Lawrence type either.

Possibly you could check up all this against my own character and temperament and find a comical inconsistency—as if I were condemning my own weaknesses mercilessly in Lawrence. In part I would concede this charge, though I'm really quite the opposite type—my emotions work in reverse from his. I cannot make this clear at all; but it is true. In the first place my emotions have to start with imagination—a cerebral start—and secondly, I can[85] afterward see what they did to me, how they colored my ideas, or submerged my ideas. And everything in the world isn't charged with emotion for me. Like Peter Bell,[86] usually a primrose is a simple primrose, a pretty object; if it has an emotional connotation I can usually say how and why. Lawrence looked at *everything* through a quivering haze of personal emotionalism. Most of the time I don't feel that the universe is much concerned with me. It was always concerned with him, in his estimation. I have no religious faculty. If I try to suppose a God, I can never get as far as supposing that God is bothering about me, individually; the most I can do is to imagine a rather ironic scheme in which we are absurd and God finds us amusing. But that is a mere intellectual concept, a fancy, to entertain myself. Not a religious feeling. I find the religious temperament interesting after it has been theologized, but not before; you see, the theology is, however cock-eyed, an intellectual approach, and that gives me[87] a handle to take hold of it. Lawrence was a religious type, but never got himself fitted with a theology.

This is all about me, rather than Lawrence. Necessarily because I admit my distaste for Lawrence is an antipathy which prevents me really explaining him—all I can explain is why I[88] shy off from him. As one might be able to say, from real knowledge: "I get mackerel poisoning, can't eat mackerel," but not know what ingredient in the mackerel caused the trouble. There are writers whom I would say myself have none of Lawrence's talent who do not annoy me; I just don't mind them. I don't think they're great or even very good, or perhaps not good at all, but they are not antipathetic to me; they are negative.

I have the secular mind, and prefer it in others. Dreiser* has the secular mind, so I never feel that annoyance at him, though I as a woman would not be attracted to him as a man, and though his complete lack of taste appal[l]s me; those things are set to one side, they don't get between me and his[89] special achievement as a writer.

Tolstoy's religiosity makes me sick, but he had also an *enormous* creative genius which was so much bigger than his religious fears that it made him create character most of the time regardless—so I forget all about his tiresome religion, even his sickening morality, in the pleasure of that vast living world he made. I can never lose sight of Lawrence's hot gospel pulpiteering. He won't let me. I do not like his style either because it is a preacher's style—unctuous, fanatical, firstly, secondly, thirdly.[90]

I wish *I* knew what goes on in the minds of men—for my purposes as a writer. I'm far from sure I know what goes on in the minds of women, except a few like myself. I am constantly astonished by both men and women; this keeps life interesting, but is rather upsetting to me when I want to write novels!

Possibly I haven't really answered your question at all. You may be able to see *through* what I have written and detect the truth I can't express lucidly. You know me fairly well, and therefore can deal with the personal equation involved. You have a great deal of intuition—intuition is intellectual, contrary to popular belief—and the kind of simps[91] who pride themselves on their intuition (like those who believe themselves to be "psychic") never have any. I have no intuition myself,[92] and have to go through the laborious processes of logic to discover anything; those processes are sadly unreliable, because to get a correct result you have to have all the factors;[93] and that is a highly improbable assumption.

Affectionately,
Pat

To Garreta Busey

Undated [February 23, 1934]

Dear Garreta,

Well, I thought I had explained to you at least twice that we are shooting the chutes into chaos, so I'm glad you noticed it; that's the way it looked to me quite awhile ago and as it gets steadily worse, I feel that I have Done My Part. Yes, three years ago, while Prosperity was Just Around the Corner, I used to sit up all night sometimes frozen with horror at What We Were Coming To, and now we seem to have practically arrived. In fact, believe it or not, the reason why Al Smith's* defeat[94] filled me with gloom and fury was because it meant we were heading for this. You may not see the connection, but I swear that was the first terrible portent, because it signified that people had *forgotten the meaning of politics as the art of government.* That was why I was so appalled and dismayed. They were voting for Prosperity, for Prohibition, for a Great Engineer, for the Ku-Klux Klan, for every idiocy and irrelevancy imaginable, but never for a political intelligence to fill a great political office.[95] It indicated unmistakably that thought had ceased, and when that happens, the roof falls in on any civilization, on a country, or an institution; on whatever is concerned. We had got utterly obfuscated by the insane spectacle of Europe, we had the idea of Saving Europe first and forgot our own proper business—and here we are.

But there I go again, I swore to shut up. It does no good, and annoys me. I must concentrate on the blue rain-barrel, which probably isn't in existence yet, I mean I don't know if it's on the premises, and if it is it will not be blue till I paint it next spring. The house is done and closed up till spring. How I'll get moved into it I blithely don't know. I have to finish my damned novel[96] first, and that will be the death of me; it has reached the stage where I die over every paragraph. Besides, I have the pip[97] tonight, and must go home and get dressed and go to a horrible party. I trust this news will strike you as interesting and amusing. I spent yesterday shopping, and what that means I will not dwell upon—standing up to confront the ravages of time, I wish I were dead; there is no point in going on forever, getting more dilapidated minute by minute, I cannot bear it, the long indignity and insult and humiliation and being dragged in the dust, and if I saw 27 rhetoric students in a mass I would turn loose a whiff of grapeshot, because it would be a far, far better thing to do than to permit them to become what they will become and are now and ever shall be—pure morons.[98] If they had any brains would they be studying rhetoric? Do I have to study rhetoric to express myself as above? What in hell and goddamnation is rhetoric? People either can say what they mean or they can't, mostly the latter. Probably they have nothing to say. I have just had a conversation with Cuppy* concerning Pericles and the City Beautiful, by telephone. From this we switched to a story called *The Postman Always Rings Twice*, which he hadn't read but I have, and he asked me is it any good, and I said it is another of those things, a stark story about bums and morons who do nothing but go to bed and commit murders; and they conduct their affairs by biting each other ferociously.[99] I said, I do not think that is True Love. He said he didn't think so either, nor does he believe that stories about such people are Art. He said that Hemingway's *The Sun Also Rises* gave some intimation of a certain fresh way of writing, but nothing came of it. I said, well, what could you do with the alleged theme—the sex life of a eunuch may sound like something to write about but if you think it over you will see that it simply isn't. There is a catch in it.[100] He said that did sound reasonable. So we rang off.

I do not care what becomes of the proletariat; I hope it starves to death, en masse.[101]

With this I will leave you; but am I right?

Affectionately,
Pat

P. S. I bought three dresses, in each of which I look worse than in the others; one is yellow crepe, which can't wear till midsummer; another is striped like an awning, and also for midsummer, and looks still worse; the other is brown polka dot and it indicates what has happened to my figure in the last eighty years. I never had but one reason for living, as I have often told you, and now that is out of the question.

To Burton Rascoe

Undated [July 1936]

Dear Burton—

Why, yes, I've always thought and still think that Aldous Huxley's* books are among the most repulsive, well, I may say *the* most repulsive if one considers only those which purport to be literature or to be intellectual productions. I do think they have a vile quality; I guess one can't use that adjective in print in such a case, as it must be a matter of opinion, but I have intimated it in print, as far as the proper conventions of criticism will permit. I am sure this review of mine[102] must have been inadequate, to give you the impression I had changed my opinion. You know you and I are frequently against the current in our opinions, not always on the same questions of course, but we don't go much with the crowd. Then when we have said a thing two or three times, maybe we rest on the record, let it go as said, and are asked, why didn't you say so? When we did say it quite awhile ago and had come to take for granted that it was understood. I remember writing specifically once that Huxley is always an ill-bred writer, as he takes advantage of a supposed intellectual position to secure "shock effects," by the use of disgusting passages. I should have reiterated this; it was not enough merely to intimate that a squeamish reader had better beware. I agree with you that he has steadily lost what bright and amusing quality of style he had. And *at best* he has always seemed to me second-rate. . . . Taking over the daily column—and in the dogdays—is a difficult task; I really need time to hit the right tone, when I change over to anything.

What Huxley lacks is taste or breeding. I meant, in that review, and then forgot, to remark that Cabell* put the whole thesis of *Eyeless in Gaza*—the skeptic confronted by the final reduction of a materialistic view of the universe—in one paragraph of *Jurgen* (where Jurgen goes into the wood with the Brown Man). That was artistry. Well, then I simply forgot to say that! After thinking of it the day before. . . . Of course I don't think the Cogito paragraphs are anything but disgusting. And utterly beside the point of Descartes.* I didn't mean to be lenient, but rather indifferent—to imply that for those who like Huxley, here is his new book. So I don't think anything has happened to either you or me; it was merely a specific failure on my part to convey fully what I do think. . . . I didn't know that Beppo was Clive Bell,* but the parallel with Proust* was obvious.[103]

I always thought that Mary Austin's* partial failure (for she failed only partially) was because she got the notion that she had a powerful intellect, and tried to work from it; whereas her gift was deep instinct and a genuinely literary quality when she chose to work for that, instead of trying to be a Great Thinker. She had just a good average intelligence, and that rather narrowed by a touch of the middle west provincial puritan clubwoman uplift temperance stuff—the desire to Do Good. But a kind of greatness in her personality too, something large and splendid about her, and very feminine, as it should be in any woman's gift or personality. She wanted to be a prophetess or sibyl, and the authentic impact of her rich femininity secured her some followers whose devotion confirmed her in that mistaken ambition.

I was really glad to get your criticism. It is a useful reminder, to keep me in better balance. . . . I don't think it can be an accident that so many beginning writers who have been associated with you in their beginnings blossomed out so successfully thereafter.

My God, it's hot.

Pat

To Burton Rascoe

Undated [late summer 1936]

Dear Burton—

That was all right; I had already bought the magazine, and got the money's worth. You did a good job with all the literary Holy Rollers.[104]

I wish you'd criticize my stuff any time you like. There's always sense in your editorial point of view—I mean you speak to the point of what the writer is trying to get at, not merely to substitute your own opinions, or rather, not confusing the two issues, as most people do. . . . I'm ag'in you about Yeats,* as you probably know; I think perhaps you are irritated or alienated by his profession of aristocratic principles—a term which it is difficult for us to allow any value. Certainly the very word is alien to all my natural and ingrained feelings. But I think that in the same article you have a paragraph or phrase which indicates, by analogy, how you and I can approach or appreciate Yeats's aristocratic faith—I mean where you speak of a parish priest, etc. As in the case of the priest with Catholicism (you and I couldn't be Catholics, you see, but the priest is), Yeats conceived his aristocratic creed as a discipline for himself, and really lived up to it—one might say that he simply wanted a word to express the discipline he felt morally obligated to impose on himself and live up to for the sake of his poetic genius, and he chose to call it aristocracy. As Shelley chose the words republican or even atheist to express the obligation he felt toward freedom for his poetic genius. In neither case is it really a political or social system they mean, but an attitude of mind and spirit; but as they have to call it something, they choose the word or system whose ideals (whatever their realities) are akin to that attitude. The sometimes appalling manifestations of the "republican" peoples in fact—our recent conventions, for instance[105]—still do not invalidate Shelley's passion for liberty.

But you have really said what I am saying above, in another connection, in your article, the part of it exposing the fallacy of those "selfless" theorists by contrasting them with anyone who actually does live for something beyond himself—all I wish to add is that it takes in Yeats; he has lived nobly. And I think his estimate of Moore* is essentially sound, though limited by the fact that he grasps literature *only* as poetry, and therefore does not appreciate the merit of *Hail and Farewell* on another plane, a very curious plane of "cat and monkey" but *literature* of cat and monkey none the less.[106] In it Moore utilized his own worst qualities (spite, malice, jealousy, mendacity, showing-off and even caddishness) in the genuine service of literature, a feat like that of Boswell* turning *his* weaknesses (snobbishness, thickhidedness, excessive sociability to the point of pushfulness and toadyism, the busybody spirit, mutability in his own life and therefore subjection to the things of the moment, and what else you please) all this he actually managed to utilize as tools for his biographical trade, and turned out a magnificent job.[107] Two very strange literary paradoxes. Or so it seems to me.

If I could use my faults to as good effect I'd be a genius too, I'm afraid. As it is they get me nowhere! Gosh, I must do some work.

Pat

To Burton Rascoe

Undated [late summer 1936]

Dear Burton—

No, of course you didn't have me in mind when writing about Yeats*; you don't write that way; but simply I knew you'd be aware that I think Yeats is the greatest poet and the greatest man now living—I should say, the greatest man I know about, for a man I would consider great might be obscure in his lifetime; and I don't consider Napoleon, for instance, a great *man*.[108]

What struck me as comic right after I'd mailed the letter—I'd have sent a postscript but hadn't time that day—was that I really learned the point of view I expressed from you! I do not mean my opinion or estimate of Yeats in particular, nor any one thing I said, nor that I took it from anything you ever *said* or wrote specifically, but something more difficult to define, a modification of my own too-logical and dogmatic tendency, a more inclusive attitude in appreciation, discarding non-essentials or symbols or theories as such, and considering rather what a man has made out of his given materials and point of view. It was your editorial attitude showed me this; and the result of it, which proved you were *right*, beyond argument. You might be wrong on any given point, here and there, as anyone may be, but that was immaterial in the same way that the specific wrongness on a given point of either fact or opinion was immaterial in any writer, when the body of his work had its intrinsic values. This is a stodgy way of stating it, but the best I can do at the moment.

I can believe what the Colums* say about Yeats—I think perhaps it was because Yeats recognized those failings in himself that he felt the necessity of his "aristocratic" discipline, the acceptance of poverty, for instance, and finding a use for it as a mode of schooling his romanticism into more austere forms, supporting himself through the ordeal by the "aristocratic" virtue of pride. . . . As a matter of fact, I do not think that any system in operation really has any distinguishing virtues, but we need labels. I think it is more than probable that a system in operation tends to destroy the very virtues that it claims formally and needs most—in fact, it claims and defines those virtues out of its particular need of them rather than its possession of them. An aristocracy perishes without personal pride, disinterestedness on the basis of its own privilege, courage, and so on. A republic perishes without honesty, etc. Yet it is an obvious fact that the founders of this republic actually possessed the supposedly *aristocratic* virtues in greater degree than any aristocracy ever did—they had distinction, elegance, intellect, courage, disinterestedness (i. e., little wish for power for its own sake), manners, everything.

So Yeats decided to be "aristocratic," because he was poor, without influence, and naturally and humanly envious of Moore's* privileged position—I can quite believe it.[109] But as he did really sustain his poverty with pride and refuse to compromise on his poetic gift, I think he justified his chosen principles for himself. In *Dramatis Personae* some of his remarks on Lady Gregory* seem to me factually absurd—seeing her as the Great Lady (like Castiglione's Duchess[110]), attributing it to her being a Percy, God bless us!—on his own account of her, she seems to me a Victorian bourgeois do-good and rather stingy with her benefactions at that, but evidently he really saw her as the Duchess and thereby *made her serve that position*, as Don Quixote made the kitchen wench into his Lady; so it is right that he should praise her.

Yeats indicates in his Autobiography that he felt socially inept as a boy—partly because he was such a big boy, bony and probably awkward; and undoubtedly the more so because he was very poor. I think it is amusing that he felt socially as Moore seems to have felt among artists and writers in his youth; whereas Yeats of course only felt at home among artists and writers, being bred among them, in the world of ideas and craftsmanship. Thus Moore wanted to be a poet, which Yeats was; and I daresay Yeats would have liked to be one of the landed gentry; but it was a good thing he wasn't.

Even as a person, Yeats impressed Moore powerfully, another slight confirmation of my belief that Yeats really is a very great man with all his faults. Molly Colum[111] says Yeats makes that immense impression personally, so much so that she could never quite be sure how she estimated his poetry apart from himself—words to that effect, when I said that his poetry made that enormous impact on me. Yeats seems to me to be a center, and Moore peripheral to others—do I mean peripheral? Well, whatever I mean—Moore could make fun of the superficial aspect or mannerisms of Yeats, but had to stop there; he could not belittle him. There are a few men who have that size which defies detraction—it's what Washington had, his special quality, which in Washington's case is rather baffling because you can't pin it to anything else specifically; he had just a good intelligence, ordinary commonsense principles and ideas, and so on, but greatness per se, as a man.

I do not think Yeats is unjust or malicious to Moore in *Dramatis Personae*; it is a fine portrait sketch; and there is an *absolute* truth in his estimate of Moore's style (Moore always derived his style, changing it several times, it was never strictly his own as Yeats's style is his own, for Yeats *could not* write in any other way); and Moore never *quite* hit the middle of the note; also his writing, being an artificial style, did disintegrate at the end, as Yeats said. But Yeats failed to allow that Moore really accomplished something (chiefly *Hail and Farewell*) with that made style—this is where absolutism is too absolute, in literature. Both artifice and pure naivete can be literature of the second rank, and Yeats could not conceive of anything but the first rank—there it was as a shining mark and you either hit it or you didn't. A bullseye or nothing. I also think he overestimated Synge's* permanent value, for the reason that he recognized that Synge was a true original, and aiming at that center mark; but Synge died too young, before he really achieved what he seems to have been capable of doing; and Yeats gives him credit for his potentialities as if they had been accomplished; whereas Moore accomplished all he was capable of, and Yeats simply cannot perceive the nature of that kind of an accomplishment, therefore he is not unjust or malicious but is unable to see a prose accomplishment because it has no poetry in it; or a fine accomplishment of the second rank because it is not the first. He reveals his predilection or standard in discussing the Irish orators—passion was what he appreciated, the instinctive poetic quality, not rational statement or persuasion by fact and reason, which is admirable oratory too and much better for strictly practical purposes—for getting men to do something sensible, politically.

Good God, how long and boring this is—throw it away. I must do a review.

Pat

Notes

1. Among the reviews Paterson was doing for publications other than the *Herald Tribune* are "Rewards of Virtue in the Spring Novels," *McNaught's Monthly* 3 (May 1925) 159–60; and "Rags to Riches in the New Novels," *McNaught's Monthly* 3 (June 1925) 190–91.
2. *Crossed out:* I don't know of any great satire that doesn't concern itself somehow with politics.
3. *Crossed out:* playing l----g--.
4. *Crossed out:* ward heeler.
5. A probable reference to Galatians 1–2.
6. *Crossed out:* Anatole France did his best.
7. The two books, both by Paterson, are *The Singing Season* (1924), mentioned also in Paterson to Fischer, April 23, 1925; and *The Fourth Queen*, which would be published in 1926.
8. *Crossed out:* Like enough, I daresay. Lee is Herman Lee Meader*; Edna Richmond was his girlfriend or companion (see also Paterson to Fischer, February 16, 1933).
9. "Egbert" was Emerson Whithorne* (identified in Paterson's letter to Fischer, February 16, 1933, where Paterson mentions his marriage).
10. *Crossed out:* accepting the fashionable bunk.
11. Jocularly British version of "daresay." *The Constant Nymph* (1924) was a well-regarded and very popular novel by Margaret Kennedy (1896–1967).
12. A mistake for *She Wanted to Know*, originally *Si Je Voulais* (published in Paris in 1924), by Paul Geraldy (1885–1983), translated by Grace George. It was then playing at the Belasco Theatre.
13. *Processional: A Jazz Symphony of American Life* (1925), by John Howard Lawson (1894–1977), American playwright who would later become one of Hollywood's leading communists.
14. Hyperbole: Paterson was thirty-nine years old when this letter was written.
15. A phrase popularized by Warren Harding in his campaign for the presidency (1920). He desired a return to the comparative calm that existed before World War I.
16. German: housewife.
17. This person has not been identified.
18. Brickell's wife Norma survived.
19. Paterson had rented accommodations in which she could write, somewhere in the countryside.

20. Rollo is the protagonist of a long series of children's books by Jacob Abbott (1803–1879). Jonas, a young hired hand who features in these books, is insufferably edifying about every small detail of life. He becomes the instructor and judge of the other boys.
21. Rotary is a network of local service clubs for business people. A "Rotarian" is a stereotyped "community minded" small businessman.
22. *Never Ask the End,* then in progress.
23. *Crossed out:* becomes visible.
24. This apparently refers to a scene in Chapter 14 of *Never Ask the End.* It is followed in Chapter 15 by a dinner scene (see below) in which family histories are provided, though without any bounty jumpers or Aunt Elizas.
25. Someone who accepted a bounty to join a Civil War army and then deserted.
26. Gannett* was the new book reviewer for the *Herald Tribune*; see page 92, note 18. The new book by Woolf was *The Waves.* Paterson said it was "a novel for novelists, mainly interesting as an experiment. It seems to us an unsuccessful experiment, but that does not destroy the technical interest" ("Turns," November 15, 1931).
27. Since 1922 Paterson had been living in a tenement apartment—decent, but a tenement—at 508 W. 34th Street, New York City. In July 1931 she moved to another apartment in Manhattan, but moved back to 508 W. 34th in December 1931; see pages 154, 156, 161–62, below.
28. Quotation from *Pelopidas; or, The Deliverance of Thebes,* by Edwin Atherstone (1788–1872), British poet and dramatist.
29. Europe had contracted immense loans from America in order to fight World War I.
30. A period of economic distress comparable to that of the depression of the 1930s began in 1893.
31. Paterson probably refers to Senator Borah's demands for radical change in the European war reparations and debt payment system. American banks, and the American government, were deeply invested in what were in fact bad debts.
32. The expression, which sometimes employs three tailors instead of nine, originates in a story about a group of tailors who gathered on Tooley Street in London to draft a statement of grievances to Parliament. The petition began, "We, the people of England."
33. *Crossed out:* It might give you something.
34. Paterson would remember this as "the most horrible party [she] ever wandered into. . . . [N]othing happened at the party; it was the atmosphere that was so ghastly. Sinclair Lewis remarked that it was the end of the lunatic 1920s, the prohibition era" ("Turns," December 1, 1935). Horace Liveright (1883–1933), founder of Boni and Liveright and the Modern Library, was a publisher of distinguished books. He married his second wife, actress Elise Bartlett (1899–1947), on December 8, 1931; on May 2, 1932, she filed for divorce. He was a party giver and an alcoholic; she died of the effects of alcohol.
35. When Lewis was working in a publisher's office he rejected Paterson's first novel, with impressive style; and she respected him ever afterward: "Sinclair Lewis IS America. He is uniquely, completely, representatively American, 'blasted for the sins of the people.' [A frequently quoted passage

in *A History of European Morals from Augustus to Charlemagne* (1869), by Irish historian William Edward Hartpole Lecky (1838–1903) refers to the prostitute as she who is 'blasted for the sins of the people.'] An amazing phenomenon; he is a human receiving station for all the cross-currents and confusions and absurdities of a most distressful country. It isn't that nothing escapes him so much as that he escapes nothing; he can't help hearing what people say, seeing what they do and remembering it forever after. What is most amazing is a kind of sweetness, gentleness, gayety and goodwill in his nature that persists in spite of the frightful ordeal to which he is subjected. He inspires affection; he attracts any one who comes within his orbit, and he has no defenses. We wouldn't accept the penalties of such a gift even if it brought with it the Nobel Prize once a year" ("Turns," October 19, 1924; December 1, 1935).

36. "My book" is *Never Ask the End*; the disorganization is presumably that of Paterson's moving from apartment to apartment (see note 27, above). For Cuppy's book (mentioned below), see the following letter.
37. Will Cuppy's *How to Tell Your Friends from the Apes* (1931), which he dedicated to Paterson.
38. *Jurgen: A Comedy of Justice* (1919), a novel by James Branch Cabell.*
39. Nickname of Will Cuppy.
40. This may have been the genesis of Rascoe's *Titans of Literature* (1932).
41. *Gentle Reader* was a magazine of reviews, distributed through bookstores, that began publication in late November 1931.
42. Louis XV of France is supposed to have said, "After me, the deluge," meaning revolution.
43. *Never Ask the End.*
44. *Crossed out:* content.
45. *Crossed out:* This, you see, means making trivial things count, for youthful lovers, as you know, are absurd, artificial, cheap.
46. See note 27, above.
47. Rascoe and his wife Hazel were in California.
48. Into "Turns with a Bookworm."
49. The deadline for Paterson's column was over a week before it appeared in the Sunday *Books* supplement of the *Herald Tribune*, occasioning many jokes and comments by her about events that she described as about to take place having already taken place by now, and so forth.
50. *Never Ask the End.*
51. *Crossed out:* eighteen hours.
52. A novel (1932) by Howard W. Roper.
53. Sears, Roebuck & Co. published a huge mail-order catalogue that went out to millions of potential buyers.
54. A very favorable review for *Herald Tribune "Books."*
55. The subject of this allusion has not been identified.
56. Burton Rascoe's wife.
57. Paterson frequently echoed James Forsyte in John Galsworthy's* *Forsyte Saga*, who claimed that nobody ever told him anything.
58. The Guild was the Literary Guild, which regularly supplied its subscribers with books chosen by its editorial committee. The Guild dinner took place on January 25, 1933. According to the *New York Times* (January 26, 1933),

Mrs. Roosevelt spoke about books for children and "advise[d] care in picking titles for youth."

59. Probably *The Golden Vanity*; possibly *If It Prove Fair Weather*. Though Paterson wrote her columns quickly, she followed a different practice with her novels. Of the difficulties of authorship, she wrote: "We have known exactly two people who simply loved writing, enjoyed it, wrote with fluency and without compulsion. They've been at it for twenty years and have not yet achieved publication. Their stuff is simply terrible" ("Turns," March 24, 1929).
60. Anne Parrish (1888–1957), novelist and art collector, was married to industrialist Charles Albert Corliss (1868–1936), whose sister Florence was married to Thomas W. Lamont.
61. *Never Ask the End.*
62. An editor with the Frederick A. Stokes publishing company and later with Doubleday.
63. Paterson wrote this in Ulmann's copy of her novel *The Road of the Gods*: "For Doris Ulmann who knows the worst already, so this can do no harm[.] From the author Isabel Paterson" (book in editor's collection). "Knows the worst" may be a joking reference to photographs that Ulmann took of Paterson.
64. From her trip to Europe.
65. Paterson was a night person. She ordinarily stayed up very late, reading and writing—when "the world at large is minding its own business," "statesmen are snoring profoundly," and "even Huey Long* is silent" ("Turns," June 30, 1935). To put it in another way, getting active before eight a.m. "is all right if you like staying up so late" ("Turns," August 9, 1931).
66. The house she was having built in Stamford, Connecticut.
67. *Crossed out:* it's too much.
68. See note 27, above.
69. A lodge of sorrow is a Masonic ceremony in honor of the dead.
70. *The Tale of Genji* is a Japanese work of fiction written by Lady Murasaki in the eleventh century. Paterson was very fond of this work and followed its publication in successive volumes of the translation by Arthur Waley (1889–1966).
71. *The Golden Vanity.*
72. Frank Farley (c. 1890–1951), American representative in Europe for Paramount Pictures, Lillian Fischer's husband.
73. Of Lippmann's concerns about "the Good Society" Paterson wrote: "He began by believing that everything could be fixed for everybody forever. Don't ask us how come he thought that; he just did. Therefore, he argued with himself, why not do so? And he set about it—at least, he was commencing to get ready to begin. But the more he worked at the world the worse it grew. So he began to think, why is this thus? There must be something wrong with the original specifications. If it can be fixed, why can't I fix it? He worried that around till he saw it in reverse. If I can't fix it, nobody can. Hence the book" [*The Good Society*, 1937] ("Turns," October 3, 1937).
74. *Cross out:* makes me gag.
75. *Crossed out:* I wish people were not so.
76. *Crossed out:* you find that it is not any the capitalistic.

77. According to an old expression, "if you give poor people a bathtub, they'll just use it to keep coal in."
78. *Crossed out:* Well, I got a lot out of life, I've liked it.
79. Owney Madden (1891–1965) was a New York gangster involved in many enterprises, including the Cotton Club and the Stork Club. He presided over bootlegging territory in Paterson's neighborhood, Hell's Kitchen.
80. *Crossed out:* And when I'm asked to save the god damned banks, I don't care if they bust, so that's that.
81. *The Golden Vanity.*
82. "Foundations of the world," "foundation of the world," "foundations of the earth," etc. appear at several places in the Bible—for instance, Job 38:4, Ephesians 1:4, and Hebrews 1:10.
83. The "maid" was a woman hired to come in at certain times, assist at dinner parties, and perhaps clean the apartment. The contractor was building Paterson's house in Stamford, Connecticut. "Wop" is now universally regarded as a derogatory term for "Italian." Paterson clearly did not regard it in that way. Her Italian American friends, in her neighborhood and in the *Herald Tribune* press room, were among the few people she consistently felt comfortable with and enjoyed (see page 247, note 34). She complimented the culture of Italian immigrants and denied the need for a "melting pot" ("Turns," January 24, 1943). In 1994, the editor interviewed Jerre Mangione (1909–1998), an Italian American author who knew Paterson and whose work she praised. Mangione, who was very sensitive to anti-Italian feeling, repeatedly stated that he never detected any of it in Paterson.
84. Origen (c. 184–c. 253), Christian theologian, is said to have castrated himself.
85. *Crossed out:* think them over.
86. The protagonist of William Wordsworth's poem of the same name.
87. *Crossed out:* an approach.
88. *Crossed out:* can't get near him.
89. *Crossed out*: peculiar.
90. Old-fashioned preachers numbered the parts of their sermons in this way.
91. Simpletons.
92. This statement is strongly contested by Paterson's references, elsewhere, to psychic experience; see WD 121, 202–203.
93. *Crossed out*: which is against all probability.
94. Paterson was an enthusiastic supporter of Smith's candidacy for president in 1928.
95. *Crossed out:* They might just as well have been hiring.
96. *The Golden Vanity.*
97. Menstrual pains.
98. One of the subjects Garreta Busey taught at the University of Illinois was rhetoric. The hero of Charles Dickens's *A Tale of Two Cities* (1859) says of his approaching execution, "It is a far, far better thing that I do, than I have ever done."
99. Pericles, Athenian political leader (c. 495–429 B.C.), beautified the Acropolis with distinguished works of architecture and sculpture. *The Postman Always Rings Twice* (1934) is a novel by American writer James M. Cain (1892–1977).
100. *Crossed out:* He said it would seem so.

101. Lest readers take this remark without irony, here is Paterson on her own social position: "The books that baffle us are those addressed to the proletariat, such as the novels of John Dos Passos.* Being a proletarian, we get hopelessly lost in his highbrow modern narrative labyrinth; and are particularly puzzled by the fact that his people don't seem to be greatly occupied by any kind of work" (March 27, 1932).
102. A review (*New York Herald Tribune*, July 9, 1936) of Huxley's *Eyeless in Gaza*, a novel to which Rascoe had objected in a letter to Paterson of the same date. Rascoe called it "the vilest, most repulsive book I have ever read." To cite an example of Paterson's previous remarks: "Aldous Huxley's sales are stimulated by the provocativeness of his books, their near-obscenity, and then checked at a certain point by the same factor. He is read for being shocking and not read for being too brutal" ("Turns," May 18, 1930).
103. In Chapter 8 of *Eyeless in Gaza*, a character reads his own ruminations—"*Cogito ergo sum* . . . But why not *caco ergo sum*? *Eructo ergo sum*? . . ."—a parody of the "cogito ergo sum" ("I think, therefore I am") of René Descartes. Cabell's *Jurgen: A Comedy of Justice* entertained and scandalized America in 1919. Rascoe's letter of July 9 had discussed the Bell and Proust parallels. In "Turns," July 19, 1936, Paterson makes the observations—about Huxley, Cabell, and shock effects—that she neglected to make in the review of July 9. She argues, among other things, that the rationalist-skeptical view of the universe has to be reductively "materialistic" and ought to be rejected: "The great writers always met [the issue] without equivocation; and their real answer was the literature they produced. Their answer was, in effect: 'You say that's all there is to life? Well, here is something more.'"
104. The article to which Paterson refers has not been identified. Rascoe associated foes of literary modernism with "Reaction" and "literary Ku Klux Klanism" (*We Were Interrupted* [Garden City NY: Doubleday, 1947] 158), but the "Holy Rollers" (the term is a derisive name for Pentecostals, when regarded as primitive religious enthusiasts) may be a different group.
105. The Republican and Democratic conventions of 1936. Paterson attended the latter (WD 229–230).
106. *Hail and Farewell* is a three-volume memoir (1911–1914) by George Moore. "Cat and monkey" is a European fable, present in many versions, including one in the *Fables* of Jean la Fontaine (1621–1695), about a monkey who persuades a cat to pull chestnuts out of the fire and then takes them all for himself.
107. Boswell's* *Life of Samuel Johnson.*
108. Paterson would later change her view of Yeats as a man: "It is very nearly incredible that W. B. Yeats should have found any excuse for Fascism, and consorted with Fascist apologists; but the fact is brought out in Joseph Hone's* biography of the poet (the title of the book is *W. B. Yeats* [1942]). There was the man who wrote with burning intensity of the champions of freedom—of Burke* and Grattan* and John O'Leary* and the "wild geese" who chose exile rather than submission—yet he could rationalize the meanest and most trumpery type of dictatorship when it was before his eyes, loud-mouthed and posturing for forced applause. This is a sad and terrible thing; for Yeats was a very great poet and, most strangely, his genius would not betray itself; not a line of his poetry praises anything base. Surely this

age must have retreated from reason until it has lost not only sight but memory of that faculty" ("Turns," February 21, 1943).

109. Yeats's associate George Moore came from a family with land, money, and political position.
110. A reference to *The Book of the Courtier* (1528), by Baldassare Castiglione (1478–1529), Italian diplomat and humanist. The Percies were a prominent noble family in medieval and early modern England.
111. Nickname for Mary Colum.*

26

Letters, 1940–1949

To Robert Selph Henry*

Robert Selph Henry was an historian and an expert on railroads. He recognized Paterson's importance and cultivated an intellectual correspondence, which continued until Paterson's death.

Undated [received September 30, 1943]

Dear Mr. Henry—

Thanks for the enclosure;[1] as a matter of fact, it does interest me. Because I have seen that question of alleged discrimination in freight rates against Southern industry brought up by Southern politicians rather recently, in terms not very far from secession talk. Of course I could guess that he might be talking in terms of mileage alone (as if that were the only proper measure for freight rates), but I had no information to judge by; so what struck me was the political application of the alleged grievance, which might in possible future circumstances matter a good deal. Therefore I remembered the item. It struck me as a symptom of real sectional disaffection. And even if it were plumb crazy, that also would be a disquieting business. So far as I can observe in reading history, alleged causes and real effects have a screwball relationship. As for a most remarkable instance, the Bostonians threw that tea into the harbor apparently because it was to be sold to them *cheaper* than just the same kind of tea was sold in England! So help me, it really was offered on that cheaper price. But of course the specific *price* was not the basic grievance; and you have to go behind the returns to discover what they were kicking about, or why in effect they declared they would fight rather than pay less for their tea! The lower price was due to a lower tax in the Colonies than in England; and the real issue was the authority for the taxing power; and the *immediate* cause of the ruckus was neither of those things, but the fact that the tea was shipped by a monopoly company and was to be consigned to and distributed by the government-nominated agents of that monopoly *exclusively*, which made the local merchants mad, because theretofore they had at least bought their (wholesale) tea on general even terms, nobody excluded from the buying market.—At this point one pauses to pluck straws from one's hair,[2] muttering vacantly. Or you could look up the freight rates on strait-jackets, in carload lots, from here to there. I think there could be a legitimate differential in shipments to Washington from any point—reduction in charges for volume.

I am sure you will enjoy the Wellington* book, since you have a rightful excuse for reading it anyhow, and it is full of rich stuff. I'm going to read your study of Forrest* with real interest, when it appears.[3] I have no doubt you picked him for particular reasons as a military subject, and I don't know anything about his military ideas or exploits. However, I think the American Civil War must contain in its history the most complete exemplification of all phases of military and civil strategy and relations ever known to mankind; and it also affords the fullest record in detail.

Wellington's deserved fame as a soldier, a very great military intelligence, I think has never been understood or appreciated for several reasons—I venture these tentatively, subject to correction; you may find my opinion all wrong—first, that nobody except Wellington himself had any appreciation of the time element involved in military effects, and even less idea of the relations of the military power to the civil order (the supply line is the physical tie-up); and finally, where Wellington's military genius was best displayed in a sequence of actions related to his general ideas, was in the Peninsular War.[4] And unfortunately for him, a strictly military expert, Sir Charles Napier, having all the technical information at command and nothing else, no savvy what it *meant* in larger terms, wrote a History of the Peninsular War in six or eight volumes, of such stupefying dullness that from the date of its publication no human being has known anything whatever about the Peninsular War.[5] It was buried then and there under six tons of solid rock, as by a landslide. But Aldington,* in *The Duke,* so far as I can judge, has dug out the main outlines of Wellington's performance; they seem to me very clear and comprehensible, and very illuminating.

In the American Civil War, I think the one thing that has never been *understood* is Sherman's* march to the sea. I will take one detail first, not the main issue. Sherman *got there* as a *transportation expert,* an ex-railroad man.[6] If the accounts I have read are correct (perhaps they aren't?) he took his army by a supposedly impossible and certainly difficult route along a great swamp, partly through it—a terrain which would have constituted a natural defence of the region from anyone but a railroad man who knew how to apply his knowledge. He put through a roadbed, corduroy, his army marching on it as it was laid, and it was laid at a rate of five to ten miles a day (maybe faster?) by relay gangs of soldier-workmen moving up constantly by sections from rear to front, just as many men to the gang as could work effectively together like section crews, felling the swamp timber and laying it down for the men and wagons.

But he lived off the country (like Napoleon, as Wellington explains in the memo I mentioned[7]). That is to say he needed no supply line for that one military exploit—and it could not be a method for fighting a whole long war. Therefore the possible *deduction* from his success is gravely dangerous in military theory.

Further, the strictly political implications are most terrible. Southerners felt those implications, but nobody has yet pointed out what they were—why Sherman appeared to Southerners as little short of a devil in person, although the man himself was a high-minded, highly civilized and very decent person, of fine intelligence. Nevertheless, that kind of war is not civilized warfare. It is literally barbaric, by which I do not mean that Sherman committed cruelties—he didn't—I mean it is the method of warfare pursued in the conditions of a barbarian culture. Therefore it is bound to evoke profound horror when it is resorted to in a civilized age or nation; people rightly feel that perhaps nothing will be left of civilization if that is once started. They felt so when Louis XIV ravaged the Palatinate;[8] and even Louis did not quite dare to go on with that kind of warfare. The French were shocked. The fact that Napoleon's method of warfare was barbaric was disguised by the sentiment for liberty which originally sanctioned the French Revolution; had Napoleon been the commander of an army for any long-established government, his performance would have had no disguise, and the world would have been horrified. He was excused on a false plea. But the fact that his method of warfare was barbaric ensured his ultimate defeat, when the available surplus supplies were used up; the loot, in brief. . . . But Sherman's march was historically of dark significance in that it was the first introduction of that kind of warfare in our own particular civilized region. The Southerners were quite right in *feeling* the shock. I wish we may not all learn the unhappy lesson in the same way, in the future.

Nevertheless, nobody understands even Sherman's strategy yet, aside from the political connotations of his reliance on living off the country. Look at the Germans in this war. You'd think they never heard of Sherman, although I believe the American Civil War has been the textbook study of Europe ever since it happened. The Germans adopted the barbarian method of loot to supply their armies, at least as a supplementary source. And then they had no idea how to *fight* in accordance with that condition! Are they crazy—yes. Look at what they did. They put millions of men under arms, which is nonsense anyhow. Then they moved into Russia with a front extending from the Baltic to the Black Sea, which is insane. It could not be supplied[9] *properly* for more than one season (as Wellington will tell you); nor beyond a certain distance, so they were over-extended before they got to Moscow, and simply *stopped* about thirty miles short of Moscow by inertia. That is a fact. They had got to the end of their string. Well, what the hell, if they were going to try Sherman's method of supplying an army by what they could grab (which was Napoleon's method), couldn't the imbeciles see they must also use his strategy or tactics to get the only results it would yield? Why did they not make a drive as Sherman did—from Moscow to the Black Sea, with the fastest moving army they could organize, of whatever size that might be, and rip Russia in two as Sherman ripped the South in two? Had they done that, they could have moved up an army of occupation on the heels of the raid, to hold the section they had sliced out, which would have included the Ukraine. But oh no, they moved their armies and fought as if they had a continuous source of supply for an indefinite time—the incredible chumps.

Really, the human race is rather discouraging. It doesn't even know how to carry out its villainies, let alone its good intentions.

And I don't know why I have afflicted you with all this, except that it is my misfortune to be interested in the general principles of anything and everything; and hardly anybody else is, so I take it out on a few people. I assure you the present effusion calls for no reply. Especially as you have a book to finish last July![10]

Sincerely,
Isabel Paterson

To Ayn Rand

Paterson met the novelist Ayn Rand (1905–1982) in late 1940 or early 1941. They became close friends, and Paterson exerted a strong influence on the formation of Rand's opinions. In late 1943 Rand moved to Hollywood to write screenplays, and lengthy letters passed between Paterson and her. The correspondence grew difficult on both sides. Expressions of deep intellectual respect and warm personal interest alternated with displays of resentment and charges of misunderstanding. Intellectual issues were inconclusively debated. Rand could not understand why and how Paterson could maintain a belief in God; Paterson was irritated by Rand's willingness to pronounce on philosophical and historical issues about which she had read very little. Rand preferred deductions from first principles; Paterson insisted on the claims of history and experience. Paterson was disappointed by prevailing intellectual tendencies, and was sometimes ill and embittered; Rand was feeling the optimism of her first popularity with readers, and was starting to want disciples. In 1948 Paterson visited Rand in California, and the two women had a climactic quarrel, all but ending their relationship.[11]

This edition includes two letters from Paterson to Rand that exemplify the tenor of the correspondence as it changed during the mid-1940s. The first letter has to do with a visit Paterson was invited to pay to former President Herbert Hoover after he read The God of the Machine. *Paterson had always disliked Hoover, opposing his policies for the same reason she opposed those of his successor, Franklin Roosevelt—he was, she thought, trying to make government the engineer of American life. She found little essential distinction between intervention as practiced by Hoover and intervention as practiced by Roosevelt, except that Roosevelt had larger support and was better able to institutionalize himself and his programs. She had little interest in Hoover's view of himself as a defender of private enterprise.*

November 30 [1943]

About Herbert, I guess he is just another of those things. He has a suite at the Waldorf Towers, not living quarters (so far as I saw), not particularly an office, except for two secretaries. Lunch served in one of the rooms, no other guests; he left the door open on the pretext that he was going to smoke! If I didn't mind. So the two girl secretaries could doubtless preserve his virtue if it came to the worst. I am sure he is a mortally timid soul, but I dunno why. I can hardly remember anything he said alas, because he didn't say much in substance. He uttered some distinctly restrained compliments, as that I had "made a contribution." None of them can get beyond that; they should ask you! He talked of my "metaphors," and I said they weren't metaphors but engineering descriptions.[12] He said very well, but I insisted that was an important distinction. —Oh, he looks just like his photos, or if possible a little worse, he is really fat. He ate very little, so I suppose he knows it. He had ordered the lunch; crabmeat salad and coffee was all. I think he really might have axed me if I wanted dessert, though I don't; but I am sure he would never think of that, because he wouldn't want dessert. The lunch was all right, though he has no manners at all, I mean does not see to it that his lady guest is served, and didn't try to keep me [in] countenance, finishing his own lunch in a few minutes, while I with my well-known aplomb and sangfroid went on helping myself and eating placidly. To return to the conversation, I told him in brief but not mincing words how matters stood as between me and the blankety-blank important lunkheads in industry, and what I wished for them; and asked him how they got that way. He told me what they all tell me—they are far too busy to think, they have no time or opportunities to do so. You see how it is. They have what is called a good education, and make money, and have two or six secretaries and meals sent up, and are large able-bodied men, so it is impossible for them to think. Whereas you and I, with the extraordinary advantages we have possessed—being women, with a living to earn as best we can, and no backing, and the dishes to wash, and no first-hand experience in the engineering and industrial field, and with the aforesaid prominent men cutting our throats by endowing every triple-asterisk Pink[13] in the country and supporting the same on all the periodicals—it is obvious that we can very well do the thinking, is it not? Why, certainly. You could think, while you were in that filthy hole, Russia, in daily peril of your life, half starved, cold, alone; you could think when you got here as an immigrant girl in a second hand coat and left-over shoes and had to find a job in a strange country and master the language; you could think while reading a bushel of tripe a day and making a careful synopsis of it to pay the rent; you could think while doing a two year job in one year on benzidrine [sic][14] and a twenty-hour working day. But if you had modern technology in your head and a good job with a big corporation attending board meetings, that would undoubtedly cramp your style. But why the hell do I go over this? You know it. You know how I had every opportunity to think, especially if I didn't at all mind what it cost me; so that is all right; you and I ought to burst into loud sobs over the unfortunate destiny of those men who had no chance at all to think. The next time you meet one and he tells you that, please condole with him for me.

To return again to Mr. Hoover, I must set down the only good thing in his conversation—it was startlingly sensible, and proved that he really did get the idea from the *God of the Machine* and could apply it. He spoke of the "mixed economy," and said that was the one thing that would not, will not, work. Because if you have absolutely despotic control, everything will shortly be ground down to a poor subsistence level, and go on like that; so you can say it works, inasmuch as it just goes on that way. Or with a free economy, that will work, on its intrinsic principles, of itself. But if "controls" are imposed here and there, as the connections are really those of an engineering system, something is bound to break. It may not break at the point where the controls are apparently imposed; the trouble may occur in another spot, as would be the case with any mechanical transmission; but it is bound to break, and cause enormous damage to the whole system.

I did not expect this outburst of commonsense and an engineering statement from the Great Engineer; I can hardly get over it, even with his other remarks to keep me from entertaining wild delusions. He thought I ought to write more, to write articles maybe, rehashing my book in parts; I said where would I get them printed? He couldn't answer that. I told him some specific facts about writing in present conditions, and offered to give him more details if he were not convinced. He didn't seem to want any more.

But the hopeless thing about the meeting was that he kept talking about his own books, as if they were somehow neglected masterpieces, and as if his alleged ideas had been stolen by his enemies, and he himself very badly treated. What could I say? I saw no use in telling him his books are all dreary nothings—no ideas, few facts, no form, no writing. Like Dr. Johnson's* remarks on some bad mutton—it was "ill-fed, ill-dressed, ill-kept and ill-cooked." He was most insistent that Secretary Hull* had borrowed an idea from one of his books and put it into effect at the Moscow conference.[15] What idea? Oh, for a "transition peace." Now for the love of God don't ask me what that means—it means nothing at all except dithering about with a bunch of gangsters in control by force of arms. And it is not even important factually, because what difference will it make, with what else is coming? But that is what Mr. H. believes—I assure you he said so—to be an absolutely original idea. So I guess he feels he ought to be thought to have made a "contribution." Well, excuse me; I do not know what to do when it becomes evident that I am asked to accept such a man as an intellectual equal. I guess that is all. I doubt if I shall ever see him again, and have no wish to.

For entertainment value, I told him my own speculations concerning the mysterious conference now going on. And that brought out one fact I did not know. (I don't quite know what Mr. H. thought of my suggestion; he did say he couldn't see what Stalin would get by it when he could have everything anyway; I said yes but Stalin really doesn't know that, and would want it right now on the barrelhead; Mr. H. also said, but no such agreement would stick; I said no, but what Stalin would get would be the fait accompli, in respect of occupation; and what if the Germans were brought to terms now while the idiots in "conference" were in the bag? Mr. H. seemed to be thinking it over) . . . But this is the point I did not know. I said the first rumors said the meeting place was Cairo, but rumors for the past two or three days said Teheran.[16] And I looked at the globe, and Teheran is close to the Caspian, that is to say, practically on the Russian border. Mr. H. remarked casually, oh, Teheran is actually in Russian occupation, because the British split Persia that way—British military occupation of the South half, Russian military occupation of the North, which includes Teheran!

If that is so, gosh all hemlock, we can only wait and see. But three weeks—everyone is now figuring that that is a long time. In Teheran?

This letter will be following you to Burbank like a bloodhound, maybe on the very same train; and I must not write more than eighty pages, should I?

This afternoon that other man from Kuhn, Loeb[17] came in for a chat. He isn't much to look at, quite small and thin; but honest, he did talk sense. He was an engineer by profession, practiced it for years, railroad man (construction and maintenance and operation); is now an economist, says it is a stupid word but one has to be called something in such a job. As an engineer he said that on beginning to read the G. of M. he took it at first to be metaphor, then began to ask, as he went along, is it? isn't it description of fact? Finally on finishing and looking over it, certified that it really is engineering. I thanked him for that, and meant it. I showed him your letter to Earle Balch.* He said he wouldn't be able to write like that, but he agreed with you.[18] That was handsome. He says he doesn't know what ails those prominent men either.

John came over for supper last night, press night.[19] I told him my theory, for fun; and incidentally, I find he is becoming better able to see what's what—there is a slow continual improvement. He told me he was going to give his class in Journalism the G. of M. as an assignment to review. He said he had quoted to them (my remark): "Free milk for one group means forced labor for another," and they blinked noticeably. (*I* said *slave* labor.)

Maybe that is enough about Me. For a minute or two.

I seen your book in Marks bookstore window on Madison Ave., while walking back from lunch. It remains in the Grand Central stores, in prominent position. It came in on Best Seller list from Providence, R. I., which is a new town isn't it? However, I expect the biggest sales will occur next year, by a fairly steady climb—it has a long-pull power in it. I think its whole history will be a most interesting performance. I think probably some of your big business admirers will want the picture[20] to tie up specifically to architecture and the supposed post-war building program; there is no harm in their wish and their backing is a good thing; but what amuses me, I am sure the story, the book, the idea, the potential picture, is going to over-ride everything and get itself made in its own terms. Of course it will not be perfect, it will probably drive you crazy in process, but I do mean that its real meaning will nevertheless come through, against hell and high water. The darned thing positively has its own power. So fare you well, my bonny young girl, we're bound for the Rio Grande.[21]

Pat

To Robert Selph Henry

Undated [received January 12, 1944]

Dear Mr. Henry—

You haven't told me (I really was enquiring tactfully), are you back on the Army list with this new phase of the railroad business?[22] I would as lief address anyone correctly as not, other things being equal—I mean I have no passion for inaccuracy. But I am vastly ignorant of military etiquette anyhow. Some years ago a West Point cadet wrote me sight unseen actually inviting me to a hop; I still treasure the compliment, but I had to explain to him that I was retired or something. He then gave me a brief exposition of my status as indicated by what I had said, and it left me dizzy with the distinctions he made. I went and looked you up in *Who's Who*, which I never do; so I still don't know—that's what *Who's Who* does for me! You see, they send me a long list of questions, to which in my case all the answers are No, None, Never Heard of It, Certainly Not (the questions are schooling, college, education, degrees, honors, etc.) Honorifics are always baffling, because they are necessarily arbitrary; if there is a positive rule and precedence, as with English titles, one can grasp it easily; but in a republic it is necessarily difficult. As the Romans, who had real dignity, nevertheless would accept such names as Red-head and Nosey and Little Boots, quite as a matter of course.[23] And I remember once hearing of an Englishman (many years ago) getting snooty about all the Americans with military titles; how is it, he asked, that so many American men are called Colonel; in England, etc., etc. . . . He got his answer; an American replied urbanely: "Yes, I suppose it is different; in the United States those men are called Colonels because they fought in a war, as Colonels."

I should have remarked about Wellington,* I never noticed the way in which the battles were actually fought, because military technique escapes me. But did you read, in the addenda,[24] Wellington's memo. on Napoleon's campaign in Russia? And I could understand Wellington's general conduct of an army, how he never allowed the supply lines from England to be interrupted, and would not accept (from Portugal) more regiments than he could be sure of supplying, or men he could not be sure would be properly trained, so they'd be reliable in battle. His analysis of the composition of the armies of Napoleon, the kind of men the system of conscription brought in, and the counter-effect of that and the supply system of Napoleon (or lack of supply) struck me as wonderfully acute, penetrating. His summary of what happened in the Moscow campaign is masterly; I am not sure if his supposition is correct that an army of such size, in that territory, really could have been supplied if supplies had been paid for—I should doubt that the area had enough transport facilities and available goods for that army. I seem to remember that Napoleon started with 400,000 men. I don't know what the population of Moscow was, but it would give a clue to the transport facilities, which necessarily supplied the city. But there is a catch in the whole business of Napoleon's war-making, which Wellington saw all right—*if* Napoleon had paid his armies and paid for supplies, by regular methods—that is, out of the tax revenues of France—armies of that size could never have been put in the field at all. The country could not have sustained them. Then since such armies were paid out of tribute money from conquered countries and subsisted by requisitions, or loot as Wellington succinctly said, they were good only for a season's campaign, and were always in process of disintegration through demoralization. It is an inescapable equation, and applies today. The kind of armies that are now raised, in imitation of Napoleon, must either destroy their own country by depletion, because their pay and subsistence comes to far more than any country can yield out of *surplus production*; or they must disintegrate for lack of support. In the long run, obviously, both processes may occur; the country becomes exhausted and then the army crumbles. That will probably be the course of events in Germany, in this war as in the last war. But it really happened in Russia too; they would surely have crumbled before now, as they are fighting only on American supplies at present, while Germany is obviously crumbling, not even able to make a good defensive stand.

I suggest, that though battles may be won, *wars are not won, they are lost.*

I wish someone would write an article on the *kind* of war that is now going on throughout the world. To be candid, I could do it, because what I mean is not a matter of military technique at all; but it would be no use for a woman to write such an article. What I mean is that this is what Hoffman Nickerson* calls unlimited war—though he did not know why sometimes there is limited war and sometimes unlimited war. In limited war, civilians are not supposed to be a military objective; civilian life and property is respected. All the wars of the nineteenth century were limited war, but there were indications, manifestations, of what was coming, as in the last year of the American Civil War. All the way back through history the two kinds of war can be distinguished. The Romans were the first, so far as I can recall now without making special research, to observe the rules of limited war generally; but on occasion, when they held that a truce had been broken treacherously or anything of that sort, they would wipe out a city or a tribe in reprisal. Before Rome, you can see in Homer, in the Bible, in Herodotus, apparently there was no *idea* of limiting warfare—I put this tentatively. Then Christian ethics declared that warfare should be limited; the rule was not always observed, but it had a considerable effect. I think the subject is of historic interest. Nickerson noted the *fact*, but he associates it only with what he calls "mass armies;" he does not perceive that the method of warfare can be and was the same with much smaller armies, in given conditions. The cause is really in the political organization, and the nature of the political organization derives from certain antecedent ideas, moral, philosophical, religious. Hence "unlimited warfare" returned in the Wars of Religion; both sides would wipe out populations, as in the massacres of the Vaudois and Cromwell's* massacres in Ireland;[25] because certain fundamental concepts were no longer agreed upon.

I'm sorry—all this because I started to ask you a question of etiquette! But I wanted to mention one other thing; last week I met the manager of the Los Angeles Chamber of Commerce, Mr. Leonard Read,* and I wish you might become acquainted with him for many reasons, if you are ever out there. Or if he is in Washington. He struck me as a person of unusual natural intelligence and with a very clear view of contemporary issues; but much more than that, I think he is going to accomplish something. I thought of you while talking to him because he mentioned an effort he was making to get business men to study and understand the question of freight rates,[26] get them to think sensibly on the subject. But it wasn't only that—I can't help thinking that it would be a good thing if the sensible and genuinely informed men are in communication, it may help a little—they are going to have a tough, up-hill job in the future. He did impress me as a really exceptional individual, and I am not often impressed in that way, unfortunately.

Sincerely,
Isabel Paterson

To Ayn Rand

Monday July 30 [1945]

Dear Ayn—

I think the book is still going up; though it went back to 13 and then 12 in the past two numbers, I think it goes up to 14 again a week from Sunday—so that's all right.[27] I wouldn't guarantee this, but should sa[y] it has a good chance of reaching the very top—fifty-fifty chance at least. Let's hope so. I sent you those numbers because they were a high mark and with you being out in the country and maybe not subscribing, and a delivery strike here—I did not know whether you'd see them otherwise or not, and did not want you to miss them. Well, yes, I did tell you so, and I remember it made you pretty mad! . . . I see your book in the bookstore windows every day. Sometimes I thought you might have been more tactful complaining to *me* that you would not be satisfied with less than a hundred thousand, seeing that my own book could not sell at all; much like a millionaire orating to a tramp about crumpled rose-leaves, which is not the best audience or occasion for such a grievance. After all, it appears to me that one could be a copper-riveted individualist without being a solipsist. You can look that one up in your philosophy books. But your book sold itself; I'm sorry to say I was not able to do anything for it; and there it is.[28] You're entitled to all the satisfaction you get out of it. I wouldn't even undertake to say exactly what the sale means, beyond the obvious fact that you have a real fiction talent which will always sell, and which is what I judge by in saying a book will sell; it's a strictly professional judgment. I hope it won't be too long before you will have time to get at the next novel, which will also be a big best seller; I'll predict that now. Of course, what I say above doesn't mean that I attach no importance to the sale in respect of the ideas—I think your work is immensely important on that score—but I do not know now if that has anything to do with the large sale at present.

It doesn't seem to be much use saying anything—we are not talking about the same thing. Certainly you are under no obligation to write letters. What I found almost incredible was that you wrote me a long letter of your own accord, nominally asking my advice about your buying a house—I know one doesn't really ask advice in such cases, it is rather a manner of speaking—I did answer it, and you never acknowledged it. I think if you speak to someone who answers you might make a sign that you heard. A person is not an object or lamp post, to be regarded as always "there" for your convenience and having no other existence. Then you telephoned me, in July, and said would I come to visit you—quite an undertaking these days—and said you would write next day, though you had not acknowledged my last two letters, and I DID NOT EVEN HAVE YOUR ADDRESS. But then you did not write; and phoned again *in the middle of September*, to ask if I was coming out! In the circumstances, I cannot imagine what you actually could have expected. And for you to tell me you find it difficult to write letters does not seem relevant to me. You said you did not get my second letter, I presume it went to your old address, because you had not given me the new one nor told me when you moved; so then you asked *me* to try to trace it. Why? You might conceivably have taken the trouble to enquire for it yourself if you wanted it, but was I to go out there and look for it? It is that sort of thing I do not understand. I repeat, if you find it disagreeable to write letters, then don't; but that is hardly the point when you actually do write one which calls for an answer and then ignore the answer, or when you say specifically you are writing next day, and let it go for six weeks, though you were asking me to take the trouble to go all the way to the Coast. I might have done so, but hardly in the given case, when you offer an invitation in such terms.

That is not a question of misinterpreting what you say in a letter. It is a course of action, which I am unable to understand—especially as you don't seem to see it yet. What you wrote afterward amounted to, "I am afraid you must be angry, but it is very hard for me to write letters; I have to take so much trouble over them;" but nothing at all about the occasion, the attitude—that is what I mean by the ungenerous heart. It is someone saying: "But you know I think just as much of you as ever, I think of you just the same."[29] My answer is, "Probably so, but it isn't very much; and I shall not be just the same." However, I suppose this is really no use.

Lonsdale* must have a lot of sense—I am sure what he said is true; you will get your own way and make an impression on the whole movie business. I would not say it is quite a waste of your talent, unless on inferior stuff, or unless you never saved out any time to write your next novel—in the latter case it would be tragic. But you don't have to be submerged; and I think most likely it was useful for you to take that contract this time. May even have helped put over the book in the best seller list, to some extent; which is important. I mean you becoming a figure in Hollywood, as I may say I have heard from other sources is the case.

Let me say emphatically, I think it might be worth while for you to get back to New York for a visit this year. Leonard Read* is hoping you will. I think you might meet a few people here perhaps, useful for your own purposes—and fortunately you can make a real impression on them, with your beauty and charm and success—no, never mind protesting, I speak impartially enough, and other people say the same. You might just as well accept it and accept the benefit of it. If I had it I would. It might be even more fun to find yourself a beauty at your age than at eighteen, when one hasn't sense enough to appreciate it. You had better come and make an impression on a few people Read might dig up, help him in telling these Godforsaken big businessmen what they are doing.... By the way, you see England is now completely sunk. That's the finish. I suppose you did see that news, though in fact you are right not to annoy yourself with reading the papers regularly. It *is* "monstrous."[30] And I see hardly anyone, because I do not propose to discuss cannibalism as a mere difference of opinion. . . . I think that within about three years England will be under a Terror. (If not invaded—by German troops under Russian command.) This may be too extreme as a prediction, but I think it a possibility, even a high probability.... Well, they all do get what they ask for. Fly head-on into the Empire State Building with a B-29.[31]

When I began to read the philosophers, rather casually, mostly in scraps, they struck me as a bit weird too. But I suppose, to be fair to them, one must envisage the whole problem of systematic thinking as from scratch—for humanity to do it at all, the whole apparatus has to be devised, and the long process of discovering or constructing logic, and arriving at principles—to begin with, even the concept of a principle was an amazing feat—how would you *begin*? You have to remember that. By temperament I heartily dislike Plato; he is the very father of all "intellectual" Communists and Planners;[32] but I suppose it is necessary to put aside that emotion and consider how he came to be, in the history of humanity.

The "frightening kind of rationality" you find in the philosophers is precisely your own kind.[33] When they had strung some words together in the form of a syllogism or other logical construction, they thought that had to be so—without asking if the facts which constitute the necessary premises are so. All men are mortal; Socrates is a man; therefore Socrates is mortal. That is a good syllogism, but its truth depends on the premises being true—that men are mortal, that Socrates is a man. Logic is an instrument for dealing with whatever you can get into its measure. For after all, what *is* a man? The syllogism cannot tell you. It assumes him, simply as being something that can be put into a class; that's all.

Plato reports Socrates as saying that the community, the City, had a right to take his life, even unjustly, because the City was the same as his parents. There is the assumption first that parents actually have a right to take the life of their child for no cause, and second that the collective is the same thing as a natural parent. Neither true.

The main error of the philosophers generally was their inability to really perceive the creative element in men. Because it won't go into any of their systems. (Plato consciously ruled it out of his Ideal State, as he had to, for it was a state made by measure and therefore a slave state).

But you, extraordinarily, assume that "if God exists, man is a slave".[34] (I don't know if you know that was Bakunin's* statement too.)

Why? Your assumption there is actually that a creative mind necessarily makes a slave of any person less creative who also happens to exist. Does it? If that is so, you have no proper grievance against your reviewer (Guerard), who said that a world of Roarks was Fascism (I do not recall the exact wording, but that was his meaning).[35]

I believe your specific argument is that if God exists, he *can* arbitrarily interfere with what you are doing.

Well, so can I. I could even kill you. Does that make you a slave? Or, for the matter of that, a tile could fall from a roof by chance and kill you! Does that make you a slave? If it does, do you propose to deny the existence of the material universe, for your thesis?

What does a creative mind do? Enslave others?—Or does it not, by its very nature, actually enlarge their freedom, so far as they care to avail themselves of it?

Is the creative, per se, and by its own nature, oppressive?

In lesser matters, you talk a lot of "reason," but frequently don't use it, because you make assumptions that are not valid. For example, you assume that the order of events or inventions in *time* is somehow an order of value or merit. You have[36] been annoyed, because I am not interested in movies and don't like the radio, when apparently you think I ought to because they are "modern." Essentially, intrinsically, the radio is a step backward from print as a means of communication, because it spans only space and not time—the great advance was made when a medium was found which spanned both space and time, and that is the *written* language. But you don't see that. The written language also is the highest instrument of thought because a printed page can be consulted by the individual whenever he chooses, kept available, checked and compared; it permits reflection. No *auditory* gadget can ever be an advance on that, for those intrinsic reasons. Therefore essentially the radio is a step back. There is no more sense in insisting the new must be better than the old, than in believing the old must be better than the new. (Including architecture).[37]

In your philosophical assumptions you ignore the fact about this country—even when it was founded, it was actually less "modern" than the contemporary European fashion in thought. It was really a counter-revolution against the political ideas drawn from the "scientific" philosophy that began with the Renaissance, the atheistic philosophy, which France (later) followed to ruin.

A thing is neither true nor false because it is old, or because it is "new." But you have adopted the "humanistic," "scientific," theanthropic philosophy. It will work out as it did work out—in what we have seen happening. It has to.

However, perhaps the human race had better destroy itself, judging by its present performance. I can't say I care any more. The present exhibition is too revolting; it has become infinitely wearisome, by its very atrocity. I do not know how to account for anyone or anything ever having appeared different. That is most puzzling, but I give it up. One hears no sense anywhere. I don't know whether these conditions can be worse for you or for me, as I seem to remember a sane world in contrast, and you only hoped for one. But if you can enjoy life at all, having a chance now to do your work, I hope you will; and I don't say that you won't accomplish a great deal, perhaps make a difference, in restoring sanity—if you don't persist in that one fundamental error. Well, if you do, I can't help it . . . You went through all this horror before. I hope it really isn't quite so bad for you this time, since you can do your work, and then you have someone—you have Frank.[38] It is nice of him to remember me. Believe me, I cannot wish you anything but good, even when I think perhaps the human race had better be wiped out, on its own showing. I have to recognize in my acquaintance a few on whom, shall I say, I have no right to make such a judgment. . . . Did you meet Muriel Welles?[39] She is going to England for a year. I tell her she'll see there what this thing means. She doesn't want to be a slave. I think it is all right for her to go, because she had it in mind for a long time (to go to Oxford for a year), and I am in favor of anyone doing what they decide to do for their own reasons.

If you don't get *[Herald Tribune] "Books"* to see the best seller list, let me know and I will send you the later ones. . . . In spite of my frame of mind, I'd like to read your next novel, *The Strike*.[40] I really think it would be sort of high explosive, intellectually and emotionally, a historic event. I wish you were writing it. Am sorry to say I think you will, for the time being, be disappointed in the visible results and sales of the non-fiction book when it appears,[41] though I do not take that as a measure of its value or effect; I think it needs to be written. But it will not have much sale, most likely. You must be prepared for that. Whereas the novel will sell furiously. Also it will be a good novel. You will be really famous. It will be amusing then to think you used to come over and help check proof. By the way, Mildred often asks about you.[42] But that is not because you are famous. Other people will remember for that reason. . . . Linda[43] says you got some more swell clothes and look marvellous.

Pat

To Robert Selph Henry

Undated [received September 12, 1945]

Dear Colonel Henry—

Now I do hope you will come to New York before the end of September, because Ayn Rand is here and will be for the rest of the month. I want you to meet her—I think it's rather important for her to meet a few people like you (if there are any). And I say flatly *she* is *very* important. If you can make it at all, save out enough time to talk to her. Incidentally, you'll like her.

If I wanted to be mean, I'd say you might as well take the time off from railroading; a day off, at least—what's the difference, one wreck more or less in the present circumstances? She was delayed getting here by two different wrecks on trains just ahead!

However, as you know, I am the most amiable person in the world, so I never say these things. Like Warren Hastings, I stand astonished at my own moderation.[44] I'll be seeing you in Outer Mongolia; and please give my regards to Senator Hickenlooper.[45]

Sincerely,
Isabel Paterson

To Robert Selph Henry

With this letter Paterson enclosed a newspaper column satirizing a radio program sponsored by the du Pont company in its "Cavalcade of America" series. The program told the story of a "Middle European" who journeyed to America and found that communist propaganda had misrepresented it. The places he saw were lovely, the people he met were lovely, and he decided to stay. One of du Pont's chief executives was the libertarian Jasper Crane, about whom Paterson comments on pages 85–89,* above.

Undated [received September 6, 1946]

Here's a fair exchange for the clipping you sent me.[46] Can you guess who was responsible for this radio program? I know—it was my friend Mr. Crane—he told me that half-witted idea himself. His notion then was to get someone to write it as a novel! (Doubtless you are aware that is how novels are written; some half-wit has what he believes to be an idea, and imparts it to a novelist, a novelist being a person who has no ideas of his own for novels but gets them from a Du Pont. Isn't it so?) I was so embarrassed by the juvenile absurdity of the notion that I didn't know what to say, though I really tried to explain to Mr. Crane that novels are not written exactly that way; but I guess he didn't believe me.

So he must have got some yes-man to dish it up for him in a radio script—or could he have composed it all himself?

And he gets the raspberry from the capitalist press his advertising supports.

Looks to me as if my own constructive program for lynching our Big Business Men as destroyers of capitalism and enemies of free enterprise is in a fair way to succeed in the not too distant future. I am working on it and will let you know from time to time how it progresses. You can keep your other eye on the Grand Canyon.[47] May I count on your good wishes?

IMP

To Burton Rascoe

Undated [1947]

Dear Burton—

Of course I'll be there; thanks. Miss King wrote a very kind letter, which I got along with yours.

Also I hope to snitch a bit of your remarks on Flynn et al, if I can get it by. Flynn does seem to have more brains, by nature, than his baboons—i. e., candidates.[48]

I want to see *Plain Talk*, for your reviews. Wish Levine*[49] would get you to edit the magazine; he could make it (that is, you could) into an important and paying magazine. I think he's a good journalist of his kind, but shouldn't suppose he has any specific talent as an editor—any more than I have, for instance. Only I know I haven't, and he might fancy himself—I should mention, though, that I like him, so I don't want to depreciate him, and say this only to you. Yes, you do remember correctly what I once mentioned about Hearst.*[50] I wish I had always been as explicit, for I know now that sometimes I just didn't actually explain my position at all. For instance, about that young man John what's his name;[51] it wasn't that I couldn't "get on with him"; practically, we just paid no attention to each other: he didn't seem interested in anything about the place, or to want to take any part; so we had scarcely any attempt at communication. But what I specifically thought was not right in the situation, a mistake, was the government arrangement by which he came there—the beginning of all that has been going on since. Someone getting a government pension or allowance to "learn" a job—a vicious absurdity. One learns to do anything only by taking it on as a real job, positive work which must be done and is done for a living wage; that is the necessary connection. I just thought it was all sort of dumb and wrong. There *wasn't* any job for him there; and if there had been and he had had the ability to do it, the only proper thing would have been to hire him, and for him to be paid by the outfit he worked for. I think he was to "learn to write" or something! By osmosis, maybe? I do not remember or never did know just how come he was wished on you, and he did strike me as rather a natural no-good of a neutral, inert kind; but didn't give him much thought beyond that, and getting bored with the sight of him. But specifically, I mean, the root of my attitude was a political principle!

Be seeing you,
Pat

Notes

1. On September 27, 1943, Henry had sent Paterson a "pamphlet" he had written about railroad freight rates.
2. A probable reference to Ophelia in Act 4, Scene 5 of Shakespeare's *Hamlet*. Compare Paterson's reference to herself at the start of her June 11, 1933, column: "Ophelia will now stick a few more straws in her hair and go through her weekly mad scene."
3. In 1944, Henry published a military biography of Nathan Bedford Forrest, noted for his strategy of mobile warfare. The Wellington book is Richard Aldington's biography, *The Duke* (1943), which Paterson had recommended to Henry in a letter received on September 24, 1943. *The Duke* was a book that Paterson had a hard time liking in detail. When Aldington writes that Wellington was so busy being a general that "for three years he never slept out of his clothes" (169), Paterson puts in the margin, "Don't believe it." When Aldington speaks of Napoleon's "marvelous intellect" and suggests that "his plans and projects were more grandiose than ever" (246), Paterson writes, "A marvelous intellect doesn't make 'grandiose plans and projects.' Small minds do that." When Aldington remarks that "the English cut off King Charles I's head for making a collection of pictures and projecting a palace by Inigo Jones" (283), Paterson writes, "This smarty style is very tiresome."
4. The long series of conflicts (1807–1814) between Napoleon and his opponents over possession of the Iberian peninsula.
5. An inaccurate reference to *History of the War in the Peninsula* (1828–1840, often published in three volumes), by Major General Sir William Francis Patrick Napier (1785–1860), brother of the more famous Sir Charles Napier (1782–1853), British commander in chief in India and also a writer.
6. Before the Civil War, Sherman had been vice president of a railroad in California.
7. A memorandum, included in Aldington's book, that was mentioned by Paterson in her letter to Henry, received September 24, 1943.

8. During the War of the Grand Alliance (1688–1797), Louis XIV of France devastated southwestern Germany, burning many towns and villages.
9. *Crossed out:* for.
10. Henry had written Paterson (September 27, 1943) that the deadline for his book on Forrest had been July 1943, but he now hoped to get it done "this fall."
11. The story of the Paterson-Rand relationship is told at length in WD 218–22, 287–89, 302–314, 334–35, 351, 357–59. Rand's side of the correspondence has been published in *Letters of Ayn Rand*, edited by Michael S. Berliner (New York: Dutton, 1995) 173–218.
12. Paterson was plagued with suggestions, by both sympathetic and unsympathetic readers, that when GM speaks of "circuits" and "structures" and so forth, it is using metaphors instead of descriptions, general symbols instead of specific images.
13. A series of asterisks was often used by newspapers to replace an unprintable word. A Pink is a near-communist.
14. To support herself, Rand had read and reported on material that might be used for movies. To meet the publisher's deadline, she had worked long hours during her year-long completion of *The Fountainhead*. Several times in the correspondence, Paterson mentions Rand's use of benzedrine (Paterson to Rand, January 19, 1944 ["Stop taking that benzedrine, you idiot. I don't care what excuse you have—stop it"]; March 7, 1944 [Rand is "get[ting] over taking the benzedrine"]; June 7, 1944 ["If you take any more of that benzedrine I will come out there [to California] in person and spank you to a blister"]).
15. The Moscow Conference of Foreign Ministers (October–November 1943).
16. The Cairo Conference took place on November 23–26, 1943, among Churchill, Roosevelt, and Chiang Kai-Shek. The Teheran Conference took place on November 28–December 1, 1943, among Churchill, Roosevelt, and Stalin.
17. A prominent investment bank.
18. On November 28, 1943, Rand had written to Balch, publisher of GM, encouraging him to advertise the book and calling it "the greatest book written in the last three hundred years" (*Letters of Ayn Rand*, 101–104).
19. Press night was the night when *Herald Tribune "Books"* was printed, and Paterson stayed in the office to deal with proofreading and last-minute problems (see note 42, below). At such times she and her guests often resorted to the *Herald Tribune* cafeteria (Muriel Hall, email to Stephen Cox, October 31, 2000). John is John Chamberlain,* who later reprinted three sections from GM in a textbook, *Living, Reading and Thinking: 56 Essays in Exposition*, ed. John Chamberlain, Benfield Pressey, and Reginald E. Watters (New York: Scribner's, 1948).
20. The film version of *The Fountainhead* (1949), for which Rand wrote the script.
21. Paterson quotes an old sea shanty about sailing to Rio Grande do Sul, in a part of Brazil associated with gold.
22. Henry had been a field artillery captain in World War I; later he became a lieutenant colonel in the Army Reserve. The new phase is doubtless the demanding task of operating railroads during wartime.

23. "Rufus," the name of many important Romans, means "Ruddy" or "Redhead"; "Naso" in Publius Ovidius Naso (Ovid) means "Nose"; Caligula means "Little Boots."
24. In Richard Aldington's* *The Duke* (see notes 3 and 7, above).
25. In 1655 and other times, French-speaking Catholics massacred the Vaudois, a sect of Protestants; in 1649, Cromwell's Protestant troops massacred many Catholics in Ireland.
26. Freight rates were regulated by the government.
27. "The book" is Rand's breakthrough novel *The Fountainhead* (1943). "Numbers" are issues of *Herald Tribune "Books,"* which published a weekly list of best sellers.
28. Paterson is being modest. By this time she had noticed *The Fountainhead* nine times in her nationally circulated column in *Herald Tribune "Books"* (WD 311–12, 401n49). The novel had not been a favorite of reviewers, and Paterson's comments undoubtedly helped it become a best seller.
29. On July 26, 1945 (*Letters of Ayn Rand* 176–80), Rand had made similar remarks. She had also reported (see below) that Frederick Lonsdale had complimented *The Fountainhead* and predicted success for Rand in Hollywood.
30. Britain had just elected a socialist government. In her letter of July 26, 1945 (*Letters of Ayn Rand* 179), Rand had said that she found current editorial opinion "monstrous."
31. On July 28, 1945, an Army Air Force B-25 (not a B-29) crashed into the Empire State Building. The plane had been lost in the fog.
32. A reference especially to Plato's *Republic*, with its utopia of philosopher kings.
33. In her letter of July 26, 1945 (*Letters of Ayn Rand* 179), Rand said that she had been reading ancient philosophers and a history of philosophy and referred to "a frightening kind of rationality about the reasons for the mistakes they made."
34. Paterson is quoting or paraphrasing a letter from Rand that may no longer be extant. In her reply (August 4, 1945 [*Letters of Ayn Rand* 183]), Rand says, "You state my assumption as 'If God exists, man is a slave.'" She then argues that "an omnipotent being, by definition, is a totalitarian dictator. Ah, but he won't use his power? Never mind. He *has* it" (184). In her present letter (July 30, 1945), Paterson probably alludes to Michael [sic] Bakunin, *God and the State* (various printings, 1890– , reprinted Freeport NY: Books for Libraries Press, 1971) 22: "If God is, man is a slave."
35. Albert Guerard (1914–2000), American novelist and writer on literary subjects, then on the faculty of Harvard, reviewed *The Fountainhead* in the *Herald Tribune* (May 30, 1945). On the evidence of Rand's next letter to Paterson (August 4, 1945 [*Letters of Ayn Rand* 183]), Paterson's reference to Howard Roark, hero of *The Fountainhead*, infuriated the novel's author.
36. *Crossed out:* told me.
37. *The Fountainhead* glorifies avant-garde architecture and satirizes period-revival styles such as the neoclassical. Rand responded (August 4, 1945, *Letters of Ayn Rand* 180–82) to Paterson's critique of her views about newness and oldness by saying, correctly, that those were not her views.
38. Frank O'Connor (1897–1979) was Rand's husband. As a young woman, Rand suffered great hardship in Bolshevik Russia; later, she had great difficulty establishing herself as an author in America.

39. The future Muriel Hall.* Paterson used her influence with former Canadian Premier R. B. Bennett (see note 8, page 91, above) to help Muriel attend Oxford for postgraduate work.
40. Rand's original name for the novel that became *Atlas Shrugged* (1957).
41. In her letter of July 26, 1945 (*Letters of Ayn Rand* 179), Rand had discussed the difficulties of writing a book that she began in 1943, *The Moral Basis of Individualism*. The book was never published.
42. It was part of Paterson's job to spend one night a week checking proofs of *Herald Tribune "Books,"* periodically going down to the composing room to work with the printers. Friends formed the custom of dropping in to "help" her (see note 19, above). How much work they actually did isn't certain; they were there to converse, and to listen to Paterson's conversation. Mildred Andrews Wall worked in the office of *Herald Tribune "Books."* She was one of Paterson's enduring friends.
43. Perhaps Linda Lynneberg, a friend of Rand (Rand, *Letters of Ayn Rand* 185, 187, 364).
44. Warren Hastings (1732–1818) was the British governor-general of Bengal and the subject of a seven-year trial for corruption, after which he was acquitted. Hastings is often thought to have made the remark in question, but it was Robert Clive (1725–1774), his predecessor in India, who said, "I stand astonished at my own moderation" about taking money.
45. Bourke Hickenlooper (1896–1971) was a Republican senator from Iowa (1945–1969). Henry's office was in Washington, DC, in proximity to senators with funny names.
46. The clipping that Henry sent has not been identified. With this letter Paterson enclosed a clipping of John Crosby's* column, "Radio in Review," *New York Herald Tribune*, September 2, 1946—a hostile review of the "Cavalcade of America" episode.
47. In a letter to Henry, received on August 28, 1946, Paterson had referred to the Grand Canyon as "an excellent place to prospect just now. One might almost find a spot of refuge in it; or if not, I can't think of anywhere else."
48. Miss King and her invitation remain unidentified, as do Rascoe's remarks on Flynn. Flynn is Edward J. Flynn (1891–1953), Democratic Party boss of the Bronx and nationally prominent Democratic politician; author of a memoir, *You're the Boss* (1947). Paterson discusses that book in "Turns," September 21, 1947, suggesting that political bosses are indebted to reformers for increasing the size of government and therefore the amount of "gravy" that the bosses can enjoy "lapping up."
49. Isaac Don Levine, editor of the anti-communist journal *Plain Talk*.
50. Conceivably this refers to a passage on page 84 of Rascoe's memoir of the 1920s, *We Were Interrupted* (Garden City NY: Doubleday, 1947), concerning a Hearst editor's customary appearance in formal dress.
51. Rascoe's *We Were Interrupted* tells the story of John Armstrong, an eccentric war veteran funded by the government to learn a trade, which turned out to be learning to write for the *New York Tribune*, Rascoe's employer and Paterson's. Rascoe said that "Armstrong and Isabel Paterson, for some reason I never bothered to learn, didn't get along at all; and for about eight months they shared the outer office without ever speaking. They would glare at each other when Armstrong came in and that was all" (137–38).

27

Letters, 1950 and After

To Muriel Hall*

Undated [January 14, 1950]

Dear Muriel—

My goodness, it is curious to see you now begin to look for those books *I* looked for years ago—which do not exist! But I should think it rather a hopeful sign. A few people realize what is missing; when that happens, presently the knowledge will be supplied. Of course I found bits and scraps of information to put together slowly; but it is a fact that I found least of what I was after in formal history.

And *God of the Machine* should have been written in six or ten volumes but I had no time and now never shall have energy to do it over. In that scope, the development of Roman, English and finally American representative assemblies for government (senates, parliaments) should have been examined and explained successively in their principles and operation, with a few sideglances at such variations as the Italian city states, and the reason why the French Revolutionary Assembly (by the way it was elected and constituted) could not possibly function for free government and was bound to lead to a despotism, as it did with Napoleon.

The mutations of the British Parliamentary system (including the Lords) would of course be immensely illuminating if properly understood. I see the *principles* and the major *elements* of its operation, but am extremely short of specific information about its particular history, chronologically; and no book I ever saw supplies that. I mean, such books will doubtless give you successive actions of Parliament to a certain extent, but not the vital information of what lay behind the actions and made them effective. And sometimes the actions don't make sense, are not intelligible, for want of that other information. For example, Henry VIII *seems* to have had despotic power over his

Parliament. Had he really? No. He could terrorize it to some extent by threats or punishment of individual members, but the *real* power was in the Parliament, just the same. The historic fact which attests that is the necessity he was under of getting Parliament to settle the succession and make him Head of the Church. He could do neither himself. But what was the nature of that power of Parliament? It is not a matter of words, but of physical realities, when it exists at all. Well, it was in the direct relations of the members to the land and the money (commerce) of England. They *did* represent those forces. In that case, how did Henry even have the partial power to terrorize anybody? Same as in Rome at the end of the Republic, *his* power was by temporary purchase—that is, by the distribution of confiscated property, which gave him an unofficial party while he lived; but then you see, once the property (Church lands) was finally all handed over to purchase support, and the title confirmed to the new owners by a little time and general consolidation of the ranks of new owners with the old lay landowners, that terroristic power of the Crown naturally ceased and the Parliament was just that much stronger by the property acquisitions, against the Crown. Hence the Stuarts could not do what the Tudors did, and when they tried, they learned it dearly. (Elizabeth still held the balance, because of the fear of reverting to a Catholic regime which would have meant turning the tables on the Protestant confiscators; that gave Elizabeth a solid party. 1588 really ended that; the defeat of the Armada).[1]

The truth is therefore that since the Reformation in England the power of Parliament has been absolute in principle, and has even been asserted as such: "Parliament can do anything." Nobody could think of any principle or theory of limitation. When you happen to read of the execution of Sir Thomas More* no doubt you get a vague impression that the King ordered his head chopped off, for opposing the power of the Crown. In fact, *Parliament* tried and condemned and executed him, for refusing to take a particular oath acknowledging those absolute powers of Parliament—especially the power of Parliament to *make* the King head of the church! Certainly it was the King who wanted to be head of the church, wanted the succession settled in a certain line, wanted More brought to book, and sicked Parliament on; but my point is, he could not do those things himself, and in getting them done by the authority of Parliament, he inescapably acknowledged and confirmed that power in Parliament. It *was* there. In 1688, just a hundred years after the Armada, it could no longer be terrorized at all by a king; it could make and unmake kings without even a drop of bloodshed.[2] But even then it was not *in fact* a *despotic* power of that body (only in theory), because in fact the physical power was in the forces the members represented, the land and commerce, and their material attachment was to the forces, the interests, not to the parliamentary body as such. That is no longer true in England; the members of parliament in the main have now *no interests* outside their official positions; nothing to check their absolute exercise of the absolute power. The check formerly is easily understood; most of the members of parliament were either actual large land-owners or were nominated by such landowners; or were directly representative of large commercial interests; when it came to legislating or to executive action, they would and did act *in the interest* of their private connections, not of "the government." *They* had to pay the taxes. If property were to be confiscated, it would be *their* property.

Oh, lord, I am making this very dull and not very clear. The general truth I am driving at is necessary relation of forces and forms; and that is what history has never shown, because historians had no clear idea of it. Nobody had. Methods of government have been largely improvised, jury-rig (jury rig means a makeshift), ex-post facto; something had to be done and they set up some instrumentality by guess and by God. The interesting thing would be to study that succession of pragmatical devices and show why they worked if they did work, and why not if not, in the light of general principles. The long story of the English parliament would be peculiarly instructive. I haven't got the information I should have on it myself. For instance, I don't even know what was the difference between county members and borough or private members (they were the same *in* the House); how did it originate, etc. How did the Parliament even get started? I daresay that is a well-known story in a way, yet I confess I hardly know. The Knights of the Shire were "summoned"; they were under compulsion to attend, frequently they did not want to! How did that come about? I suppose Trevelyan* explains, but I can't remember or don't know! Of course the major force in English history which acted (as a force) to create parliament (the Commons, I mean) was money, i. e., the fact that England was a commercial nation. That force acted[3] toward the power of King and Commons jointly at first, because the King always needed money to stand against the great landed gentry (the Barons); so the King had to rely on the commercial interest; but when the Crown had at length reduced the power of the Barons, the Commons retained the real power which they had only lent, as it were, to the Crown; so in the next struggle, the Crown lost.

It is a story of the energy relations of static (land) and kinetic (commerce, money) forces, expressed in changing political institutions and relations; and when the hook-up was not sound, not mechanically correct, the result was civil war, terrorizations, or trouble of some sort.

Looking at it in this light, you might get some useful factual information from Trevelyan, as to the historic changes in those relations, the actual methods of nomination, election, and operation of the Commons, etc. But such information becomes intelligible only in the light of general principles, and when read conjointly with other facts outside the strictly political record. For instance, how was it that Charles the First could not hold his own by force against Parliament, and yet so soon afterward Cromwell* could and did walk in on the House with a corporal's guard and close it! Historians will talk drivel about the power of "the people," etc. In fact, Cromwell had an army, an army actually created by Parliament but over which it had no adequate means of control. The King had had no such army; England never had a standing army before that time, and was very cautious of having one afterward. Why could not the despotism Cromwell exercised be carried on by some successor? Because there was no means of supplying such an army for an indefinite period; the lack of adequate supply was just the reason Parliament had had no control over it, and why that army must dissolve in due course. Those are force relations. The power was again found to be in Parliament as soon as that army dissolved. General Monk* took a standing jump from a sort of melting ice-cake (the army) to meet Charles II as the parliamentary power resumed and required the Crown again as "dead center" for its function.

Now I think if you mull over these main points gradually, you may make some sense of what history there is; or at least get some gleams in it, and find it really interesting. For my own part, I have never been able to force or hurry my mind to understand anything; I have to read for pleasure and see what I see as it comes to me. Of course I do want to know, and without wanting to know, I daresay nothing *will* come to one.—I may add in regard to parliamentary institutions right now, that their present "absoluteness" is the positive reason why in the comparatively near future they will suddenly become absolutely powerless, as it were overnight. They are destroying their own means of action, which is money! Our Federal government will go that way.

I guess that's enough.

Pat

To Muriel Hall

Dated "Tues." [June 7, 1950]

Dear Muriel—

>> The maxim that children should be seen and not heard was based on immemorial experience—in brief, *all* children are predominantly bores in conversation. That is no measure of their actual intelligence—not as if they were adults. It is just that they have not yet acquired the accomplishment, as they have so much else to do first in getting their mental equipment in good shape. Their business at that age is to *acquire* information, not to impart or exchange it (hence also their disinclination to answer questions); and the things they say are generally simple utterances or the obvious because they are also *acquiring* the use of speech, merely running scales, learning grammar and pronunciation. It is, however, distinctly useful to them if their seniors talk to *them* on an intellectual level, for they understand quite well on that level long before they talk up to it. The old rule which practically silenced children while they were growing up had pretty good sense in it, the more if the children at the same time could listen to intelligent conversation. However, that rule was for children in company, not with mother (or nurse), so you needn't feel worried either way, if you can stand up to the boredom.—There was sound good sense in most of the old rules for children, though too often they were *applied* stupidly or cruelly, which I do not mean to extenuate.

Yes, certainly ticks exist only in a certain climate of a definite degree of dryness. E. g., there are ticks in North Dakota, but not in Connecticut—they live in Texas too but not in Oregon—I daresay there are none in Northern New Jersey.[4] They are the same kind of ticks in North Dakota, and incidentally they are found only on the dryer areas, which there means the higher ground. Drat them. But at least you had some indirect benefit from this Noah's weather. If it is still wetter than usual in the fall, they will probably disappear early.

Yes, "corruption of blood"[5] was, as you indicate, merely the legal term for "collective" guilt. As custom or law it is ancient barbarism. I do not know if Roman law admitted it in anything but "treason"; I think not. More barbarous systems imputed collective guilt for almost any offence—I mean that the family was held guilty for any crime of a member of the family, and was punished in varying degrees. The *strictest* meaning of that particular term in English meant that all direct descendants of anyone "attainted of treason" lost their civil status, whatever it was (for instance, if a nobleman was guilty, the title was extinguished)—descendants could not hold office, etc. (They might, of course, be pardoned and the civil status restored later). Also entailed estates could be confiscated, forfeited. It is a broad subject, the whole transition from barbarism to civilization in legal forms; but that is one most significant aspect of it. Of course Russia really has *no* law or laws, nothing but arbitrary despotism, but what they actually do corresponds to the laws of barbarism, though without the benefit of even barbaric law as it is not settled or limited to even that code, any code.

Incidentally, I do not know if the penalty of "corruption of blood" is not still *legally* possible in England; or if it has ever been debarred by law or by repeal of laws. It tended to fall into desuetude there, even before the American Revolution; that is, it was less and less often enforced throughout the centuries before. It had always varied somewhat in England, according to the stress of the times. If you have ever wondered why old-time victims of treason trials in England made such humble submission before execution, well, one main reason was that they hoped thereby to give *their* families a better chance of royal clemency, the remission of forfeiture of estates, titles, civil privileges of any kind. The King could always grant such remission if he chose.

There have been innumerable variants of the incidence of "collective guilt" in law; I daresay it would fill a huge book.—In France under the Regent a nobleman (Count Horn) was convicted of ordinary murder and sentenced to be hanged (this was sometime about 1725 or 1730)—and in fact he *was* hanged.[6] His remotest family connections and many other nobles begged in vain that the Regent would (not pardon him but) alter the sentence to beheading. Why? Because if he suffered the regular "felon's death" by hanging, *all* the members of his "house," the Horns, a great family, would actually lose certain privileges of the noble order; for instance, numerous noble Chapters of Canonesses would be closed to their womenfolks, etc.—But this is a long way from where we started on the subject. The crucial contrast now is in such present cases as you cite.[7] And I may add that Russia alone *never emerged*, in either principle, theory or practice, from that barbarism. Under the Czars, right up to the end, families could be and were punished for the guilt of members, though less ferociously than the Bolshevik practice.

The fundamental difference in law made by the American Revolution is little understood, never really mentioned in the ordinary history, and I must add it has never been *fully and consistently* put into effect either, throughout the whole body of our laws (since Jay's* interpretation and decision was actually reversed on that very point[8])—such basic historic changes in thought never do take *full* effect immediately—but it is a vast change of the utmost importance none the less; and if the human race survives, it can be only by going on with that change. It is precisely a change of basis from existing by permission to living by right.

I put in a call for you once or twice (last Friday once) and happened to miss you both times—not at your desk, and I didn't like to bother you. Be seeing you soon.

Affectionately,
Pat

To Muriel Hall

Undated [August 26, 1952]

Tuesday—but I don't know when you'll get this

Yesterday, after you had gone, someone else came in, and told me that in yesterday's *World-Telegram* there was a front-page demand that Eisenhower should now actually say something! Perhaps you've seen it; I didn't see the paper. So this campaign is becoming curiouser and curiouser. The Scripps-Howard papers did all they could to get Eisenhower as nominee, didn't they? Perhaps I am mistaken, but I seem to remember that was the case. Eisenhower never has said anything, as far as I know; but they would have him, they got what they wanted; and now, like Chinaboy,[9] they seem to find their doll stuffed with sawdust. Really, I may have to take back my remark that this will be a dull campaign, if they go on getting louder and funnier. Please keep me posted on further developments if any, in the same line. Fried mush.

By the way, I'm afraid I was thoughtless in speaking of Bernard Shaw's* father (his being a drunk) in front of X.[10] I'm sorry I didn't think in time, or I would not have mentioned that fact. However, I suppose it is impossible that such allusions should never occur; and perhaps some time you can find occasion to explain to those children that they need not feel any personal reflection on themselves from family distresses, in general. Perhaps it would be helpful to them to be assured that *all* families have similar misfortunes among very near relatives. Usually we just don't know other people's circumstances or troubles in detail, that's all. I think children seldom know or realize that fact, their experience being limited; and they are apt to be sensitive on such points. X is a nice child, and I daresay she has good sense enough to understand and follow your advice if you tell her not to feel that family difficulties really reflect on her personally. And anyhow, practically everyone else is in the same boat, one way or another. It *is* sad, but there again, nobody can get through life without some very sad experiences, yet they are not the whole of life, nor even the greater part of it. She's pretty and attractive and that's a great deal. She's very nice to Becky,[11] isn't she? >> I was glad Becky made quite a hearty supper of bread and butter and apple sauce. You see she knows and likes what is good for her, which is unusually fortunate since some things do not agree with her. She looks fine and healthy, and happy.—What I was really thinking about, as exemplified by Bernard Shaw's case, is that children need to be *loved.* It is a need like the need of sunlight. Obviously we are not made to live in sunlight twenty-four hours of every day; therefore children are fully capable of profiting by discipline, of enduring inevitable difficulties, sorrows, normal hardships, e. g., the stormy aspects of existence, if they are loved—just as we get through the seasons well enough on our norm of sunny days and find the stormy seasons bracing, a natural part of our environment. It is equally natural that children should be loved; they are, in fact, lovable. I suppose all this sounds very platitudinous; but some platitudes are perfectly true; so I will mail this anyhow and risk boring you. (A little boredom is on the cards for all of us!)

Love to everybody.

Pat

To Muriel Hall

After completing The God of the Machine, *Paterson became interested in the works of philosopher and historian Etienne Gilson.* As part of a discussion of Gilson and the "revival of medieval studies" within* *the Roman Catholic church, she commented on the opposition of the nineteenth-century papacy to liberalism and modernism.*

Dated "Tuesday" [February 1, 1955]

Dear Muriel—

>> That encyclical caused much commotion; Protestants denouncing it as reactionary, and "liberal" ("Modernist") Catholics taking to cover, most of them making submission, a few, very few, leaving the Church.[12] I think it is fair enough to say it *was* reactionary, even in a technical sense; at the same time it is equally fair to observe that "modernism" really was incompatible with Catholic doctrine, and therefore the Pope was morally bound to squelch it—as Pope. "Modernism" was not a formal body of doctrine but a general tendency of thought, which naturally came out differently with different proponents, and slightly fuzzy altogether. It was a consequence of the impact of science in the 19th century on the minds of educated Catholics—one of those attempts at "reconciliation," you know. Be that as it may, the Pope said: "Back to Aquinas,"* hence such institutions as St. Michael's in due time.[13] And on the other hand, a side effect of "Modernism" actually was the arousing of lay Catholics to an intellectual approach to their own religion and philosophy, instead of leaving it all to clerics. Vide Gilson, and others. Action and reaction are equal and opposite, so Newton said. I doubt if they are exactly in human affairs, but at least they tend that way; and Newton only spoke of physics. I guess I ought to say that I don't think the Modernists would have got anywhere if left alone, though they had some very brilliant men among them, and that very great scholar Lord Acton.*

I might add that the "liberalism" of the period of that "reactionary" encyclical—Protestant "liberalism"—was a damn sight worse than reactionary; it was the theoretic approach to the stateolatry of today, our enslavement to the state. The original and true Liberalism, the movement for actual liberty, was already dead and its clothes stolen by all the alleged reformers whose panacea was continual and increasing political interference and suppression of individual freedom and rights.

Now I wonder—an idle, not serious, fancy—why some of us got born in the eighteen eighties to set ourselves against the drift of our age? I mean Gilson, du Nouy,* *and* me. Maybe others I do not know.

If you read Gilson's *Unity* (etc)., you may chance to wonder, did I derive from that what I wrote in *God of the Machine contra* Descartes.*[14]

Swelp me, no, when I was writing my book I had never heard of Gilson, much less read anything of his; and what I figured out about Descartes was honestly my own view, unaided. I was simply surprised when I found Gilson's exposition. I picked up Descartes first in reading about Pascal,* and saw in a flash that the Cartesian attempt at a mathematical philosophy was one of the most important (and fatal) influences in modern thought. Important, of course, because Descartes really was a high mathematical genius, and therefore influential even when he was wrong.

Also you may note that Gilson as a young man (and he is just two years older than I, or to be exact, eighteen months) began to wonder what was in between the ancient classical world and our own time—felt sure sumpn[15] must have been happening. That very speculation occurred to me, as more than a passing notion; set me trying to trace the connections of ideas.

Du Nouy rejected the mechanistic deterministic view in science at about the same time, apparently.

By the way, when Aquinas is eulogized—and I admit he was a great mind—never forget one thing, which is seldom mentioned. (I'll say he must be in hell for it.) It was *he* who furnished the argument for exterminating heretics, as a "social" duty, a right of the "community."

Oh, though this is a trifle of our own times, that Papal encyclical against "liberalism" was brought up against Al Smith* when he ran for President. Funny. I have no idea whether or not it influenced any votes, against him I mean. >>

Pat

To Muriel Hall

Undated [March 5, 1955]

Saturday
(won't be mailed till Monday)

>> In case the information is any use to you, that Chinese method of teaching children *not* to read[16] was first propagated in this country by that old blatherskite Amos Bronson Alcott (father of Louisa M.).* He tried keeping a "school," a few children, in his home (he didn't like work). He called the method "say and see." I do not know if the notion

originated in his own mush-brain or if he borrowed it from some European nut-hatchery of the period; it seems to have been his own, but he had read or heard of the Froebel-Pestalozzi kindergarten notions abroad, and I don't know what all *they* tried.[17]

Of course the primary trouble is that parents care so little about their children, and mainly want to dump 'em anywhere, anyhow—until they are old enough so the boys can be shipped off for slaughter and insurance collected.—In this age of print, when it is actually part of the landscape, all children should be taught to read at home, before they are five years old; a simple task when thus taken in time. The children need not be expected to read advanced books, but to *read*. Teaching one or two or three children is such a short job—a few minutes a day for a few weeks or months. Slightly more trouble and time with a large class, because all children do not learn with equal aptitude—not any branch of learning, naturally. So the reading should be taught first and save some years of expense in schools. By learning so early, reading seems to the child as natural as speech—which actually it is. They should be taught and learned at practically the same time, as elementary necessities in respect of use (though they are also the most advanced technologies with aeons of intellect involved in their development. As I have told you, babies have all the brains, intellects, they are ever going to have; that is why they really begin *learning* at the point of highest development of knowledge.) I suppose I shall not live to see these simple truths recognized.

All well here; hoping you are the same.

To Muriel Hall

May 5, 1955

I guess the Amphibolos has a good right to figure alongside Cyrus Griffin, though I have actually come across A. once before, in some book, the name of which I forget.[18] I'll just keep quiet about it, especially as I did not remember his name either, but only the contraption.

You never told me you had met the Duke of Windsor. Poor little shrimp, he had not a grain of royalty in him. I hope your Grand Duchess was more like it.[19] —Anatole France* wrote that we really get our notions, our mental images, of aristocracy and royalty from the stage, from actresses who might have been born in the gutter. I don't think that is quite true; I think probably we get the idea from a few historical personages who happened to be born (or elevated) to those ranks, and who also had some personal qualities which beseem the part. Would not both Becky and Diana[20] figure perfectly as Grand Duchesses or queens, although they are not a bit alike in most ways? The very way they carry their heads would do the trick. The Grand Duchess Marie* of Russia (I met her twice)[21] was up to her original position, but it bored her—as being a queen bored Marie Antoinette. That was their times; they came on the scene too late to be interested in something that was no longer real, being on the verge of dissolution. But Marie Antoinette is nevertheless still the figure of a queen; she had it, in spite of being rather a foolish woman. And by the way, when I was young Americans simply were not interested in royalty or aristocracy as such; literally, they wouldn't cross the street for it. That's because North America was then *really* republican, and really could not think in any other terms. Simply, nobody cared. A few female "social leaders" with money enough would "entertain" visiting titles, but nobody else paid any attention. It seems to me we looked on them as something like the bones of an extinct species. Inaccessible, as you say, but also unreal. Queen Victoria certainly existed, and yet she was rather a legend than a human being; and Edward VII wasn't a king in the same sense she was a queen.

I think anyone left of my generation must be somehow unreal to other people now. Aren't we? There is a funny kind of transposition, too. In some context I can't recall, Hilda[22] said to me: "You are a lady," meaning a lady by class, you understand. And Ayn Rand once remarked: "You seem to me like a Grand Duchess." She did not mean that she had known any Grand Duchesses, but the idea she had. I did not try to explain to Hilda, but to Ayn I said: "I think what you mean, an attitude, not exactly an individual attitude, is nothing but what American women in general had, in my time." Of course the general attitude of a period, being general, cannot connote the character of any given individual; and the result may be rather weird. Two examples are Eleanor Roosevelt and the Aged P.[23] Mrs. Roosevelt has money and a factitious position to support her attitude, but not *one* personal qualification, neither brains nor beauty nor wit nor moral sense; the factitious, extraneous facts impress the other idiots, but to rational people she is a kind of monstrosity. The Aged P. has just *nothing*; so you don't quite believe she exists at all. Your mother, you know, had her immense common-sense competence; so you recall that with her first stroke, which disabled her from her natural role, she abdicated consciously. What has happened to me you'd have to judge for yourself; perhaps I don't know, and at least I can't tell how it strikes other people.

Why I wandered off into this letter I can't imagine. Partly because here's the typewriter, and partly because you set me pondering on time's revenges. Because of course I was born and brought up as far from being a lady in the *class* sense (much less a Grand Duchess) as anyone could be and still belong to respectable people, "poor but honest." Yet here's the world turned upside down and grand duchesses looking for jobs—I hope she got one if she actually wanted it.

And stopping in the middle of this, I went into Princeton to the Univ. Library and called by request on the chief librarian, Mr. Dix.* Thought he'd be an aged barnacle, but he's a good-looking well-bred man under fifty, a Virginian, very nice. In the course of conversation Ellen Glasgow* was mentioned. I said I supposed he had met her—I knew her. He said no, he wasn't important enough then! Bless my soul, the old girl would have been delighted to admit a personable, literate young man to her calling list, I'm certain. Can it be that most everyone has some queer notion of what *other* people think or are like? I suppose so.

I will send this because it is now written. It is just possible I may get into New York before this letter reaches you, but probably not. I really have got someone working on that trench now, and perhaps should stay and watch him! Oh, two of my rosebushes have tiny buds on them! Cuttings from your garden, the first batch, two winters ago. The Mermaid[24] is not robust yet, but at least alive.

Be seeing you; love to all,
Pat

To Muriel Hall

Undated [May 13, 1955]

Dear Muriel—

Of course the Man did *not* come on Monday, but he appeared Tuesday for a couple of hours and next day sent his nephew, so the trench is now nearly filled in at last. If I really had to, I could do the rest myself, but the Man is to come again on Saturday for the remaining bit of shovelling. Which of course he won't, though I don't care now.

Ted[25] told you, I daresay, that we went to Mettler's Woods and saw cut stumps in numbers. Ted said they were the work of beavers. Splendid woods, certainly, though to my mind no better than on your mother's farm, only rather messier with down timber.

The way presents get shuffled around, you shouldn't have been surprised that I made off with the book given you on Mother's Day; but I sent it back Wednesday faithfully.—I hope Becky[26] likes the shopping bag. I thought she could use it for carrying her fancy dress around; apparently little girls do that.

Can't say I like the world depicted in most modern novels, including Nevile Shute's.* Lately I read C. P. Snow, *The New Men*, which rather gave me the creeps too.[27] The people don't seem quite human to me—something missing in their works. No feelings. I know you're told that they have but I don't believe it. Shute's is a war novel. And he says (and makes it credible) that they had the time of their lives in the war; I believe that. Yet at the same time they can't stand it when it hits *them*. I realize fully that in the past human beings, certain societies, have liked war better than anything else—savages, barbarians, half-barbarians like the Vikings; war was the great sport for them, the peak of living. They had few mental resources and craved excitement instead. Otherwise they were bored. But they were quite ready to take the consequences. These people aren't. They haven't got the ethics; I'd say that they haven't got any ethics, civilized or otherwise. They are entirely empty. They crack up.—Well, these reflections are a bore—inane.

Oh, I have just found a local place name to identify Bishop Berkeley's house near Newport: Paradise Rocks.[28] Seems to be sufficiently well-known. Paradise Rocks isn't the name of the house or farm, but nearby.

Pat

To Muriel Hall

Undated [June 5?, 1955]

Dear Muriel—

The book is *First With the Most Forrest,* by Robert S. Henry* (Bobbs-Merrill); I believe it is still in print.

The reference is in Chapter XIII, *Pages 198–199*. But note first Page 193—"What does he (Bragg*) fight battles for?"[29]

At the moment I can't recall similar instances, except the famous one of Nelson* putting his telescope to his blind eye and saying he could not see the signal—a signal to stop fighting, I suppose.[30] I can't give you book and page reference for that, as I have no Life of Nelson.

It is possible that some British Army officers resigned at the time of the Revolutionary War, rather than fight America, but I do not know for certain; I can think of only one man who said he wished he had but did not, and durn it I forget this name—so that's no good. It would, of course, have been possible to do so without incurring any penalty. Just as Robert E. Lee resigned his Federal commission when the Civil War began, because he could not bring himself to invade his native state Virginia. He wouldn't have been punished for that, you know. An officer simply has the privilege of resigning when he pleases, as far as I know. This doesn't bring up any wild question of his resigning right in a battle, because he is not excused from duty until his resignation has been accepted, in form.

I think the ethics of an officer's whole duty are not likely to be understood by many persons, as it doesn't ordinarily come within their scope of study or experience. Also there is an inevitable margin of conduct which cannot be reduced to specific rules. A private solider of course cannot resign. (All that I am saying must be understood as relating to the military traditions and regulations of Western civilization—Europe and America.) The margin of conduct for a private soldier can't be fully regulated either; e. g., he must obey orders, but his orders have to allow too that he may be beaten back *in battle*, and he isn't punished for that. I mean, when a regiment "breaks," gives way, under attack, nobody is punished. Generally, the private solider is punished only if he doesn't go forward when he is ordered to do so.

But an officer has definite responsibilities of a different kind, calling for the exercise of judgment. In battle, to be sure, or in military action generally, he must obey superior orders. At any time he can resign only by formal notice. But there is the special ethical problem of the commanding officer in the field, receiving orders from Washington (supreme headquarters). Such orders cannot be given in battle, obviously. They are orders for this or that large movement or line of action. He is on the spot; suppose then he receives an order which his immediate knowledge tells him will be disastrous if carried out. Very well, then he can still resign, by wire, in protest.

But suppose he considers that general order so bad, so disastrous, that it will be gravely injurious to his country. His resignation will not prevent it being carried out by his successor; nor will his resignation inform his country of the danger.

HIS DUTY IS TO HIS COUNTRY.

He may then choose to disobey the order, on his own judgment.

Such disobedience renders him liable at least to recall and demotion and at worst to courtmartial and a sentence which could actually extend to the death penalty. (The latter not very likely, but still legally possible, I think.)

Now it is precisely the grave risk he is taking *personally* that makes it *ethical* for him to disobey if in his judgment his country will suffer if he does not. Same as the risk he is obliged to run of being killed in battle, you see. He may not, ethically, put his own safety or his own career ahead of the well-being of his country. And the particular reason why he might choose ethically to disobey rather than to resign is just that his punishment, whether recall or courtmartial, is the only way he has of making known to his country the danger he sees, or thinks he sees, to his country. He can't say anything otherwise, that is, he can't speak publicly. The risk he runs shows that he does think the matter very grave. It is his last resort, naturally.[31] Such circumstances are rare, and possibly some men would actually dodge the issue anyhow; so it is not to be expected that instances of a man in high command openly disobeying orders because he thought them inimical to his own country would occur often.

I allow that MacArthur's case was not *likely* to bring him to a courtmartial or any other punishment than recall; but it *could* have had worse consequences for him than merely the loss of command.[32] Further, to be recalled from command in a war is no light matter to an officer anyhow. It has the appearance of a decision that he is unfit for command.

Apparently the way it looked to MacArthur is that he was being ordered to fight a war and at the same time forbidden to fight to win. That is, his orders were, or seemed to him, to mean, that he must keep his army in position to be slaughtered while he was forbidden to allow them to fight back *effectively*. In that case, the only rational and moral judgment is that he was ethically obliged to do whatever he could to inform his country of the situation at his own risk—and that is what he did. He had a duty to his country and a duty to the men under his command. An officer may subject his army to all risks for a commensurate chance of winning, but *not for nothing*. (That idiot who led the Charge of the Light Brigade should have disobeyed the order.[33])

Reverting to Forrest*—whoever consults the book should read the *whole* of Chapter XIII; otherwise the reason for Forrest's insubordination will not be seen. What made Forrest so mad was that Braxton Bragg, his Chief, time and again refused to let Forrest (or any of his subordinates) get any results from their actual victories.

To Muriel Hall

Dated "Friday" [December 7, 1956]

Dear Muriel—

Could you phone and find out for me how is little Andrea Spinelli; I think she was to have that appendicitis operation on the 19th, and I hope she is getting better.[34] You've got their phone number, Fairlawn 6–7158; I expect her mother would be at home any time that isn't hospital visiting hours.

Nothing special here; I had a chill last week and got over it. Cold and windy today and wind always makes me gloomy and cross, but I know that is it, so I don't attribute it to anything else. I have got a volume of the pomes of Edna St. Vincent Millay;[35] would you like it to keep? I had her Sonnets anyhow, so don't feel like keeping a duplicate. Looking over her work, it seems less in volume to me than I expected—I think Elinor Wylie[36] really stands a little ahead of her as a poet, but still E. M. *was* a poet. Strange little down-east[37] Yankee she was, small, thin, sharp-featured, an authentic Yankee twang in her speech; but she had personal charm none the less, like a little wild crab-apple or wild plum. It's the darnedest thing to think of that dough-faced homunculus Edmund Wilson* as her lover—I suppose he was, among others. I guess the love affairs of poets are best left unexamined. Old horse-faced Wordsworth and his French girl stagger the imagination.[38] Be that as it may, do you want the book?

Oh, Harper's do *not* want mine[39]—I understand that the characters are too well bred for them. Not enough booze and bedding, I guess.

Hope the Senator hasn't got the sniffles again, poor lamb; and that my darling Becky is well, and John forging ahead, and everybody beamish.[40]

Love to all,
Pat

P. S. I noticed in obit of the unlamented Marshall Field[41] that he seems to have owned Simon & Schuster publishing house. I thought they were fishy, but didn't know Mr. F. was the fish. God damn the rich.

To Muriel Hall

Dated "Next day" [May 24, 1957]

Great heavens, it *is* two chapters![42] I must break it, and proceed. That doesn't mean rewriting, praise be; it just happens sometimes one doesn't see the proper break beforehand. The journey down is one chapter by itself. The time in Annapolis, the actual honeymoon, is another chapter. I wish someone who really could write a novel was writing this novel; it might get done in a reasonable time, and maybe even done right. —I have to write you these letters to preserve my sanity, and never mind yours. Of course you need not pay any attention to them; you just happen to be walking through the woods in the hunting season and get shot. Correction of one statement above, probably if someone who could write a novel was writing this novel, he (or she) wouldn't; they'd know better. And that goes for a hell of a lot of alleged novels that actually get published in the contemporary crop of fiction.

Well, the moral is that I must get on with the job. When it is done, no doubt *I* shall know better.

Mrs. S. is at home this week, taking part of her vacation, and cleaning house.[43] Discomfort seeps through the air. She has a gift for it. She has repainted some of the kitchen all over again. That wallpaper didn't stick, in spots, and she is fixing that, too. She has tidied shelves and corners; but the rubbish remains, I mean miscellaneous junk, such as the aquarium on my beautiful walnut chest of drawers; that doesn't bother her; it only bothers me. The "sunroom" remains uninhabitable with its jerry-built pingpong table etcetera, and will remain so no matter how hot the weather gets, so nobody can sit there in the cool of the evening. The pingpong contraption rests on two of my own small tables and an ash-tray stand of mine, regardless of their being mine. I am inclined to think that a well-spent life might consist largely in getting rid of junk. If ever I get into a decent house again I will work on that. I will not have an unlimited number of cats, and dogs. Fish shall stay where they belong, which is not in any house. What is the ocean for, not to mention Lake Superior, the Mississippi River, and various other damp spots outdoors. I ask you?

I must tell you the most screwball event, and then I request you solemnly to tear this up. Mr. S. thinks he has discovered how to tri-sect an angle.

Now I can't say that someone might not discover that; the whole of geometry had to be discovered, and I don't know that there is any law of nature which prevents the trisection of an angle (like the Second Law of Thermodynamics which forbids the invention of a perpetual motion machine). Also if an angle can or could be tri-sected (a question I am not competent to answer), well then, such things have sometimes been discovered by screwballs; I suppose that lies in the laws of chance, with odds of billions of zillions against each individual screwball, and indeed with the same odds against highly trained geometers; nobody can know how it will come out. The really screwball part is that he thinks this will give him[44] fame and recognition, and that your alleged magazine might have an article about him; he sees that with the headlines and all![45] Calm yourself, *that* notion will get no further—I convinced him that Henry Luce* and his minions and his public wouldn't look around if every angle in the universe were trisected simultaneously. At least, I hope I convinced him. I explained that if anyone did tri-sect an angle, the best the person could hope for would be a paragraph in *Nature* or *Scripta Mathematica*, periodicals with several subscribers each and totally unknown to the general public. So I trust you will hear no more of this.

Don't you think the peculiar mania of this age (which to be sure does not exclude all other possible manias being endemic) is the idiot craving for "publicity"? that is, simply to get one's name and silly face in print, for any or no reason at all? It seems so to me. As with public manias of all ages, of course not everyone is affected by it; I mean only that it is the particular mania of the time, the most manifest symptom of something wrong, the surface sign.

Personally I stick to the good old yearning to make money, but as there is no real money to be had, I am sadly frustrated, and might as well write the kind of novels I do write. I think John means to get rich, for which ambition I admire and sympathize with him. You must bring up Thomas in the same faith, the faith of our ancestors.[46]

If this novel goes on distracting me, I'm quite likely to make Ted read the dubious chapter for a judgment of taste; it seems to me his writing is naturally free from vulgarity—don't you think so?

Love to all, and I do hope I won't afflict you with any more of my distractions.

Pat

To Muriel Hall

July 20, 1957

Dear Yo-Yo,[47] the thermometer riz to102 today, so I thought I would write and tell you maybe you'd better *never* come back, much as I should miss you-all. I have sometimes wondered if the final cause of the Fall of Rome was not the Roman toga. I mean, a Roman cit. of any social standing *had* to wear it. And a toga was simply a long *woolen* blanket, draped around the manly form in many folds, very difficult to keep in place as well as very hot on a nice Roman summer day. So one such day, the Ides of August, the Roman cit said the hell with it and quit the job. Gibbon* lived in England and Switzerland; he had no idea of the thing.

It is just as dry at present as it is hot. Not a flower will grow. One lonely tomato achieved ripeness, but it was no bigger than I can't think what; well, about an inch in diameter.—I have just been reading in a book about Julia Ward Howe and her family, something of Joseph Bonaparte's estate in Bordentown, quite interesting.[48] He had a *lot* of land. You may like to read the book sometime, from the library; I got it from the library. (The connection with Julia is that her sister married Adolph Mailliard who was the legitimate son of the illegitimate son of Joseph Bonaparte.) The most diverting thing in the book is the part revealing the private life of Julia's husband. Dr. Samuel Gridley Howe was a famous philanthropist, a reformer; he dashed about liberating Greece from the Turks, founding Institutes for the blind and for idiots, etc., etc. Julia was an heiress in a modest way. Dr. Howe grabbed all her money, spent it as he pleased. It infuriated him when she wrote and printed anything. He was enraged if she got any publicity; he wanted it all. He couldn't quite stop her, because she too was a born Public Character, but he made life pretty miserable for her. Furthermore, he carried on affairs with other women, apparently females on his staff at the Institute; at least, he carried on such affairs in his office. When he became senile he told his wife, and besides he left documentary evidence of his divagations. He was a regular Do-Good. He blamed his affairs on the ladies concerned. It is all extremely edifying. I do not know exactly why Julia did not bash him with a rolling pin, except that she couldn't cook. She had red hair. How is your young coppertop?[49] He is a lamb.

Love to all,
Pat

The title of the book is *Three Saints and a Sinner.*[50]
I am getting on with the novel, really-truly.

To Muriel Hall

Although her relationship with Ayn Rand dissolved in 1948, Paterson was warmly interested in the appearance of Rand's novel Atlas Shrugged *(published in 1957, and commercially successful ever since). The idea for the novel had come to Rand after a conversation with Paterson in 1943, and Paterson had encouraged her during the work's early stages. Paterson had meanwhile been writing another novel of her own,* Joyous Gard, *which is still in manuscript. Toward the end of her life, Paterson renewed contact with a number of friends with whom she had been out of touch. One of them was Ayn Rand. In 1959 she called Rand and sent her the new novel, perhaps hoping that Rand could help her get it published. Shortly afterward, Paterson visited Rand's apartment in New York. They talked for a while, quarreling over philosophical issues.*[51] *They never met again.*

Dated "Thursday" [September 26, 1957]

Dear Muriel—
I've been reading an advance copy of Ayn Rand's novel. I should think that if any periodical can get material for some personal feature on her, the public will be eager to see it. The book is sensational in itself and I expect will be a "sensation" on publication. I omit strictly critical literary judgment on it here—by no means implying that it has no literary merit but just sticking to the particular point of news interest. To me it will be curious to watch its reception by the literary critics; but whatever they may say, I don't think they can do much if

anything either to the sales or the public impact which I think it must have. Her previous novel[52] had no breaks at all with the reviewers, not much advertising, and no big sales record of any previous book by the author to help with the booksellers, so it took some time to hit its stride in sales; but it went over just the same. With this one, Random House will certainly put on a big advertising campaign, the book-sellers will be stocked up, etc., etc. Of course it would be deplorably cynical of me to suggest that those facts will affect the attitude of reviewers and literary editors, so let that pass. The good old N. Y. *Times* has got permission to review it on the Sunday before the publication date, so the Trib. will do likewise. I shouldn't wonder if they gave it the front page of their book review sections, though I cannot predict this. John Chamberlain* will do it for the Trib. and I presume will give it a favorable review. I don't know who for the *Times*, or how they may handle it.[53] All this is very edifying to me, as you may suspect. (Publication date is Oct. 10).

I rather anticipate that the book will be a chunk of high explosive to "public opinion." It is quite possible that it may have a definite effect on future events, like *Uncle Tom's Cabin*. You will note that I am judgmatical, not bursting out with adjectives; I am giving an objective opinion, as nearly as possible, in respect of news value. Ayn has had very little personal publicity; she isn't interested in personal publicity except insofar as it can help the sale of her books. But I think the public will certainly be much interested in hearing about her, and the best time to *get* good "feature" material from her would be now, i. e., before publication, as she will wish to get as good a send-off *for the book* as possible.—To say the least, it really is a remarkable novel, she has an extraordinary talent, hardly comparable in kind to any other.

I hope your house is still standing, with Thomas[54] at large. The agility, speed and tireless energy of one-year-old[s] must be seen to be believed. He was lots of fun. Love to all, specially Becky.[55] Isn't she an elegant creature?

Pat

To Muriel Hall

Dated "Sunday" [October? 1957]

Big rain this afternoon; you must have run into weather on your trip.

I've just had an invitation to the wedding (Oct. 26) of the oldest daughter of Robert Henry—that's the slim pretty dark girl. I don't know why it's a surprise to me that it's at a Presbyterian church; I guess I can't think the Henrys are much like John Calvin.[56] Groom unknown to me, someone named Norman Burkey Musselman, also an odd combination of names. Oh, dear, how fast people grow up and get married and da capo.[57]

I have returned Ayn Rand's novel; I can't think how you'll ever get time to read it; but I fancy it will have an enormous continued sale, partly among people who don't read many books—this is not meant as a depreciating sneer, but simple fact. Sort of an *Uncle Tom's Cabin* public, I anticipate.[58] The Eggheads will be furious. She has astounding power of invention, that is, of constructing a *story*; I wish I had. Really, I should never have tried to write fiction. I can never see any human life as rounded out to a plot-story, which is not to say that I object to those who can. The events of real life are often wildly improbable. Shall we drop in on the Duke of Bedford for tea at 2/6?[59] Tourist rates at Woburn Abbey. You must know that the Duke of Bedford was the byword for bloated wealth two centuries ago. I must say that I rather admire the present Duke for getting enjoyment out of his present enterprise, I think that is actually more dignified than resenting it. Same as I like young Thomas's[60] attitude toward life; all he asks is a chance to get at it! You were almost alarmed by the vigor of his attack on the pots and pans; but you must realize they were the first objects with which he had a free hand.>> Well, how I have wandered in these remarks, and that is just my point, life is infinitely more various and complex and incalculable than I can even suggest in fiction. In a word, it beats me. If ever I get that last chapter[61] done, maybe I will know better than to write another novel as long as I live.

Love to all,
Pat

To Muriel Hall

With this letter Paterson enclosed an illustrated article, "Is Your Child Fit?: Fitness Begins at Home," by Bonnie Prudden, published in the* Herald Tribune.

Undated [October 21, 1957]

Dear Muriel—

Now here is something you will thank me for—advice about your child. Part of it, to be sure, is too late, but just do the best you can. For instance, you'll notice you should have begun "immediately following birth," that is, not your birth but your child's, *immediately*, mind you, when mother is at the top of her form and baby is naturally rather confused. But you missed that chance, of stretching his arms and legs, which if you had done your duty would now be elongated to I don't know what extent. Ad you should never have let him sit comfortably—what are tacks for?—but let that pass.

He has now begun to walk anyhow. Note that you should take him to the woods "where he can run free." Then just go home and forget about it. I'm afraid, knowing your child, he'll be hot on your track, but it's worth a try.

If he does follow you home, all right, "help him to climb and balance on every available object." Then he'll "do it without your help," and I expect you get the idea.

If that doesn't work, buy him roller skates. The article says, "when you are planning your new driveway," but you've got a driveway. Fine. A driveway "can be used as a roller skating rink, a basketball court, a place to bounce a ball and for all games requiring chalked ground markings"—in fact, for practically anything *but* a driveway.—But I overlooked a preceding instruction, you must put down a mattress somewhere. Meantime you have won the child's confidence. I daresay you have lost your job too, but what of that? The mattress then, I guess it should be put down in the house. All right, walk the child around the block until you are exhausted—he won't be. Then lead him to the driveway, and give him his roller skates, a basketball, chalk, etc. Then you go in the house and lie down on the mattress. The milkwagon or garbage truck ought to be coming any minute. That will be about all.

Except that when you venture hopefully outdoors again, you'll step on a roller skate right on the front steps and land in the pachysandra[62] with a fractured clavicle; the milkwagon will be a wreck on the driveway; and young Thomas will be bouncing his ball on those curved front windows that are almost impossible to replace.

So finally you wire to Washington for a detachment of paratroopers and start again, from scratch. Remember that Fitness Begins at Home—or else. And that child of yours just won't be fit, he simply won't take exercise, if *you* don't make him do so.

The survivor can write a book about it.

Pat

To Muriel Hall

Dated "Tuesday" [October 22, 1957]

Good heavens, I am so annoyed because the Queen has taken my ferry ride from Staten Island to the Battery, and just as I am in the middle of writing that chapter.[63] It was *my* idea and nobody else's and people had no right to steal it, not even queens—I've had it in mind for years, ages, aeons. In fact, I think I have a first lien on New York harbor, though I will let a few people like you and family see it as a favor. (To me, the Morans really own it, but they gave me a special privilege.) I've never had any spite against the Queen, but she isn't even writing a book and could just as well have kept off my ferry. It is too bad.

I am about half way through that interminable and unwriteable last chapter. As I am sure it will never be done, half way through does not signify. It is an Achilles-and-the-tortoise problem,[64] impossible to bring to a conclusion. But I just had to complain to someone about my ferry, and I hoped you might understand. I want sympathy.

All these visiting royalties are a curious repetition of the period when Rome was changing from a republic to an empire and full of kings and queens from all over, either as guests or being led captive—not much difference in historic significance which role they played; what it denoted was the sheer dominance of Rome. And incidentally the death of the republic.

I notice that both the Governor and the Mayor squoze into the same car seat with the Queen, regardless of mashing her flat.[65] Harriman grins as if he had the colic. Wagner just looks like a lump of lard. They should have punched each other's heads.

I write all these letters just to keep from working. I used to have someone—Elizabeth [sic] Sanxay Holding*—to read my ms. bit by bit—but she died, poor dear. (That had nothing to do with it; everyone dies.[66] I noticed Josephine Pinckney* of Charleston died lately, much younger than me. She had a terrible crush on Wendell Willkie.* She was 100 per cent First Family of Charleston and S. C. generally—*the* Pinckneys. A lady is apt to fall for a travelling man, but he can't fool a hotel diningroom girl.[67] If I don't happen to have told you about her, ask me. Him and his green pajamas! She would even listen to his radio speeches.

Pat

To Muriel Hall

Paterson remained interested in Ayn Rand's novel Atlas Shrugged *and its prospects for success.*

Undated [November? 1957][68]

In the very first place, any kind of reading matter that will sell at all has an intrinsic time cycle of "returns" from the first lot sold—the period of time varying in accord with certain factors in the book itself. A newspaper, you know, is limited practically to one day by the nature of its contents; even if by chance you hear of and wish you'd seen something in some newspaper of yesterday, you simply won't take the trouble to dig it up! But if it is still on the news stands and you see it, you'll buy it on someone's say-so. Periodicals also are generally limited to the time-cycle of their publication intervals and availability on the news stands; after that they're extinct.

But books have no such *arbitrary* periods; *their* "time cycle" of additional sales varies with the type of book, speaking generally; and within such classifications by type, it varies with the intrinsic factors of each book. E. g., you certainly know that[69] whodunits as a class have a pretty short selling life anyhow, yet there are a very few exceptions.

Now with novels in general, the period it takes to get "returns"—oh, bother, I had better state clearly what I mean here by returns. I mean the copies bought on word of mouth recommendation from the *first* lot of readers, *or* (which is only a variation of this kind of recommendation) on a sort of general, in-the-air, in-the-news-mediums, discussion of the book, controversial or otherwise;[70] *or* by a properly *timed* advertising rally, big advertising put out just at the calculable period of the first pause. The *second* lot of readers are those who constitute what I call the returns of the time cycle on the given book. That is, the second, third, etc.

Now some very popular novels have a time-cycle for returns of no more than a week—a very short period. Those are the lighter kind of novels (but they must be good enough of their kind, mind you), which the average reader can get through in a day or two (*I* can read 'em in an hour or two!). That kind of a book hits the best seller list on its first sales (if the author is already known) and then moves off the list, moves down it gradually instead of building up.

But if a book takes a week or two instead of a day or two for the average reader to get through it, then the time cycle for returns will be commensurately longer. Yet if it has the potential of a best-seller it will "build" by geometrical progression and hold onto the best seller list accordingly. And if it happens to be by an unknown or little-known author, then it won't hit the best seller list until it has had time to build; the time will be a multiple of the return cycle.

Here I may remark that I have never even heard of any publisher who perceived these simple principles of his trade and had gumption enough to advertise at the right time to put a potential best seller over the slump when it was a book with a longish time-cycle. What's more, I don't *expect* ever to hear of any such publisher. They just let a book of that kind go down in the trough of the wave and are they surprised when it does come up again! The "return" demand always catches them out of stock; and you needn't pretend *you* don't know *that* story.[71]

Well, now, I'll get down to cases. *The Fountainhead*[72] was by a practically unknown author. It had no chance of getting good reviews, and it got lousy reviews. The first printing was 7,500 copies, and the publishers advertised on publication just what they thought 7,500 copies was worth. They didn't have plates made![73] They ran out of stock, a hiatus of two or three weeks.

I told Ayn it would sell, nevertheless, but that I reckoned it would take about two years to reach the best seller list. I figured that on what I judged its time-cycle to be. As it proved, I was almost *exactly* right! But I must state emphatically I didn't expect to be so exactly right, I was giving only a rough estimate, and really assumed I might be quite a bit off in the *time*, though I was pretty sure otherwise, e. g., that it would sell and build. . . . I judged that the reading time for the ordinary reader would run to about six weeks, average; and made my estimate on that, even allowing for the "out of stock" contretemps too, I expected that. And I knew that those publishers (B.-M.)[74] just wouldn't advertise very heavily, at any time.

Now we have *Atlas*. I am reasonably sure the publisher did a notable job of pre-publication promotion; I don't think any other publisher could possibly have done more or better. Also with the selling record of *Fountainhead* it was easy to place heavy stocks in the bookstores. I have heard the advance sale to bookstores was at least 50,000 copies; and that I would expect. Perhaps it was[75] more, I forget now, though I did hear the correct figure from a reliable source. I believe the first printing was 100,000. Sales out of bookstores, to readers, ran about

65,000 in the first month; and publishers ordered a second printing (25,000 I think) to be got ready.

The reviews, as I expected, were bad; at least, any that I saw or heard of—John Chamberlain* in the H.-T.[76] an exception, pretty good, but on the whole a bad press. No way to prevent that, of course.

Now you say that the sale to readers went to 80,000 and then "suddenly stopped." Well, 80,000 is a hell of a lot, for *an initial sale,* isn't it? Tell me what other novelists come up to it—not many, I should think. So now it is in the trough of the wave.[77]

And that novel (*Atlas*) has intrinsically the longest return time-cycle of any I can think of at the moment. I should think it *might* be as long as three months instead of three or six weeks; while the first demand has been pretty well saturated at 80,000. I can't judge how long it would take the average reader to read that novel, because it is really hors concours.[78] It is not only of enormous length, but cram-jammed with "story," with action, nothing to skip except one unfortunate stretch, most unfortunately in the worst place, a speech sixty pages long! And certainly dull to the average reader. However, it is skippable, and I daresay most people will skip most of it. Even so, there's over a thousand pages left of densely packed *action,* not skippable. About four times the length of an ordinary novel, no, five times, in wordage; and ten times as much action, plot. That's why I can't figure it, because it's not a simple formula of addition, but Nth power calculation. The only thing I can be sure of is that it's the longest time-cycle for returns of any novel I can bring to mind. Far more complex than *War and Peace,* and I believe a lot longer (haven't made actual comparison).[79]

Now I haven't seen the various literary periodicals, except H.-T., Books,[80] so I really don't know if the publishers are *now* giving it an advertising push—are they? They should, but maybe they aren't. Wish you'd tell me.

What advertising I did see wasn't very attractive, in my opinion; in fact, I thought it notably poor, for reasons I could give, but will omit at present. Don't think I ever saw less effective copy.

The book itself has one rather grave technical defect (besides that boring speech)—I mean a defect which will detract from the interest of the average reader. I must confess I can't calculate how much. The defect is that the theoretically central character in the book, the Number One hero, simply doesn't *appear* in it until very near the end! That's pretty bad. Maybe the subsidiary heroes and the heroine will carry it anyhow. I don't know.

There is another handicap, but external. That is, I find good reason to believe the great fraternity of eggheads and deadheads, "Liberals" and Commies and bureaucrats, are carrying on a deliberate campaign to kill the book if they can. To be sure, with 80,000 copies sold to readers, a campaign of suppression can't be called successful; but I suppose it could have some effect temporarily on sales.—There was no such campaign against *Fountainhead,* for the simple reason that eggheads in general never read anything but what their fraternity tells 'em to read—they don't read independently, as individuals—so in fact they really didn't know there was such a book as *Fountainhead* until it had racked up its huge sales, and gained its durable momentum. But *Atlas,* they've rallied against at once. They are ganged up in close ranks.

I may as well mention now what's wrong with the advertising, it is negative and colorless. Most of the ads say: "Story of the man who said he would stop the motor of the world—and did." Silly. One wants to read about someone who made something go, not someone who stopped it. And the ads give you no hint of the astounding "story interest" of the novel, the wild adventure. Those ads were deplorable.

With all that, I do expect the book to go on selling under its own steam. It is really, faults and all, a remarkable, an extraordinary, an amazing novel. If you haven't read it yet you should. You don't have to like it, you don't have to concur with it 100%, but if you don't read it, you'll miss something; and you certainly will have no right to talk of it, because only reading it can give you an idea of what it actually is. And it darned well is Something. I might remark that the first part of it is the poorest.

Now for gosh sake why don't I get onto my own job? I think I have got that final chapter[81] under way, and something ought to give—it or me! Maybe both?

Here goes.

Love to all,
Pat

To Edward Hall*

Dated "Friday" [November 22, 1957]

Dear Ted—

Well, we all have our problems, such as genius.[82] I think you missed the main point—you must make him secure. I don't know if there are good reformatories in Jersey, but you could look them up, and be prepared. Until then, I expect the old house will stand up, at least the frame. Just keep an eye on the banisters, electric light fixtures, etc., for the time being.

Me, I am suffering from shock. Today I went into the University Library,[83] and a new youth was obliged to ask me my status. I always forget when the new crop comes in. I said "guest," and he said of course he ought to remember, and I said, no reason why he should; but he said: "I do remember your name." I said, oh, do you, what is it? He said "Carrie Peebles."

What would *you* have done if told your name was Elmer Svenstrom?

Ordinarily I should assume it was useless to deny the charge, but you understand I had to sign my name on the library cards. I took the only course open to me, I said: "Impossible, there is no such person." We had a slight argument, he said there *is* a Carrie Peebles and she looks like me. I said again that nobody could possibly look like me, fortunately. He said she *did*. We got nowhere, even though I explained that Carrie Peebles could exist only as a minor character by Sinclair Lewis* or the heroine of a novel by Louis Bromfield, probably both.[84]

He let me have some books anyhow, under my alias, I mean the name you know me by.—If you suggest I made this up, you ought to know that it is unnecessary to invent anything of the kind; it happens.

Now if you will run off that Vassar item[85] I want to wish it on Mr. Buckley.* I have just stuck him for an article by me. (On teaching young geniuses to read[86]).

I hope to see you all on Thanksgiving—I hope.

Pat

To Robert Selph Henry

August 28, 1958

Dear Robert Henry—

If this letter runs to length, just give it the once over and lay it aside for your leisure. Your letter[87] prompts me to some comment, and a shadowy suggestion. The latter first—why do not men of intelligence and information in the present contingency discuss among themselves the truly grave difficulties of the times, their causes—political science, in short? That is what the Founders did for a generation or more before the Revolution; and without that long preliminary exercise of intelligence, there could have been no United States. If there had been insurrection, it would have come to nothing but bloodshed—no other issue. They formulated principles, axioms, and deduced their application, in advance.

You mention in your letter why Southerners, in heroic defiance of grammar, prefer the designation "War Between the States" to "Civil War."[88] But (excuse me if I am too blunt) it is erroneous in fact and in logic. Well, that wouldn't matter two pins if the problem had been fully and finally settled by the War (whichever you call it—Civil War even as a general term is a contradiction in two words). And it is quite true, as you say, that the South had a constituted *government,* set up with the consent of a majority of the governed (at least, I suppose a majority, on the evidence); the same authority by which the USA was set up. Very well, in that case the war was between the Confederate and the Federal *nations,* not the separate States, or the several States, *as such*; that is, as political entities. No *State* declared war—or made peace.

However, the real intention of the phrase "War Between the States," I have always taken as being a claim that the Confederacy was fighting for "States Rights." Am I mistaken on this point?

If I am not mistaken, then the claim is erroneous. It was the Slave States that in fact—by the agency of the Federal Government—positively infringed the very "right" they[89] professed to be defending. They claimed that "state sovereignty" included the power to make a man a slave and hold him as a slave, a chattel, a piece of property, belonging to another man.

Now I ask you, if the "sovereignty" of a certain territorial entity is adequate to assert and maintain within its borders that a human being *is* a slave, that is, to determine his status arbitrarily and to assert that he is "property" *by territorial law,* what "right" has that State got to dispute the equal claim of an equal political entity (another State) to jurisdiction of the same nature over *its* territory? Such equal power in another State, must in equality be sufficient to determine that on the soil of a free state every human being is free by natural right.—Yes, I know very well that the Constitution did[90] allow the recapture of fugitive slaves from free soil. I am not disputing that. My specific contention simply is that the very provision of the Constitution to that effect, on which the Southern slave States relied for legality, *destroyed the grounds for the claim of "state sovereignty,"* and did so specifically on the question at issue—slavery. You can't have it both ways.

I mean you really *cannot* have it both ways, not even if you get it into a Constitution; the inherent contradiction in principle will make all the "practical" means inoperative and finally, if the effort be persistent, the issue will be violence. And you may call the violence the War of Jenkins's Ear[91] if you prefer to do so; the principles and the facts will remain forever what they are and were. The Slave States denied to the Free States the very[92] attribute of "sovereignty" which they claimed for themselves. To put it rather impolitely, they did not know what they were talking about nor what they were doing, when they insisted on and got the Fugitive Slave Law.[93]

I don't know—I have never discovered any historical evidence to show—whether or not the Founders were aware that the proviso in the Constitution for the recapture of runaway slaves on free soil must be unworkable. I suspect they rather avoided considering the point, with the excuse that they certainly did hope for the gradual extinction of slavery (by State action) and had some reason for the hope; so if that had come about, the problem would have disappeared. And there was no chance of getting a Constitution, a Federation, at all, if they did not tacitly allow slavery for the time being and leave it to the States. The most and best they could do was to leave an opening for the abolition of the *importation* of more slaves from abroad; and that hope was fulfilled. But I am afraid it was fulfilled mainly because the slave-owners perceived that the slaves they had would bring higher prices at sale if there was no "foreign competition."

Now what I mean by political science is the true knowledge of causes and effects in political organization and action. What I have written above is an illustration by one tremendous problem in history, on which we happen to have all the data. . . . I might add that I do not impute to the South any peculiar moral obloquy; they *were* stuck with a terrible problem, and if they did not understand it themselves (for the underlying problem was actually the growth of democracy, which is also unworkable),[94] neither did anyone else; and the South had it right in their lap.

Now let me advert to your saying that "we'll probably dissolve our economy without civil disorder," as you intimate "the British" have done. My dear man, that is absolutely impossible. Mark, I don't say we shall or must "dissolve the economy"; I am only saying that nothing of the sort can possibly occur without fatal disorder, to an extent and in detail beyond imagination. And we can have grave disorder without going to the point of dissolving the economy. Your example of "the British" is not parallel; you overlook the plain fact that *England has done it on the dole from the US.* On whose dole are we to do it? To draw a true conclusion, you have got to take *all* the factors into account, neither omitting any nor tacitly assuming something that does not exist.

Even the Roman Empire lapsed into internal servitude *on tribute money,* from its conquered provinces. There is no such factor in our situation. . . . Our "dole" to England, and the tribute paid to Rome, alike supported the respective administrations, bureaucracy, and army, to reduce the citizens under a "police state."

You've just seen a repetition, with France and Algiers,[95] of the *mechanism* that operated when Caesar came back from Gaul. Good heavens, the French had a million men in Algiers. Too heavy a load for the extensor to handle—it reversed the leverage.

Reversed leverage forced the Federal government to issue a blanket amnesty to the Confederate soldiers even though the latter had surrendered unconditionally, and were beyond question *legally* guilty of treason. (So were the Americans in the Revolutionary War, but they won and were out of the jurisdiction.) The Federal government simply couldn't try and execute all those captives and all the civil officials of the Southern States.

The South cannot now be compelled to "integrate" the schools. And again, I may add, they are taking the wrong remedy—the public schools simply should be abolished, the state has no business whatever to touch education, by subsidies or otherwise. *That* is what is wrong.

The mechanical form of the error in passing the Fugitive Slave Law was that it created an uncompensated thrust. You do that with any machine and it will tear it apart.

Can't I get *anyone* to understand? . . . I wish you Civil War buffs of the Round Table would get on to the third day at Gettysburg and discover who won it—and then devote your time and thought to why and how they ever got to fighting there. (If "the third day" is inaccurate I accept correction.[96]) The men who fought the Civil War may rest in peace—"They are forgiven as they forgive all those dark wounds and deep; Their beds are made in the lap of time and they lie down and sleep."[97] But if they had done more thinking they'd have had less fighting to do.

I wish I had someone to discuss these things with—I live a solitary life—but I shouldn't take it out on you, and will desist. I hope the subject itself has sufficient interest for you to partly excuse me.

- - - - - -

Muriel Hall just now called me on long distance, and incidentally said she had been reading your *Forrest*[98] (which I lent her for vacation reading); she found it fascinating. She hopes as much as I do to meet you and your wife again; the day you gave us remains in memory as a rare pleasure.

Best wishes always,
Isabel Paterson

To Robert Selph Henry

Dated "January ? 1959" [late January 1959]

Dear Robert Henry—

Thanks for the historical item, "West by South."[99] As a general rule or principle of history, I'm not sure I would concede the importance of genuine turning points to actions (small or great) which occur on the periphery of a large scale or field of events in continuous history. I think they may be in one sense *significant* (i. e., visible signs) without being crucial. That depends on the forces back of them, I think—and such forces may be far back indeed, either in time or distance or both. This is really my *view* of history, very briefly stated.

But I do approve in principle and in any instance such evidence of local (in this case Southern) patriotism. And I would like to say expressly that I don't mean "sectional" or "factional," when I say local. I am convinced that *local* patriotism is the enduring, *holding* element of national patriotism; it is not divisive *per se*; and without it nations perish. I am afraid there is not enough of it now in this nation. Patriotism is not an artificial sentiment; it is entirely natural, and begins literally at home—with the countryside, the region, that you stand on and know as your own. That is the center; the radius may be the breadth of a continent; I believe Washington felt it for the whole continent, from Mount Vernon. Lee was a little narrower, he had not the scope of mind—his feelings were more powerful than his intellect. . . .[100] Incidentally, of course I don't think there was anything like a "conspiracy of the slave power,"[101] although there were suggestions from this man and that of a kind of slave empire (including the West Indies); but those were quite desperate notions, all in the air, unorganized and actually incapable of being organized. I am open to argument and evidence, but the more I read of the South before the Civil War, the stronger becomes my impression that Southerners generally and considerable slave-owners especially simply did not know *what* to do; so they began and fought a war of desperation for a cause they could hardly bring themselves to admit. They ought to be a lesson to us now; *expediency will not work*. The moral law *is* an absolute; it *does* work. But I can never judge them harshly, because I ask myself, if I had been in their position then, one of them, would I have been able to see any better than they? I am afraid not; it has taken me a lifetime to think it through.

Yes, I think there is much in your suggestion that what takes the gimp out of our business men is that they do not know the rationale, the moral justification, of their position, their function—their money! I have known them pretty well; I do not find them insensitive. Nor do they lack natural intelligence, as a rule. But as one very able man once remarked to me, business is carried on by the short view, from day to day. And they have long been confined to that short view, entirely engrossed in business. That is their defect, which is our ruin. Well, I don't know what to do about that either. All I have accomplished so far is to hurt their feelings dreadfully, without enlarging their perspective. (If it would amuse you, remind me and I'll tell you some funny examples!)—By the way, what do you make of this shake-up in the Republican Party?[102]

Revising a book which has been some time in print strikes me as a tough job.[103] Well, easy does it.—I'm thinking of spring already.

Isabel Paterson

To Edward Hall

Dated "Tuesday" [February 24?, 1959]

Dear Ted—

Thanks for the *Columbia* piece—herewith returned for the files or whatever.[104] It's true that people simply don't seem to get mad—or not enough people—any more, on just occasion. However, I do think there was a lot of wrath about the Mikoyan business that had no public outlet for expression; and I think our business Big Shots who welcomed M. have been made aware of it to some extent, enough to leave them squirming.

Alas, no—Holt rejected the novel. I have to go in and see about it next week, but can't think right this minute where to try next. I was speaking to Ayn Rand by 'phone and she asked to see it so she has got the MS at the moment. I guess she won't like it either.

It would take a very long explanation to explain why not—it would be on "ideological" grounds, of course, even if she thought it was well written (she might think that). Talking to her, I realized how impossible it has become to communicate with her at all. (If she read this sentence she would have a fit!) . . . It's the darnedest thing, but professed atheists (one of whom she is which) are really more bigoted than any adherents of any religion, except perhaps Whirling Dervishes.[105] Ayn has got the phrase "A is A,"[106] which she recites at intervals like a good Moslem saying "La illah Allah" (if that is the correct expression.)[107] I fancy she'd spin at 1200 rpm if I mentioned that atheism isn't news to an American; that we've always had a few atheists around, and nobody minds. In fact, H. L. Mencken* made a prosperous career as a writer though he was an avowed atheist; and the public respected him as a good prose writer and a gifted polemist and didn't give a damn about his atheism—calmly ignored it. Ayn wouldn't understand, and I guess would be infuriated by the American tradition on that point, which derives from the "separation of Church and State" political axiom—its social expression is the attitude that your religion is your own business. Looks as if Ayn meant to spend the rest of her life, and perhaps some money, mainly in the effort to propagate atheism. I'm sure she'll get no further with it than Benjamin Tucker* or Brann* the Iconoclast did in the 19th century (they both ran little magazines to spread their peculiar faith in No-God.) Nobody ever interfered with them. I think they got subscribers mainly by printing clerical scandals—preacher elopes with soprano choir singer, you know. . . . Well, anyhow, Ayn has got a following, and I suppose is happy with it. And people will continue to buy *Atlas* for the story. She said it continues to sell about a thousand copies a month—I wish any book of mine would do likewise. Oh, I should have mentioned that it would seem she has decided, or is on the verge of coming to the conclusion, that I am not rational. That worries me a lot. On the other hand, she really seemed to imply that I *could* write novels like hers if I tried—it isn't talent, but Reason that does it, you see. I guess I'd better stop at this point, but I trust you get a dim idea of the situation. But I forgot to remark that of course atheism does make that esteemed Christian publication, the N. Y. *Evening Post*, get its dander up. Maybe this clarifies the issue.

If there are no atheists around to throw me out, I may venture to Montclair this coming week-end and parley through the grille at

101 S. M. Avenue.[108] Is that all right? I rest my hopes on Thomas; he might let me in, merely to see who is dat?

Love to all,
Pat

PS. Even the *Saturday Evening Post* did give the Big Shots who entertained Mikoyan a slap on the wrist last week—but naming no names and omitting the State Dept.[109]

Notes

1. The Spanish fleet that was intended to conquer England.
2. In the Glorious Revolution, which began in 1688, Parliament and the forces it represented ended the reign of James II and started that of William and Mary.
3. *Crossed out:* to create.
4. Muriel Hall and her family were living in Bloomfield, (northern) New Jersey.
5. Article 3, Section 3 of the United States Constitution: "The Congress shall have Power to declare the Punishment of Treason, but no Attainder of Treason shall work Corruption of Blood, or Forfeiture except during the Life of the Person attainted."
6. The incident of Count Antoine Joseph van Horn took place in 1720, basically as Paterson narrates it, although the punishment he received was breaking on the wheel, not hanging.
7. This reference is unidentified.
8. The reference to John Jay is obscure. Paterson may be thinking of an objection that Jay made while chief justice of New York to an act of the legislature that he thought was in effect a bill of attainder because through taxation it imposed "penalties, not incurred on conviction" of crime. The legislature made the enactment anyway. (See Walter Stahr, *John Jay: Founding Father* [New York: Hambledon and London, 2005] 86).
9. The reference is obscure. Dolls were often made of china and stuffed with sawdust.
10. A teenaged girl, named in the letter.
11. Rebecca Hall.*
12. Elsewhere in this letter Paterson remembers the name of the papal encyclical to which she refers as *Rerum Novarum* (Leo XIII, 1891), but her discussion is directed either to the encyclical *Mirari Vos* of Gregory XVI (1832) or to the *Quanta Cura* of Pius IX (1864) and its associated "Syllabus of Errors."
13. "St. Michael's" has not been identified.
14. Paterson refers to Gilson's *The Unity of Philosophical Experience* (1937) and to her strictures on Descartes in GM 145–46. "Swelp," following, is a jocular form of "so help me."
15. A jocular form of "something."
16. Paterson strongly advocated teaching children to read by the phonetic system, resisting a then-fashionable idea of teaching them to memorize whole words. The latter method, she thought, treated words in alphabetic

representation as if they were Chinese characters, representing words as a whole.

17. Friedrich Froebel (1782–1852), disciple of education reformer Johann Heinrich Pestalozzi (1746–1827), is known as the founder of the kindergarten.
18. Amphibolos is a kind of ambiguity; the Oruktor Amphibolos was a steam-powered vehicle; there are other possible connections. Cyrus Griffin (1749–1810) was the last president of the Continental Congress. Muriel was presumably doing research on these topics in her job with *Life.*
19. The Duke of Windsor (1894–1972) had been King Edward VIII of England and had abdicated in order to marry a woman who had been divorced. The reference to Muriel's grand duchess is obscure.
20. Becky is the Halls' daughter Rebecca.* Diana is the daughter of Mr. and Mrs. Sanner, who rented half of Paterson's home near Princeton, New Jersey.
21. In January 1931 and February 1934 ("Turns," February 8, 1931, February 18, 1934).
22. Hilda Perlman was the Halls' Finnish housekeeper and cook. She did not like Paterson.
23. The Aged P., or Aged Parent, is a character in Dickens's *Great Expectations*—a male character. The pronoun "she," below, may be a typographical error; or Paterson may have confused this character with another, which is unlikely.
24. A flowering plant, either a bracteata rose or an azalea.
25. Edward Hall.*
26. Muriel's daughter Rebecca.*
27. *The New Men* (1954) by Charles Percy Snow (1905–1980) concerns scientific efforts to develop an atomic weapon. Snow was a British civil servant, politician, and novelist but was trained as a scientist. Paterson had been highly favorable to Shute's novel *An Old Captivity* (1940), was friendly with him personally, and might have been expected to sympathize with his ideas on many issues (Paterson, review of Nevil Shute, *An Old Captivity,* February 18, 1940; "Turns," December 22, 1940). Her comment about him is perhaps directed against what he portrays and not against his portrayal.
28. George Berkeley, bishop of Cloyne (1685–1753), was an Irish philosopher. He lived in a house in Middletown, near Newport, Rhode Island, from 1729 to 1731, while engaged in the project of founding a college in the New World. In 1955, Muriel Hall drove Paterson up to Newport "as a lark" to find Berkeley's house. It wasn't open that day, so they looked in the windows (Muriel Hall, interview, 1994). Paradise Rocks is about a mile distant.
29. Henry's book on Nathan Bedford Forrest* (Indianapolis: Bobbs-Merrill, 1944) 198–199, tells the story of Forrest's refusal to follow an order by his superior, Braxton Bragg, to place himself under the command of another officer, and Forrest's gross insult to Bragg as a "damned scoundrel." On page 193, Henry quotes the remark made by Forrest about Bragg's failure to follow up on Forrest's victories: "What does he fight battles for?" Henry adds that most of Bragg's soldiers saw him "as a savage and irascible tyrant, for whose strictness and severity there was no compensating habit of victory."
30. At the Battle of Copenhagen (1801), Horatio Nelson was signaled to withdraw, and the incident that Paterson describes took place.
31. *Crossed out:* Very few officers would be likely to.

32. General Douglas MacArthur (1880–1964) was in command of United States forces in the Korean War until he was removed by President Truman (1951) after MacArthur disobeyed the president by making statements about matters of policy.
33. The Charge of the Light Brigade, celebrated in Tennyson's poem of that name, was an attack of British cavalry against Russian positions in the Battle of Balaclava (1854) during the Crimean War.
34. Andrea was the young daughter of Frank Spinelli, who worked in the press room of the *Herald Tribune*. When the Spinellis lost their home, Paterson invited them to live with her, and they did, for several months (Paterson to Muriel Hall, undated [August 21, 1955]).
35. Edna St. Vincent Millay (1892–1950): prominent American poet whose sonnet sequence *Fatal Interview* (1931) Paterson especially admired ("Turns," May 3, 1931; December 6, 1931). "Pomes" was a common jocular spelling of "poems."
36. The poet Elinor Wylie (1885–1928) was an acquaintance of Paterson and friend of her friend Will Cuppy;* Paterson used words from Wylie's "Lament from the Breton" to title her novel *Never Ask the End.*
37. A term often applied to Maine, Millay's native state.
38. Millay, who had many affairs, had one with Wilson early in her career as poet. While visiting France, the poet Wordsworth had an affair with Annette Vallon, who bore his child.
39. Harper & Brothers, the publishing company, did not want Paterson's novel *Joyous Gard.*
40. The Senator is Thomas Hall,* Becky is Rebecca Hall,* and John is John McLaren.* "Beamish" is a word in the nonsense poem "Jabberwocky" by Lewis Carroll (1832–1898).
41. Marshall Field III (1893–1956): heir of the Marshall Field department store fortune; investment banker, polo player, and contributor to leftwing causes; from 1944 the owner of the Simon & Schuster publishing company.
42. Paterson was still working on her novel *Joyous Gard*. In the completed version, the events she mentions in this passage take place in chapters 21 and 22 of the 25–chapter book.
43. Paterson had rented half of her old farmhouse on Canal Road near Princeton NJ to a family named Sanner (pronounced Sawner).
44. *Crossed out:* great.
45. Muriel Hall was working for *Life* magazine.
46. John: John McLaren;* Thomas: Thomas Hall;* Ted (below): Edward Hall.*
47. A nickname for Muriel Hall, derived from a child's mispronunciation of her name.
48. Julia Ward Howe (1819–1910), author of "The Battle Hymn of the Republic," was married to Samuel Gridley Howe (1801–1876). Joseph Bonaparte (1768–1844), Napoleon's older brother, once king of Naples and king of Spain, lived in exile in Bordentown, New Jersey.
49. Thomas Hall.*
50. This book about Julia Ward Howe, et al., is by Louise Hall Tharp (1956).
51. WD 302–303, WD 357–58.
52. *The Fountainhead* (1943).
53. Chamberlain's favorable review appeared in the *Herald Tribune* on October 6, 1957. The Sunday *Times* review (October 13) was by Granville

Hicks,* a former communist who had not given up the slashing style of his earlier years. It was highly unfavorable.

54. Thomas Hall.*
55. Rebecca Hall.*
56. American Presbyterians were originally exponents of the austerity and predestinarianism of John Calvin (1509–1564).
57. "Burkey" should probably be "Biurkey." "Da capo" is a musical direction meaning to repeat something.
58. A reference to the influential antislavery novel (1852) by Harriet Beecher Stowe (1811–1896).
59. In 1955, John Ian Robert Russell, 13th Duke of Bedford (1917–2002), threatened with ruinous taxes occasioned by the death of his father, opened the family's seat, Woburn Abbey, to paying visitors. Paterson estimates the price of a tea at Woburn Abbey as two shillings sixpence.
60. Thomas Hall's.*
61. Of her novel *Joyous Gard.*
62. An evergreen ground cover.
63. On October 21, 1957 Queen Elizabeth II visited New York and took the ferry ride mentioned. Episodes in Chapter 24 of Paterson's novel *Joyous Gard,* which she was writing at the time, involve the ferry. The owners of the Moran tugboat company were friendly with Paterson and gave her rides around Manhattan.
64. Achilles and the Tortoise is a paradox of the Greek philosopher Zeno (c. 490–c. 430 B.C.: Achilles, a swift runner, can never catch up to a tortoise to whom he has given a head start, because he has an infinite number of points to traverse before overtaking the animal.
65. The Governor was W. Averell Harriman (1891–1986), in office from 1955 to 1958; the Mayor was Robert F. Wagner, Jr. (1910–1991), in office from 1954 to 1965.
66. Paterson never typed a close to this parenthesis.
67. One of Paterson's first jobs was that of a "diningroom girl" in a hotel (WD 23).
68. The first page of this letter has been lost. The extant part begins here, with a page numbered "2." The letter is difficult to date precisely, but a general date is suggested by its discussion of the time passed since publication of *Atlas Shrugged* on October 10, 1957.
69. *Crossed out*: detective stories as.
70. *Crossed out:* or finally by.
71. Presumably a reference to Paterson's complaint that GM had been allowed to go out of stock (Earle Balch to Paterson, April 21, 1944).
72. Ayn Rand's novel of 1943.
73. Plates of type from which the book could be reprinted.
74. The Bobbs-Merrill Company, publishers of *The Fountainhead.*
75. *Crossed out:* a little.
76. *New York Herald Tribune.*
77. Bennett Cerf of Random House (see note 5, page 53, above), publisher of *Atlas Shrugged,* remembered: "It was her first novel since *The Fountainhead,* and we printed a hundred thousand copies, knowing there would be tremendous interest in it. Then the reviews came out. The critics were

hostile, as they always were to Ayn Rand, and the sale was badly crimped for a while. We thought it was going to be a failure, but the fact of the matter is: the book has gone on and on and on, through many printings" (*At Random: The Reminiscences of Bennett Cerf* (New York: Random House, 1977) 250).

78. French: without a rival.
79. *Atlas Shrugged* is considerably more than fifty thousand words longer than *War and Peace.*
80. *Herald Tribune "Books,"* which continued to be sent to Paterson after she had left its employ.
81. Of her novel *Joyous Gard.*
82. An apparent reference to the adventures of Ted's son Thomas, fourteen months old.
83. The library at Princeton.
84. While Paterson never lost her sympathy for Lewis (see page 178, note 35, above), she had lost it for Bromfield (1896–1956), a successful novelist who had been a friend in the 1920s and 1930s.
85. Reference unknown.
86. See above, pages 131–138, for Paterson's "Learning to Read," published in William F. Buckley, Jr.'s *National Review.*
87. This letter has apparently not survived.
88. *Crossed out:* Yes, I know what the point is.
89. *Crossed out:* claimed.
90. *Crossed out:* provide for the.
91. A war between Britain and Spain (1739–1743). One of its causes was an incident in 1731 in which a Spanish captain boarded a British vessel and cut off the ear of its captain.
92. *Crossed out:* sovereignty.
93. The federal Fugitive Slave Act of 1850 was intended to expedite the return of slaves escaping to free states; it increased the hostility of the North against the South.
94. Paterson had called slavery itself "the fault in the structure" of the constitutional system (GM 135); here she refers to her theory that the new ideology of universal manhood suffrage created unqualified voters and made plans of emancipation impossible to realize in the South; see pages 99–113, above.
95. Between 1954 and 1962 the French government struggled against nationalists in Algeria, then considered an integral part of France.
96. The battle of Gettysburg took place on July 1–3, 1863.
97. Quoted with virtually complete accuracy from Rudyard Kipling's poem "The Sack of the Gods."
98. Henry's military biography of Nathan Bedford Forrest.*
99. An article by Robert Henry in the *Journal of Southern History* 24 (February 1958) 3–15. Henry reviews various "turning points" in the process of Western expansion, such as George Rogers Clark's conquest of Vincennes in 1779, emphasizes the importance of Southerners at each point, but denies that the general goal was the expansion of slavery. The article is not concerned with "patriotism," as Paterson is in her reply.
100. Paterson said that she had tried all her life to dislike Robert E. Lee but had at last succumbed to his peculiar charm and interest: "Nothing could diminish Lee, not even his admirers" ("Turns," March 4, 1934).

101. Opponents of slavery often suspected that Southerners were attempting to convert the American republic into an empire supported by slaves.
102. Paterson may be referring to changes in the Republican congressional leadership following the party's bad showing in the November 1958 elections. In early January 1959, Joseph Martin (1884–1968) was replaced by Charles Halleck (1900–1986) as minority leader in the House of Representatives, and William Knowland (1908–1974) was succeeded by Everett Dirksen (1896–1969) as minority leader of the Senate.
103. It is not clear which of his several books Henry may have been revising.
104. *Columbia* editorialized angrily about the January 1959 goodwill visit to the United States of Soviet First Deputy Premier Anastas Mikoyan (1895–1978).
105. Sufi Muslim mystics who performed a whirling dance.
106. A logical principle that figures in Rand's *Atlas Shrugged* as a fundament of knowledge.
107. The expression, which has been transliterated as *lā 'ilāha 'illā-llāh,* means "There is no God but Allah."
108. Ted and Muriel Hall lived at 101 S. Mountain Avenue in Montclair, New Jersey. This is the house where Paterson died.
109. A reference to the *Saturday Evening Post* editorial, "The Kremlin Seeks More and Better American Pipelines" (February 28, 1959) 10. Issues of the *Post* were dated many days in advance of publication.

Index